LANDSCAPE DETAILING

Volume 4   WATER

LANDSCAPE DETAILING

Volume 4 WATER

Michael Littlewood

ELSEVIER

AMSTERDAM • BOSTON • HEIDELBERG • LONDON • NEW YORK • OXFORD
PARIS • SAN DIEGO • SAN FRANCISCO • SINGAPORE • SYDNEY • TOKYO
Architectural Press is an imprint of Elsevier

Architectural
Press

Architectural Press
An imprint of Elsevier
Linacre House, Jordan Hill, Oxford OX2 8DP
200 Wheeler Road, Burlington, MA 01803

First published 12001
Reprinted 2002, 2004

British Library Cataloguing in Publication Data
Littlewood, Michael
    Landscape detailing.— 3rd ed.
    Water
    1. Architectural drawing—Detailing
    I. Title
    712

ISBN 0 7506 3829 X

Library of Congress Cataloguing in Publication Data
A catalogue record for this book is available from the Library of Congress

For information on all Architectural Press publications
visit our website at www.architecturalpress.com

Printed and bound in Great Britain by MPG Books Ltd, Bodmin, Cornwall

CONTENTS

FOREWORD

It has always been my intention to produce a fourth book in the *Landscape Detailing* series, dealing with water. The success of the first three – Surfaces, Enclosures and Structures in the third edition – has prompted this publication.

In case the reader has not seen the previous publications, some parts of the text are repeated to ensure clarification for the purpose of the book.

Many landscape architects, architects, other professionals and students responsible for the production of drawn details and specifications for landscape construction works have a need for ready reference. This book has been produced to meet that need and it can be extended by additional sheets. It has been arranged for ease of copying of sheets and it is sufficiently flexible for designers to use the details for their specific requirements.

The range of materials for external works and their possible combinations for water would make it impossible to provide a definitive book of details.

It may appear that a great deal more technical expertise is required for the design of an ornamental water feature with fountains and/or cascades in an urban public place compared to a natural pond in the rural landscape. Nevertheless consultations with specialists may well be necessary for the success of both of them, particularly over time. Aquatic ecology is not to be underestimated.

It is not the intention of this book to supplant the designer's own skill and experience, which is vital to the success of any project. This is still essential in evaluating the site conditions, assessing the character of the environment and creating sensitive design solutions. It is hoped that the book, if used correctly, will allow the designer to spend more time on design details, avoiding the need to produce repetitive drawings for basic construction elements. It has been found that the details can be very useful for costing purposes and to support the preliminary design when presented to a client.

Design information has been excluded; many other publications deal with this subject much more adequately than could be achieved in this book. General comments on appearance have been given only where it was felt appropriate.

ACKNOWLEDGEMENTS

I give thanks to the many people who have supported me in some way, no matter how small, and who have encouraged me to complete this book on water details, thereby enlarging *Landscape Detailing* to four volumes.

I wish to express my appreciation to:

Anthony Archer-Wills for, not only allowing me to use the many illustrations from his book *The Water Gardener*, but also for making so many useful comments on my manuscript. Without his encouragement from a site meeting in Somerset many years ago this book would not have been undertaken. I have benefited greatly from his vast pool of knowledge!

Professor Anne Beer and student Lydal Skeat of Sheffield University, Department of Landscape, for using information from their publication *School Grounds Design Project Pack*, Parts A & B, Nature Areas.

The National Rivers Authority, now the Environment Agency, for taking extracts from their publication *Ponds and Conservation*.

The editors and publishers of *Time-Saver Standards for Landscape Architecture* for the use of material from this wonderful, large, reference book.

The CIRA for their kind permission to use extracts from the book *Protection of River and Canal Banks.*

And too many other authors too numerous to name but whose publications (listed in Appendix A) have been a tremendous source of information and inspiration.

Many, many thanks must go to my professional friends and colleagues who willingly read my manuscript and made helpful comments and suggestions – Fiona Hopes, Garden Designer; Debbie Roberts and Ian Smith, Landscape Designers; Paul Bryan, Landscape Architect/Eco-builder; Vincent Marley, Head of Landscape, Writtle College; and my very long time friend of over 20 years, Robin Williams, Garden Designer/Author. To each of you I owe a debt of gratitude for your support and encouragement.

Finally, to my technical team – the editorial staff of the Architectural Press (Sue Hamilton, Katherine MacInnes, Pauline Sones and Alison Yates), my long-suffering publishers – who have supported my work and put up with so many delayed publishing dates. Thank you for being so patient, especially during periods of illness and times of personal distress. To Peter Thomas who has produced such excellent detailed drawings from my rough sketches on his CAD system, and a very special thanks to Mary Coles for all her word processing skills and for correcting my manuscript in such a cool and calm manner.

All of the above have contributed to this book to ensure that it eventually reaches the publishers after such a long time. I hope that everyone will think that it has been worthwhile.

INTRODUCTION

The landscape details sheets have been produced in an effort to eliminate needless repetition in detailing landscape works covering hard elements. It is possible to use them without alteration, but in some cases minor modifications and additions to dimensions or specifications may be necessary. Lettering has been standardised. When a detail is required which is not available on a detail sheet, the new detail can be drawn by the designer using the standardised format, which will enable it to be added to the original collections of details and to be easily reused on other projects. Readers are invited to send the publishers copies of their own details which they think would merit inclusion in future editions of this book. Appropriate acknowledgement will be made.

Each sheet portrays a detail without reference to its surroundings. This approach has been adopted because it affords to each detail the maximum number of possibilities for reuse. No attempt has been made to recommend a particular detail for a particular situation. This remains the responsibility of the landscape architect, architect or designer.

There are, of course, a great many other details that might be included on specific projects or in specific situations. In some cases, the detailing of site elements and site structures can be co-ordinated very carefully with the architect or building designer in order to ensure a uniformity of form and material. In yet other instances, various agencies and organisations may have standard details that must be used on their particular projects.

NOTES

The notes that precede each section are intended to give only the briefest outline of main points. For more detailed guidance, the publications listed in Appendix A should be consulted.

SPECIFICATIONS

Specifications should not be written without a knowledge of the content of the relevant British Standards in Appendix C. Some British Standards contain alternative specifications that may prove more suitable in a particular case.

The task of writing specifications has now been made very much easier by the use of the word processor. Nevertheless, if a specification is to serve its purpose efficiently it must be concise and accurate, otherwise it could be misunderstood by all the people involved in the project.

So many contractors ignore the specifications and use only the bills of quantities. Probably the best way to ensure that the completed specification is satisfactory is for the designer to read it as if he or she were the contractor and could complete the project accordingly. Reference should be made to two main sources for *specification*, namely the NBS of Newcastle-upon-Tyne and the publication *External Works*. Full details of their services are given in Appendices A and B, respectively.

USE OF THE DETAIL SHEETS

The collection of detail sheets, as purchased, may, if users wish, be photocopied, punched and stored in a ring binder. The detail sheets have been laid out in such a way as to facilitate this operation. In the form of individual leaves the details can easily be traced or copy negatives can be made.

The sheets must be used in conjunctions with a site layout drawing, preferably 1:200. These may be more than one sheet, depending upon the size of the project. The layout drawings will convey all information on levels, directions of falls and setting-out dimensions. They also indicate the location of the elected details and the deployment of any finishes (see plan below).

Simple conjunction of details (for example, pond construction and a wall fountain) can be indicated on section and elevation drawings quite easily (see section on page xiii).

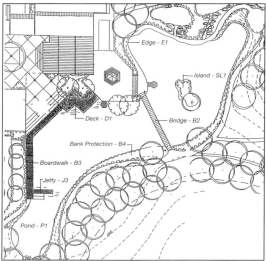

PLAN

STANDARDS

British Standards and Codes of Practice are referred to where necessary. Users of this book living in countries where British Standards are not used should delete the reference to the British Standard and, if they feel it necessary, either insert a reference to an equivalent national standard or describe what is required in empirical terms.

PRODUCTION OF NEW DETAIL SHEETS

Where the use of a detail not included in the original collections of detail sheets is required, the new detail can be produced using a standard format. This will enable it to be added to the original collection and to be easily reused. New details can be assigned a reference number by the design office, using their own reference system. The title of the new detail, as shown in the centre label at the foot of the drawing, can then be added to the contents list prefacing each section.

ISSUE OF DETAIL SHEETS

Detail sheets can be used in two ways.

A set of photocopies can be issued to the contractor of the selected details, after completion of the title panel reference, and number-stamping each detail with the office stamp. The second method is to draw or copy a batch of details, grouped according to type and identified with key numbers, onto an A1 sheet of paper and include the drawing with the contract set in the normal way.

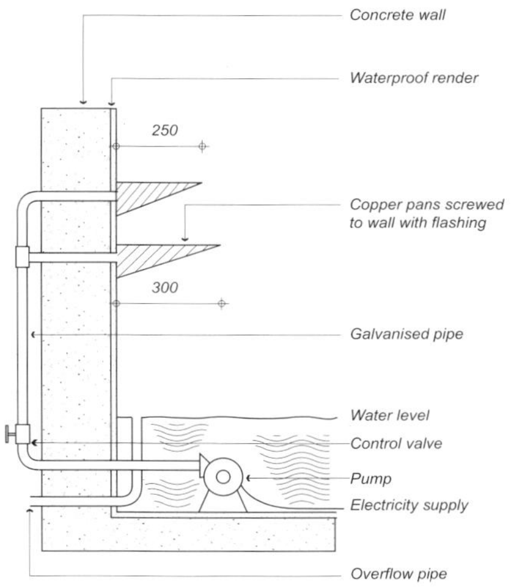
Concrete wall
Waterproof render
250
Copper pans screwed to wall with flashing
300
Galvanised pipe
Water level
Control valve
Pump
Electricity supply
Overflow pipe

SECTION

Scale 1:10

WATERFALLS
Spill pans

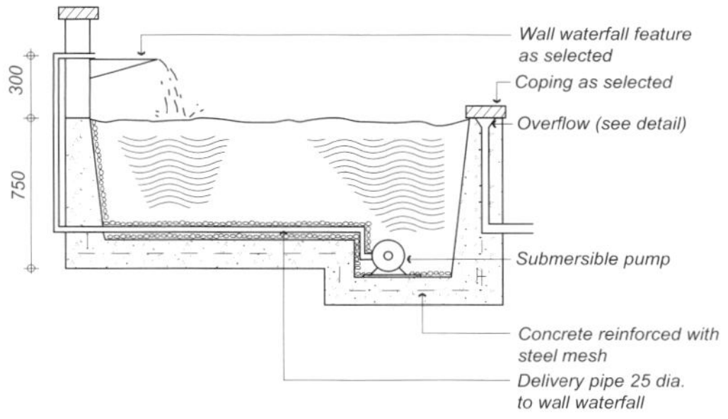
Wall waterfall feature as selected
Coping as selected
Overflow (see detail)
300
750
Submersible pump
Concrete reinforced with steel mesh
Delivery pipe 25 dia. to wall waterfall

SECTION

Scale 1:20

POND CONSTRUCTION
Concrete - rectangular

DESIGN DETAILING

The creation of good design can only come from the designer, and no amount of drawn details can be a substitute for this fact. The principles must be followed as Frazer Reekie has stated in his book *Design in the Built Environment*. To make an objective assessment of a design, or to set about the process of designing, consideration has to be given to the three aspects which may be summarised as:

1. Function: the satisfying of requirements of use or purpose.
2. Structure: the physical implementation of function by the best available material(s), construction, manufacture and skills as conditions permit, especially those of a local character.
3. Appearance: the obtaining of satisfactory visual effects (sometimes referred to as 'aesthetic values').'

Other words can be used to describe these three aspects but, on analysis, whatever words are used it will be found that almost every writer on environmental design, which may be extended to cover the built environment, is dealing with the same three fundamentals.

These three constituent parts of design are closely interrelated and each, according to the nature of the subject, influences the others. An urban composition, a rural feature or a detail that is truly well designed is one in which the creation of all three aspects have been fully considered and integrated. Integration may well be the key-word in good design. Not only does it mean the correct combining of parts into a whole but it implies, by association with integrity, soundness and honesty.

PONDS AND POOLS

INFORMAL LANDSCAPE PONDS

PLANNING

Planning is a vital part of creating a new pond in the landscape and there are many subjects to consider such as:

- legal aspects
- landscape assessment
- wildlife interest
- water supply
- water quality
- soil
- reason for construction
- access and safety
- siting/visual
- uses.

Legal aspects

Although the legal requirements depend largely on the size of the pond to be created, and its water supply, the relevant authority should always be consulted first.

The Environment Agency – in England and Wales a licence or permission is required for the following procedures:

- impounding water
- abstracting water
- making a reservoir
- land drainage
- fish stocking.

Impounding water. A licence is required before obstructing or impeding a surface watercourse by means of a weir or dam (or other structure) to raise water above its natural level. Provided a stream stays within existing banks an impounding licence will not be required. Always check with the Environment Agency Water Resources Department.

Abstracting water. A licence is needed to abstract either surface or groundwater and in some cases spring water as well. Off-stream ponds will need an abstraction licence if they are fed from a surface watercourse, even when the water is returned to the watercourse further downstream, because this is technically an abstraction. Always check with the Environment Agency Water Resources Department. Permission must always be sought from the Environment Agency before a borehole is drilled or an existing source utilised.

Making a reservoir. Structures containing more than 5.5 million gallons (25,000 m³) of water above the lowest natural ground level will need a licence from the Environment Agency Water Resources Department Licensing Officer, and require inspecting regularly by a Panel Engineer.

Land drainage. For any other work in a watercourse, including diverting a watercourse or building the pond (if it is not attached to a watercourse), and for works within a specified distance of a watercourse (this distance varies regionally), a land drainage consent will be required. Contact the Environment Agency's Fisheries Department.

Fish stocking. A consent is required to stock a pond with any type of fish. Contact the Environment Agency Fisheries Department.

The Environment Agency prefers off-stream ponds to on-stream ponds, so an abstraction licence rather than an impounding licence would be needed. A minimum of six months should be allowed for the granting of a licence.

Local Authority. Prior notification of any plans to build a pond is required by all Local Authorities. Although individual planning authorities vary in their requirements, planning permission may then be required for the following:

- ponds for non-agricultural uses, e.g. angling
- ponds within 25 m of a classified road
- ponds created by exporting soil or gravel from a site.

Protected species. Many species of plants and animals are protected under the Wildlife and Countryside Act 1981. English Nature should be consulted if further information is needed.

If an area of land is designated a Site of Special Scientific Interest (SSSI) it has special protection and English Nature should be consulted before any change in its management takes place.

It is illegal to dig up and move any species of plant unless the landowner's permission has been obtained.

Certain species of plant have greater protection and it is illegal to damage them in any way.

A licence is needed to handle certain protected species of animal, e.g. the natterjack toad and great crested newt. It is also illegal to move these animals (including spawn and tadpoles) from their native habitat.

It is illegal to release non-native waterfowl into the wild unless they are pinioned or clipped so that they cannot fly.

The British Isles has one species of native crayfish – the white clawed crayfish – which is protected under the Wildlife and Countryside Act 1981. Releases of non-native crayfish such as the North American signal crayfish can seriously affect our native populations by introducing disease.

Landscape assessment

The topography or the lie of the land (ground slope and form, catchment area) will determine the feasibility of the proposed pond as well as its optimum shape and layout. For larger ponds it will be necessary to take site levels, and draw up an accurate plan. The approximate volume of earth to be removed will need to be calculated, and a suitable site for its disposal found. Maximum water and bank levels will need to be estimated.

Services

Check the area for underground water mains and drains or service pipes and cables, such as telephone, electricity or gas, as these will need to be avoided. Check access for vehicles and machinery. Avoid any site that is known to be or to have been land drained, as this will cause great problems even when a liner is used. Above ground, pylons and telegraph poles may interfere with bird flight lines or fishing rods and should also be avoided.

Wildlife interest

The main conservation questions to consider when creating new ponds are:

- which sites should or should not be developed
- how many species already present on the site can be protected
- how a pond or lake with the capacity to become rich in wildlife can be created
- how ponds or lakes designed for angling, recreation and other uses can also provide valuable wildlife habitats and landscape features.

If the chosen area is water-logged and uncultivated, then it is very likely to be valuable for wildlife already. The creation of a pond must not decrease this value. It may be possible to compromise by creating a pond in a field on the edge of the wetland, when the two habitats will complement each other.

It is important to assess existing flora and fauna of the area before deciding on the site for the pond. Check to see if there are any statutory or non-statutory designations on the land or farm. (English Nature or the local Wildlife Trust will be able to help.) On a farm ensure that the pond will fit in with other conservation areas.

It should if possible link in with hedges, woodland, field margins and any semi-natural land to create a network of 'wildlife corridors'.

Water supply

The water supply must clean and reliable. Running water has the advantage that a constant supply of fresh, oxygenated water flows into the pond and prevents it becoming stagnant. Check that it is not polluted. The quantity available should be estimated to ensure that there is sufficient to sustain the proposed pond and for determining the requirements for the inlet and outlet. If the water level in the pond is to be maintained from a high water table, information should be obtained to ascertain its consistency, especially in the summer.

If the water level is to remain constant even in drought years the input of water must at least balance the outflow plus the losses due to evaporation and leakage. If an abstraction licence is required the Environment Agency Water Resources Department usually allow 25 mm/week evaporative loss during the summer. Leakage may be assessed by soakaway tests. The surface area of the pond would also be considered. Check that the evaporation losses in the summer do not exceed the water supply over the year.

Ponds can be placed into three categories: on-stream, off-stream and non-stream fed. On-stream and off-stream ponds have a running water supply from a stream or spring. Non-stream fed ponds are those sustained by rainwater or groundwater where there is a high water table.

There are three possible sources of water:

- surface water
- ground water
- spring water.

Surface water

Includes surface run-off, land drainage, roof and road water and surface watercourses. Look for potential sources of surface water, assess the catchment area from maps, check farm drainage plans. Water from a land drainage pipe and roof run-off may not require a licence to be utilised, but once the water is in a ditch or watercourse it becomes licensable.

Ground water

The water table may be regional or local depending on the soil and topography. Its level may vary throughout the year, and from year to year. A high groundwater table is indicated by the following:

- permanently wet areas with established wetland vegetation
- high water level in an auger hole or test pit
- an impervious layer in the soil profile.

Beware of 'perched water tables' which may be drained by piercing a layer of clay or other layer obstructing the passage of water (pan). If the pond depends on groundwater a series of test pits should be dug with a small digger or auger and the water table monitored for at least a year. If the pond is not to be lined then the level should remain relatively constant even during a dry summer. Digging a hole and allowing it to fill with groundwater does not require a licence.

Spring water

Spring water appears where water from underlying strata surfaces at ground level. It is often routed through land drains. Springs are usually a reliable source of water for a pond although they may be associated with iron ochre (see Glossary). To identify a source of spring water look for isolated wet areas with established wetland vegetation, or for land drains which flow at the same rate throughout the year.

Many springs in 'hard rock' areas such as millstone grit and limestone have a low storage capacity and may be drastically reduced at the end of a dry summer. A licence may be required, depending on the proximity of the pond to the spring.

Reservoirs

Most reservoirs work in a large catchment or run-off area on higher ground so that rainfall is collected and fed into a basin. Dew ponds are usually found on tops of hills.

Water quality

The water quality must be good or the wildlife value of the pond will suffer. Water may be contaminated by effluent, pesticides or fertilisers. Land drainage and surface run-off may be particularly high in nitrates. Spring water is generally the best supply. The water quality required will also depend on the end use of the pond; for example, game fish such as trout require better quality water than coarse fish.

Identify the source of the water supply, and beware of:

- septic tank effluent
- silage and slurry effluent
- run-off from manure heaps and farm yards
- nitrate and pesticide run-off from within the pond's catchment area.

Indicators of poor water quality include:

- blanket weed or algae
- excessive weed growth
- iron ochre
- bad smell or cloudy water
- sewage fungus – a brown coating on the incoming stream bed
- lack of invertebrate life.

Because of lack of dilution, pollution problems are more likely to be greater in times of low flow. However, in times of flood, water may enter from other sources. Be careful when designing on-stream or off-stream ponds – they will be in danger of pollution from 'incidents' upstream. It may be worthwhile to be able to isolate the pond from the stream if the risk is high. It may also be possible to plant reed-beds or create wetland areas to intercept nutrients before the water reaches the pond.

Soil

Background information gathered for the landscape assessment should include geology and soils. For the purposes of pond construction, soils can be classified into two main types, impermeable and permeable:

- impermeable soils are those which can be made to hold water; they include clay, clay loam, silty clay and sandy clay.
- permeable soils are those which will not naturally hold water; they include sand, gravel and sandy loam.

Soils consist of sand, silt and clay. Clay is the most important ingredient for impermeability, because it gives cohesion, and allows the soil to become plastic when wet. When plastic or malleable, the soil can be puddled to eliminate any pores or cracks.

Investigate the soil on site by using a soil auger over the whole area of the proposed pond, and particularly on the line of any impounding works. Before starting work, dig a series of trial holes over the area of the pond, to at least its maximum proposed depth, to see how the soil and the level of the water table varies. Look at the soil survey maps if they are available. Always obtain expert advice.

Reason for construction

There will usually be several reasons for creating a new pond, and it is important to define these precisely because they will affect the criteria for its design and also its eligibility for grant aid. A pond is created for:

- provision of habitats for wildlife
- wildfowl – for pleasure or shooting
- irrigation
- fish-farming
- fire-fighting
- amenity/ornamental
- fishing – private or commercial
- watering stock
- education.

Remember that the pond and the new habitats being created can also be managed to maintain them at certain successional stages. This will require commitment and resources and should be planned for at this stage.

Abstraction for the purpose of fire-fighting is exempt from the Environment Agency's licensing requirements.
Up to 20 m³/day may be abstracted without a licence for agricultural use for fish-farming or watering stock.

People access and safety

People will disturb the wildlife attracted by the pond unless great care is taken during the planning stages. When siting the pond always consider public access, whether people should be kept away from the site to protect the wildlife, or whether it is to be used for shooting or for the use of schools, in which case ease of access will need to be considered.

If the pond is to be used for recreation or education then hides and screens can help to avoid disturbance to wildlife. If some areas are to be trampled always make sure there are others that will remain undisturbed.

However small or large the pond, always consider the safety aspects. Generally, for a small community or school pond, as long as the pond has a consistent water supply and is small enough to manage easily, there is no need for it to be more than 1 metre deep. The banks should be gently graded, to make it less likely that people or animals should fall in, and easier for them to climb out if they do.

Ponds created for irrigation or fishing, or larger ponds which may have problems with controlling marginal vegetation (reedmace – *Typha latifolia* can be a particular problem in shallow water) will need to be deeper, so other safety measures will need to be considered, such as warning people of deep water.

Siting

A new pond should create an interesting focal point in the landscape and any possible view points from which it can be seen.

It should not be too close to buildings because of the potential disturbance from people and animals. Buildings and sealed surfaced yard areas are potential sources of pollution from rainwater run-off.

Habitat diversity will improve the potential for wildlife of a new pond, while existing wet ditches and streams can act as biological corridors and increase colonisation from one site to another.

The siting of the proposed pond should consider the various climatic conditions that are prevalent all the year round. Sun, shade, wind, etc. will all have an influence on the pond's location. It is important that a pond is not overhung with branches or shaded by tall trees and that the south side is open to maximise sunlight available to aquatic and marginal plants.

Uses

While the main consideration for the natural pond or pool will be for wildlife there are other uses which can be considered appropriate at the planning stage.

These are:

- supply of water for animals/livestock
- supply of water for fire-fighting
- supply of water for fish-rearing
- supply of water for angling
- supply of water for irrigation.

Animals/livestock. Livestock should be given access to the water's edge around only one part of the pond bank. A railed or fenced 'drinking bay' will be necessary to stop animals straying over the whole bankside and getting into the pond.

The drinking bay should have a hard surface to prevent damage to a clay or butyl pond liner or the creation of mud, which would make the water turbid, by the animals.

Alternatively water could be pumped from a pond into a nearby animal water trough.

Fire-fighting. A pond near buildings in a rural area can be used for an emergency water supply. The main requirements are:

- The pond must be capable of holding at least 20,000 litres of water.

- It must not be more than 150 m, and preferably only 100 m, away from the farm buildings.

- A hard road must lead to a firm pumping site within 1.5 m of the pond bank. The road and pumping site must be capable of supporting a fire appliance which may weigh in excess of 10 tonnes.

- A deep sump must be constructed adjacent to the pumping site, so that water can be extracted quickly from the pond. The sump must be constructed so as to prevent any clogging of a suction hose with debris or plant material.

- Any gateway on the access road leading to the pond must be at least 3 m wide.

- The pond must be clearly marked as 'emergency water supply'.

Whenever it is proposed that a pond is to be created (or restored) to serve as a supply of water for fire-fighting, advice should be taken from the Fire Prevention Officer of the local Fire Service.

Fish Rearing/Angling. Water for fish rearing requires a pH of between 6.5 and 8.5. Acidic ponds with low pH, less than 6.0 will cause stress to fish and could cause disease and death. A pond that is too acidic can be remedied by adding agricultural lime or wood ash – the amount being determined by the pH. It should be applied in spring and/or autumn.

Alkaline waters are less dangerous but in the extreme they can be toxic and sterile depending upon the local soils and geology, such as limestone quarry waters. The main aim is for a balance between the acid and alkaline elements. Manure and compost tend to balance hard and soft waters and the seasonal inflow of nutrients mellows pond water.

Oxygen levels are also crucial for the success of fish rearing. The amount of dissolved oxygen in pond water will affect pond life and vegetation as well as vice-versa. There are many methods of oxygenating water from the simple spring type bubble fountain to the large rock waterfall.

Small round ponds are best for trout as they are easy to manage and aerate provided that they are not overstocked. The minimum depth is 1.2 to 1.5 metres with 2.00 metres being the maximum. If they are too shallow weeds will appear and the fish could freeze in winter. Steep banks increase the storage capacity and discourage weeds but slopes should not be steeper than 2:1.

Irrigation. Water requirements for irrigation vary according to the locality, soil/ground conditions and climate. An average rainfall of 1–2 inches/25–50mm a week during the growing season will realise 28 000 gallons/126 000 litres or 600 gallons per 1000 sq ft./2 700 litres per 100 sq m. This should be sufficient to allow water to be replenished to the pond provided no more than 10 per cent of the total water area is taken for irrigation and without it affecting any flora and fauna.

Measuring the overflow from the pond (during a dry period) to calculate any surplus will also assist in determining amounts available for irrigation. For example, if a 25-litre container fills in two minutes, the pond will take in 112 500 litres a week, regardless of irrigation.

A pond can be tapped for irrigation in many ways. A pump can be used to move water, via a filter, to a container near the garden for manual or drip systems. Small wind pumps can be used to lift water, for example 4.0 metres in height over a horizontal distance of 10 metres: and in certain circumstances hydraulic rams could be used.

Drip irrigation is the most conservative watering technique. By minimising losses to vaporisation, run-off and deep seepage, a drip system can reduce the amount required by 50 per cent. The most efficient use is weekly irrigation as this encourages root growth and produces the strongest plants and it also avoids drenching plants, thereby conserving minerals and nitrogen.

DESIGN

There are many alternatives to digging isolated ponds to a standard design; for example, it is possible to create wetland complexes, which combine ponds with temporary pools, wet meadows and marsh lands.

If the water quality and surrounding habitat are good, a new pond will always have the potential to support a valuable wildlife community.

The wetland complex

If a large space is available, rather than creating a single pond, it may be possible to consider creating several ponds within a wetland complex, each with a character of its own. Generally, the larger the wildlife area, the greater the value of the site. The greater the number of different habitats created, the greater the diversity of species the area as a whole will attract. It is easier to achieve this diversity in a large area, but diversity of habitats is also possible within very small areas.

It is necessary to consider how this wetland complex can be linked to other semi-natural habitats nearby. The complex is more likely to be colonised quickly if there are already adjacent wetland areas. Some semi-natural areas can be created from adjacent intensively farmed or managed areas. In places where water quality is likely to be poor it is important to look at ways of reducing the risk of pollution; for example, design 'off-stream' rather than 'on-stream' ponds and consider the provision of buffer zones to reduce the risk of nutrient rich run-off into surface fed ponds.

Other wetland or complementary habitats include:

- reed beds
- willow carr
- wader scrapes
- wet meadow
- grazing marsh
- seasonal pools
- alder carr or wet woodland
- nearby streams or rivers
- boggy areas
- unimproved grasslands
- tall herb vegetation
- hedges, trees and natural scrub.

These habitats can be diversified further by varying the way in which they are managed, or left unmanaged. With smaller areas it is possible to think about incorporating features of special interest such as an acid bog area in an otherwise neutral or alkaline substrate by importing suitable material. It is possible to design ponds to attract certain species; for example, dragonflies prefer warm, shallow, acid pools with emergent vegetation and rich, wet soil conditions (they also need semi-natural areas to hunt for insects). Wading species of bird will be attracted to large areas of shallow water with suitable muddy feeding areas or scrapes.

The following drawing gives some idea of what can be created, often making use of features which are already present.

WETLAND HABITAT CREATION ALONG A STREAM

Wildlife corridor linked to other woodland and wetland areas nearby

Existing hedges protect and shelter site

Open shallow pond

Shaded pool

Alder and willow carr

Arable and grazed fields

Boggy area and reed pool

Livestock drinking point

Wet meadow and seasonal pools

Fenced-off meander

On- and off-stream ponds

The existing water source and topography will determine if an on-stream or an off-stream pond can be built. An on-stream pond can only be created by blocking a watercourse with a bank or dam, which can be complicated, and expensive. An on-stream pond is also more likely to have problems caused by siltation and water turbidity, and also by erosion at the inlet.

In designing a dam and outlet, it is necessary to calculate the average discharge or base flow of the river, so that the structures can be sized correctly. The outlet must be large enough to accommodate five times the base flow. It is also necessary to calculate potential flood flows. These are derived from the size of the catchment area and the annual rainfall. A dam should be designed and built with a spillway or other overflow device to allow flood waters to bypass it without causing damage to it or surrounding land and property.

If no alternative to an on-stream design is possible, then the legal requirements of the Reservoirs Act 1975 should be met. Consult an engineer to ensure that the dam and overflow are adequately sized for flood flows.

Off-stream and non-stream fed ponds are generally much easier to build and maintain. They do not necessarily need dams, with all their attendant difficulties, and they are less liable to siltation.

The single pond

By incorporating as many different features as possible into an individual pond it is possible to create a mosaic of habitats and species diversity within a very small area. Different types of wildlife have different habitat requirements. The following aspects should be considered:

- size and shape
- depth
- profile
- banks
- islands
- adjacent areas.

Size and shape

The larger the pond the greater the potential for a variety of different habitats for wildlife especially if the pond has the longest possible length of bankside.

If the space available for a pond is limited then it is important not to fill all of it with water. A buffer zone in which vegetation is allowed to develop would benefit wildlife. Small ponds if they are close to other good wildlife habitats are still valuable.

The outline should be irregular, with bays and spits as this increases the length of the shoreline. This will allow for emergent and rooted aquatic plants, which in turn will provide more locations for birds to feed, nest and roost. A correctly sited spit will protect the surface of the water in an adjacent bay from the prevailing wind.

There could be potential for the creation of a small reed bed in a large bay if the surface area is in excess of 0.25 ha (2500 m^2).

Depth. The maximum depth of a pond will depend upon the surface area. Small ponds may reach 1 metre if sloping banks and shallows are to be provided. Ponds over 100 m^2 should be at least 1.5 metres. Larger ponds may well have a depth of 2.5 to 3 metres.

A minimum depth of 2 metres will prevent the spread of emergent vegetation and ensure an area of permanent open water. This depth also reduces the possibility of the pond drying out in dry weather or being completely frozen in winter.

Profile. To enable the landscape pond to offer the greatest habitat diversity, a progression of depths ranging from very shallow at the edges to a metre or two at the deepest point should be provided. The maximum depth will depend on the main use of the pond: for example, for a small, easily managed pond without fish, a maximum of 1 metre would be adequate. If irrigation is the main use then the depth will need to be adjusted to provide adequate capacity.

The landscape pond should avoid steep sides and consist of very gentle slopes into the water to allow access for as many birds and animals as possible. Ducklings can only manage a step less than 50 mm high from land to water.

Shallow water varying between 150 and 600 mm is the most important ecological zone within the pond as it has warm temperatures and abundant plant growth. It is the equivalent of the woodland edge in terms of productivity and value to wildlife.

Shelf areas of different depths beneath the water will allow plants to establish their roots. A broad shelf between 150 and 250 mm deep extending to a minimum of 1 metre into the pond will ensure the establishment of the many marsh plants. A shelf at 500 to 1000 mm deep will be colonised by emergent marginal plants. Submerged and floating plants will root at a depth of between 1 and 3 metres. Marsh areas next to the pond will attract other species and shallow sloping edges can be extended in one or two places to create marshland that blends into the pond.

Banks. In large ponds, depending upon the surrounding soil, it may be possible to construct a 'cliff face' bank, ideally on the eastern or western side. This would provide nesting sites for sand martins and kingfishers.

The 'cliff' should be approximately 1200 mm above the water surface.

Where fishing is allowed then some steep banks will need to be allowed for anglers as they require access to deep water a rod's length from the bankside. Alternatively this requirement can be met by the construction of a small pier or floating jetty.

It is important to provide a variety of types of indigenous vegetation ranging from grasses and herbs, through scrub to mature trees, because these provide food for the greatest numbers of insects, birds and mammals.

When planting trees and scrub close to the water's edge, consider the shading they may cause. If shading is not required, plant trees on the northern side of the pond. The leaf fall from trees may cause problems with excess organic matter in the pond so do not plant trees too close to a small pond. It is preferable to keep trees clear of the pond for at least 2–3 metres. No more than 30 per cent of the surface water should be shaded.

Islands

An island can serve several advantages such as:

- it extends the length of shoreline
- it creates more wildfowl breeding sites
- it helps to alleviate surface disturbance of the water
- it encourages seclusion
- it protects birds from predators and humans.

Islands are better suited to larger ponds and lakes; to be completely safe for birds there should be a minimum distance of 30 metres of deep water from the shore to the island. This will prevent predators from attacking bird nests. Even where this distance is not possible, an island can still be advantageous as it will provide protection from disturbance by humans.

The best shape for an island is either a cross or a crescent with the former providing the longest possible length of shoreline and wind protection in one or more bays.

The crescent shape would be more suited to the larger pond and it is more likely to encourage wildfowl to breed. Steep sides should be avoided and gentle slopes predominant. In the absence of an island a floating nesting platform anchored to the base can be an excellent substitute (see Islands, rafts and jetties, p.188).

Adjacent areas. Many ponds are often spoiled because insufficient attention has been given to the surrounding areas. These are often too small to allow grassland, scrub and woodland to become established.

Setting aside an area of land to create a buffer zone increases the overall potential for wildlife. The amount will depend upon the location of the pond and in turn the surrounding land uses will have an influence. A pond in an intensively managed field will require more area than a pond next to or near a woodland.

The buffer zone can offer:

- reduction in disturbance to wildlife
- avoidance of any fertilisers and pesticides
- control of surrounding water running into the pond.

The buffer zone will need to be at least 6 metres wide around the fringes of a pond. It will need to be larger still where a hillside site is used or where there is high rainfall. Surrounding grassland, scrub and woodland can all play a very important part in the ecology of the pond. Grassland may be wet or dry depending upon the topography, soils and location. Dry land is ideal as a resting and feeding place for wildfowl.

Scrub is important for providing concealment as well as food for birds, mammals, invertebrates and amphibians. The size of the area will depend on the location and the space available; for example, on farmland, extensive scrub belts can be created, whereas on a small local urban nature reserve only a few shrubs can be planted. It is essential to link scrub to grassland and to woodland.

Woodland can ensure that the pond and environs produce a more diverse and stable habitat for wildlife. It should be at least 20 metres from the water's edge, as, if it is less than this, shading of the pond could lead to excessive build-up of leaf litter and nutrients in the water. Conifers should not be considered in any planting scheme involving ponds.

MATERIALS

Pond linings

The results from trial pits will show whether the pond will retain water naturally or whether an imported puddled clay or artificial lining will be needed. The cost difference will be considerable, so a thorough investigation must be undertaken.

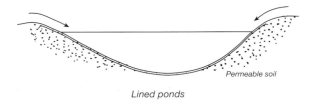

Permeable soil

Lined ponds

Linings require careful handling and laying on a stone-free base. Some materials are weakened by ultraviolet light and they require a covering of soil to protect them from sunlight. All artificial liners should be covered with soil to provide a substrate for aquatic life.

In stony or flinty soils some lining, especially the thinner ones, will require a layer of sand, or protective matting (old newspapers, carpet or underlay) beneath them. Penetration of the lining by weeds can also be a problem and weedy soils should be treated first.

Linings which require soil over them also require shallower banks (a slope of not more than 3:1 and preferably 4:1) to prevent the soil sliding to the base of the pond. This soil is also needed as a rooting medium for aquatic or fringe vegetation, but large plant species (both in and close to the pond) whose roots may penetrate the lining should be avoided.

Concrete

Concrete linings can be used where a more permanent structure is required and where the size and conditions make it economic to do so. Concrete, like clay, can be made to fit almost any shape and in America the sprayed-on concrete (Gunite process) is used extensively for free-form swimming and ornamental pools and ponds.

Provided the original construction has been undertaken efficiently concrete linings are extremely durable. They can be dried out or exposed at the shoreline without harm and are affected only slowly by erosive forces.

However, concrete on acid soils will break down eventually unless a sulphite resistant cement is used in the mix.

Cement used in concrete linings contains chemicals that are harmful to aquatic life. A seasoning period of several weeks is necessary, during which time the pond should be emptied several times, the bottom and sides scrubbed with a stiff broom and the pond hosed down.

The pond should then be filled again and left for a short time before being emptied and refilled. Bottom gravel or soil can then be added. Check the lime content, using a pH test kit; a value of below 8.5 should be achieved before introducing fauna and flora.

Concrete linings are more prone to crack due to settling, especially if the ground preparation and compaction has not been thorough, which in time causes leakages. These can be repaired with a commercial product. Extra care is required on clay soils.

Reinforcing will be necessary for any pond larger than 4 m x 2.5 m x 1m using steel mesh or bars, depending upon the complexity of the shape.

Puddled clay

This is the oldest form of pond lining and can be successfully used without any special expertise, tools or equipment. It was also used on an engineering scale to create the canal system and to line docks during the eighteenth century. It is still one of the simplest and cheapest solutions to waterproofing the bed of an artificial waterbody where the soil conditions are suitable. A clay-lined waterbody is relatively immune to leakage and the main risks of damage are from mechanically piercing the lining or from cracking due to drying out if the water level falls for any prolonged period. Mechanical damage may occur as a result of trampling stock, machinery or through driving in piles to build decks or bridges.

If the in situ subsoil has a high enough clay content ('almost any clayey subsoil will do as long as it contains at least 30% clay "fractions" and is free of stones and foreign matter' – BTCV, 1992) it will be suitable for puddling. This should be ascertained by a particle size analysis for a large-scale project, or in the case of a small pond the plasticity of the soil can be estimated by hand. Where there is no soil suitable for puddling available within the immediate vicinity, this form of construction is likely to be uneconomic as the transport of the large quantities of clay necessary will greatly add to the costs.

A properly compacted formation must first be formed, either by excavation or filling. It should contain no large stones or roots. Maximum gradients of bed or banks should be 1:2. Clay should be puddled in layers of about 75 mm if working without machinery, and not much more than 200 mm with machinery. For ponds a 150–300 mm compacted depth of clay should be sufficient where there will be no access by stock. For canal linings between 300 mm and 1 metre is recommended (BTCV, 1992).

The completed puddled liner should not be allowed to dry out. This can be prevented by covering with a protective (at least 200 mm) layer of sand, but it should be flooded as soon as possible.

Bentonite clay

This is an aluminium silicate clay with a high swelling capacity which can be purchased commercially in the form of a fine powder which is used in industrial processes. There are two forms, a sodium form, which swells to 15 times its dry volume in a reversible manner (i.e. it can be easily re-wetted), and a calcium form, which swells to eight times its dry volume but cannot be reversed on drying out.

Bentonite clays are expensive and linings formed with them are less robust than conventional puddled clay. They can only be used where sufficient depth of water will be available, otherwise there is a risk of them swelling to fill the whole pool. They do, however, have the advantage of not needing to be puddled to form an effective seal. The swelling caused by the powdered Bentonite clay can be used to repair cracks in conventional clay lining or as an additive when preparing conventional puddled clay linings (BTCV, 1992).

Sheet linings

The main materials used are:

Polythene

Polythene is the least expensive and also the least durable material and is available in a range of thicknesses. Sheeting below 0.5 mm thick is only suitable for relatively light duty applications or should be covered by a layer of at least 100 mm of backfill. A special quality is manufactured (1500 gauge) for use in large-scale water storage projects, but this too needs to be completely covered with earth.

Thicker sheeting (0.5–2.5 mm) can be used either alone or in conjunction with a concrete skin. Polythene sheeting is *not* stable in the presence of UV radiation (sunlight), although black sheeting is better than clear in this respect, and detailing must take account of this if it is used (i.e. it ought to be buried entirely). Exposed to the sun black polythene '. . . cannot be relied upon for more than two years' (BTCV, 1981). Polythene has the advantage of being relatively light, thereby easing transport and handling problems and reducing costs.

Polyethylene

Polyethylene (PE) is a more recent development, which is far more robust and long lasting than polythene. PE is less flexible than rubber liners, which make installation often impractical and expensive as more on-site welding is required. Only very thin PE (0.5 mm or less thickness) can be prefabricated into large panels, but it is more susceptible to puncture and tear during installation and the life of the lining. PE is welded together using the 'hot wedge' or 'hot air' weld method (where the surface of the plastic to be welded is melted using a heat source; then the materials are pushed together and held until cool. This type of lining cannot be repaired with a self-adhesive patch and will require a specialist membrane

subcontractor to carry out the work. The life span is very dependent on environment and quality welded seams, but if installed correctly, should last 15–20 years.

Bituminous felt

Bituminous felt can provide a relatively cheap solution when other materials are not available, but should not be used for large-scale pools or in situations where any degree of permanence is required.

Polyvinylchloride

Polyvinylchloride (PVC) is stronger than polythene and is the commonest liner material generally available and the most frequently used. Garden centres sell 0.35 mm thick PVC in a range of colours suitable for the construction of small ponds, which has a 5 year guarantee. 'Black PVC should last up to ten years when fully exposed to sunlight' (BTCV, 1981), although it is better to protect it with a covering of soil. PVC liners may or may not be net reinforced. PVC linings are available as prefabricated panels, with welding being carried out on site by hot air or hot wedge.

Butyl

Butyl is a strong and elastic hydraulic membrane manufactured in a range of thicknesses (0.75–1.5 mm) from synthetic rubber. It is tough and durable and, in comparison to polythene and PVC, is able to resist puncturing by irregularities in the formation, as well as being largely inert, remaining unaffected by ultraviolet light. Because of its hard-wearing qualities, butyl membranes are used in a wide range of industrial, engineering and agricultural situations. Butyl rubber can be joined together in two ways: by 'heat welding' (termed the 'vulcanising process') or by using a cold bonding tape (though this is now mainly used for repair work). Easy to transport (it can be rolled or folded), and with a lifespan of over 30 years, butyl rubber is usually supplied as 0.75 mm or 1.0 mm thickness.

Summary

Concrete

Advantages

- cheaper than Bentonite
- less laborious to use than clay
- can be made to fit any shape
- extremely durable even when water level drops.

Disadvantages

- more skill necessary than other liners.
- requires 'seasoning period' after construction
- difficult to repair
- concrete subject to attack by acids
- cracks under loads.

Puddled clay

Advantages

- cheap, provided suitable source available nearby
- no special equipment or tools required
- clay could be puddled by machinery where suitable access exists
- immune to leaks and decay if applied thickly
- pond can be cleaned by hand without fear of damage
- leaks can easily be traced and repaired.

Disadvantages

- clay has to be bought
- hand labour is usually used which is expensive
- clay liner could crack if not covered by water
- large, heavy animals could damage the bottom of the pond (application of a layer of gravel or other material would assist in protection).

Bentonite clay

Advantages

- non-toxic and easy to handle
- large areas can be treated mechanically
- leaks in existing ponds can be easily repaired.

Disadvantages

- expensive product
- thorough ground preparation is crucial
- not suitable for shallow ponds
- more easily damaged than clay linings
- difficult to clean bottom
- cannot be applied to steep sloping bank.

Sheet linings

Advantages

- cheapest of liners
- light weight per unit area
- easily transportable
- conforms to minor ground undulations
- minimal skill and supervision required
- can be made up by manufacturer.

Disadvantages

- puncture very easily except butyl (which can be cut with a knife)
- sheets need to be handled with care
- larger ponds require joining of sheets on site
- cheaper liners tend to deteriorate in sunlight
- slippery surface for children and animals unless covered.

CONSTRUCTION

The method of construction will be dictated by the site characteristics and with the soil type(s) determining the method of lining, while the water supply will influence the type of pond which is necessary, i.e. on-stream, off-stream, below or above ground.

Types of construction

Below ground ponds

- – water table sites
- – surface water sites.

Above ground ponds

- – impounding
- – cut and fill.

Below ground

Water table sites

These ponds rely on the natural water level in the soil. They can be built in river and stream valleys, and in sandy, gravelly and peaty areas, and are normally constructed by excavating into the water table. If the water table remains high there will be no need to line the pond, because it will fill naturally with ground water. It may be necessary to use a pump during the excavation, but if this is not practicable, excavation by dragline or hydraulic excavator should enable the construction to proceed. Bank slopes are formed as the work progresses and islands can be left where they are wanted.

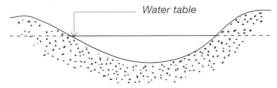

Water table excavation - permeable subsoil

Surface water sites

If the water table is too low but a reliable source of water is available from a natural spring or stream then lining may be necessary. Artificial liners of clay puddling should be used where there is an unreliable source of water or where the pond depends on rainwater from the immediate catchment. Lining a pond will be expensive so great care must go into all stages to ensure success. Where the source of the water is a natural spring, stream or water from a drainage system above the pond site, the water will need to be piped or diverted into the pond.

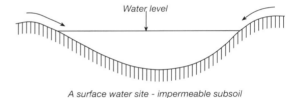

A surface water site - impermeable subsoil

Above ground

Impounding. For small ponds in gently sloping areas, water can be held back by constructing a bank no more than 1 metre high. The flooded area behind the bank can be deepened by excavation but the area of water will be dictated by the slope on the ground.

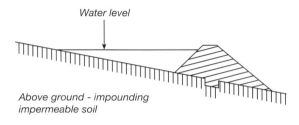

Above ground - impounding impermeable soil

A dam should preferably not be placed across a stream; the Environment Agency prefers 'off-stream' ponds to 'on-stream' ponds, because off-stream ponds do not interfere with the flow or ecology of the stream and a new wildlife area can be created nearby. On-stream ponds also tend to silt up rapidly.

If a dam has to be built across a stream it must be properly designed and constructed under the supervision of a chartered civil engineer – details on dams are given in Dams, weirs and sluices, p.172).

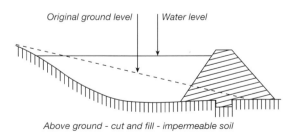

Above ground - cut and fill - impermeable soil

On- and off-stream ponds

On-stream ponds may seem more straightforward to construct but they have several disadvantages:

- the overflow from the pond must be capable of taking the maximum flow
- they have no facility for regulating flow, or eliminating or diverting polluted water
- an impounding licence will be required if the water level is raised
- they are difficult to excavate and by-pass arrangements are required
- the ponds can silt up very quickly
- there is little increase in available wildlife habitat.

Off-stream construction is therefore recommended as being more straightforward and generally cheaper.

- a silt trap can be built into the intake of off-stream ponds
- a sluice can be installed to divert or regulate the flow of water if necessary
- creating a new habitat next to a stream will increase the wildlife value of the area as a whole.

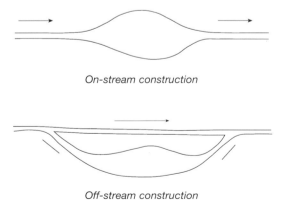

On-stream construction

Off-stream construction

Basic operations

There are a number of basic operations which have to be undertaken for the construction of a pond such as:

- site clearance
- marking out the pond area on site excavation
- impoundments
- water supply
  - inflow
- water discharge
  - overflow
  - outflow

- laying liners and detailing edges.

Site clearance

Prior to commencing excavations the site should be cleared to allow sufficient space for machinery to operate.

Any trees to be retained on the site should be protected up to the drip line of the tree (see Tree Detailing (Littlewood, 1988) for full particulars).

All scrub over the site should be removed to allow machinery to operate without any impediment and to identify marker points.

A few carefully located coloured poles marking out the area of the pond, island(s), bays and spits should enable the excavating machinery to operate successfully.

Excavation

Topsoil should be stripped first and hauled off the site or stockpiled in a pre-arranged location on site no more than 2 metres in height. If it is not going to be used for some time and depending upon the season, a green manure should be sewn all over for protection.

The removal of topsoil from the site will be beneficial to the creation of species-rich wildlife habitats. The basic rule is that a decrease in the nutrient status of the soil generally means an increase in the diversity of plant species that grow there. A rich diversity of plant species will generally mean a rich diversity of insect species, and so on up the food chain. A nutrient-rich soil will encourage dominating, aggressive plants (mainly grass and weed species), which will take hold quickly and shade out other plants of more interest, and most of the topsoil should be removed to prevent the weeds dominating the habitat.

After removal of the topsoil, excavation should recommence at the centre of the pond and work to the full depth in one operation. Subsoil should be either removed off-site or stockpiled for later use.

On wet sites it may be necessary for the hole to be pumped dry as work proceeds to prevent waterlogging. Care must be taken to avoid any pollution of nearby watercourses. Soil disposal in the vicinity of the pond may be another problem on wet sites. Wet soil slumps when placed in heaps and it may only be possible to excavate small areas at a time, which are allowed to dry out as work progresses.

Excavation/foundations

Excavations should be as near as possible to finished contours. The formation should be compacted, unsuitable (including organic) material being removed and all depressions and irregularities backfilled in layers with appropriate granular material.

The loading of the soil resulting from the creation of a water body will cause consolidation to take place and the consequent risk of settlement must be taken into account in the design. The compaction referred to above will provide part of the answer, but other precautions, including reinforcement, the laying of extra folds in a sheet liner, or use of a stronger material capable of stretching without damage, may be necessary depending on the type of construction used and the substrate in question.

The maximum gradient of the edge of the pool will be determined by the ability of a covering layer of earth to remain in position on the lining material, whereby effects of erosion by wave action need to be taken into account. The maximum feasible gradient is likely to be around 1:2.75, with 1:3.5 being recommended as preferable. (The actual gradient or gradients selected will in practice be dependent on the form and function that the edge zones are to have, and maintenance as well as requirements for the creation of various aquatic habitats should be taken into consideration. Where there will be disturbance, e.g. resulting from access to the waterbody, the maximum gradients will best be reduced.)

Stones, roots and other sharp objects must be removed from the formation, and if necessary the base should be blinded with a 50 mm layer of (compacted) sand where a sheet liner is to be used. A layer of non-woven geotextile felt is sometimes used to fulfil this 'blinding function'.

The desirability of providing some form of drainage of the ground beneath the liner should be considered to avoid the possibility of water (or in the case of filled ground, gas – especially methane) pressure building up beneath the liner (which will be impermeable to the passage of fluids from below as much as above. Where a pool or pond is constructed below the groundwater table this is essential if it is going to have to be emptied for maintenance work at any time. Otherwise the upward pressure of groundwater will be likely to deform, if not rupture, the liner when the water is removed.

Impoundments

If it is necessary to construct an impoundment to dam a watercourse, build an embankment above the level of the ground or create one as part of a cut and fill scheme, then professional advice should be enlisted; all three require care in their design and construction. More information on dams is given in Dams, weirs and sluices, p. 172.

Water supply

Inflow

Water coming into the pond can be by a variety of ways, ranging from the ornamental to the practical. The source more often than not dictates the method of supply.

Should water need to be diverted from an existing water course into an off-stream pond by a pipe or a ditch, then the Environment Agency may request a control valve fitted such as a sluice gate to ensure that minimum flow of water is maintained to the main water course.

Piped inlets should be placed pointing down stream so that water has to flow round a corner into the pond. This reduces sediment and the need for its removal.

For on-stream ponds the inlet should incorporate a silt trap, consisting of a stilling chamber with an overflow into the pond, confining any sediment into one small area, which can be easily removed.

The size of the silt trap should be according to the discharge of the stream and its sediment load. Natural silt traps can be created by establishing emergent plants at the point where water flows into the pond.

Discharge

The outlet from an off-stream pond must have a larger capacity than the inlet to prevent the pond flooding over its banks and to direct the overflow back into the stream.

Ponds which do not receive any water supply from a stream or water course will need an outlet pipe to direct any overflow after heavy rain.

Laying liners

Laying the liner requires careful consideration in terms of both design and workmanship. With large pools rolls of liner should be laid lengthwise down the slope to avoid stress on cross-joints. Black liners will expand in hot conditions and this should be taken into account when joining sheets. This should ideally be done during cooler periods of the day, or sufficient slack should be left to allow for contraction. Although most forms of liner are flexible and capable of stretching, slack should be left to allow for the possibility of settlement. There is no need to allow for large overlaps; however, the width of overlap depends on the method of joining. Care should be taken not to leave a liner on grass areas for any length of time.

Joining liners on site is frequently necessary as, although shaped prefabricated liners can be manufactured, there is a limit to the size and weight of the sections that can be handled and transported. Joining can be carried out by welding using special equipment or with the use of a combination of adhesive tapes and mastic compounds, often in a sandwich construction. Another possibility is the use of a lap joint secured in a trench. Joints made under controlled factory conditions are generally more reliable than site made joints, and the design of the liner should minimise the need for these.

Fixing liners around inlets, to outfalls, etc. requires special care. Where fixing has to be carried out to concrete or masonry headwalls, this can easily be achieved by screwing to timber battens attached to the wall and securing the membrane to the batten with laths. Sufficient slack should be left immediately adjacent to areas where the liner is fixed.

Any object, such as an overflow pipe or a timber pile, which has to pass through the membrane requires either the use of special flanges between which the sheeting can be fixed, or, more simply, star-shaped cuts can be made in the membrane as it is stretched across the end of the pipe or pile. This is then carefully pulled through and the cut points of the star are bandaged and sealed with tape and mastic as appropriate around the object.

Repairing liners provides little problem in most cases (assuming the leak can be located, which is often very difficult!). Patching is carried out in a similar manner to joining two sheets. Light gauge polythene cannot, however, be repaired very successfully.

'Soft' edge detailing for ponds

Where there is to be no masonry or concrete edge treatment, the edges of flexible sheet liners are usually secured in a backfilled trench running around the perimeter of the pool, just above the intended maximum water level. By manipulating the contours of the edge of the liner to form a hollow with its rim below the final median water level, a marshy zone for marginal planting can be created around the perimeter of the waterbody.

The same principles apply to pond liners made with clay, although it is obviously not necessary to secure the edge in the same way as a sheet liner.

The edges of the ponds and lakes are likely to be the areas most susceptible to mechanical damage and consequently consideration should be given to increasing the depth of earth cover on the liner in these areas. The possible effects of wave action in eroding this covering earth must also be taken into account and bank stabilisation measures may be required.

Bituminous construction

Close textured bituminous materials used in the construction of flexible pavements provide a more or less impervious surface, and this fact can also be made use of in constructing larger-scale water bodies. This form of construction is particularly appropriate when maintenance of the pond or lake in question is likely to require the use of vehicles. By virtue of their granular nature, bituminous materials are to a limited extent able to accommodate small amounts of settlement.

INFORMAL GARDEN PONDS

PLANNING

While for a garden, be it private or educational (school), the planning aspects may not be as onerous as for a pond in the landscape, there are nevertheless planning issues that need consideration.

Legal aspects

It may not be necessary to consult the Environmental Agency; however, it could be appropriate to discuss the project with the local planning authority. A simple pond on a flat site should not present any problem apart from consideration of the overflow/outlet pipe. Conversely, water features on a hillside could cause various factors that may affect not only the site itself but adjoining properties too. Should there be any fault in construction and leakages occur then the movement of water may go beyond the pool or pools to land lower down outside the property boundary.

Site assessment

Assessing the site (and especially its surroundings) for its potential for a pond and associated water features is an absolute necessity. An accurate survey with levels should be the first step.

Water supply

A source of a water supply will be necessary for topping up especially during dry periods. It could be advantageous to have a supply contained in a tank (above or below ground) that has been obtained from roof rainwater. Unlike mains tap water this would be free of any chemicals and beneficial for the pond. If tap water has to be used it should be sent to a storage area first so that it can become 'naturalised' prior to going into the pond.

Soil

Unfortunately the soil in many gardens will not be the original due to builders stripping both top and even subsoil prior to the building operations. What is often imported is a soil that may have come from another site. A thorough soil inspection will be necessary using a soil auger, especially where the pond is to be constructed.

Drainage test

Dig a hole 450 mm (18 inches) deep and fill with water. If all the water does not drain away in a reasonable time then there is poor drainage, or a high water table. Remove the water and dig a further 450 mm deep. If the hole fills with water, then the water table is high. Its level can be ascertained when the water stops rising.

Reasons for the pond

There is usually more than one reason for creating a new pond and any water feature in a garden. The first one is usually aesthetic – as water does bring a considerable number of attributes as so many authors and writers have stated. The second one is for the provision of habitats for wildlife followed by education and recreation uses.

Safety

Many people are concerned about safety, especially where there are young children playing in the garden or the school grounds. While measures such as fencing can be undertaken, there is still a need for children to be warned about playing in and around ponds without any parental/adult supervision. Even a very shallow depth pool can cause the death of a toddler if he/she slips and falls face down.

Services

The position of all underground, and even overhead, services including manholes, drains, etc. must be established. On no account should any excavation take place near them, and if any are in the way of the proposed pond then it may be possible for them to be moved.

Siting

Very often it is the poor siting of ponds which leads to their demise in gardens. Poor siting can make the job of properly installing the pond much harder, which will lead to problems later, and can greatly increase maintenance problems – especially where access is poor.

The points to consider are:

- Ponds require sunny, open, warm positions to avoid stagnation and maximise the number of plant and animal species that can colonise them. Ideally, a pond should be in a south to south-west facing position.

- The site should also be reasonably sheltered for healthy growth of the pond inhabitants and to stop excess rubbish blowing into the pond.

- Naturally low-lying and wet hollows are best for ponds. Not only will they look the most natural, they will generally require less excavation work and be easier to maintain.

- If the site is sloped and/or very rocky excavations for ponds will be difficult and the end result will often be unsuccessful – cut and fill operations often need to be reinforced with concrete to take the weight of a pond and the ensuing instability often leads to leaks. If the pond can't be sited at the bottom of the slope, alternatives such as a stream should be considered.

- If the underlying soil is very stony and/or hard, excavating to pond depth will be long and arduous. In this situation, a shallower bog, wet meadow or marsh might be better.

- Check the location of underground services – these will determine whether you can dig deep enough to create a pond.

- Consider space available. Ponds do take up a lot of space – this includes not only the water surface area, but the planted areas around it along with accessways and gathering points.

- The surrounding vegetation – overhanging deciduous trees cause increased maintenance problems for ponds in autumn. In addition, invasive roots from surrounding trees and shrubs will quickly disturb foundations and steal moisture. Dense vegetation around at least part of the pond, however, is essential as a link and shelter for the wildlife using the pond. There must be space for this and reasonable soil conditions to support growth.

- Consider run-off in wet weather. Avoid sites where the pond will collect polluted run-off water from car parks and rubbish areas. In turn, consider what will happen to the run-off from the pond itself. Is there adequate drainage? Will it disturb other garden features?

Location

The siting of the pond will need to consider the views from inside and outside the property, the boundaries, landform, high and low points, dips in the ground (potential frost pockets), sun's arc, wind direction, existing vegetation (its size and impact), areas of shade, sunlight and partial shade, at different times of the day and year. At least 30 per cent of the pond area could be in shade.

DESIGN

Importance

Garden ponds can play an important conservation role. Like all the small-scale wetland habitats, natural ponds are rapidly disappearing – yet they are probably the richest of all habitats in terms of the variety and complexity of the plant and animal community they support. Within this community, photosynthesisers (plants, green algae), herbivores, omnivores, carnivores, decomposers, all of the major categories from the food web can be found.

In addition, because a pond habitat encompasses both water and land elements, most of the major plant and animal groups are also represented. It is vital, therefore, that pond habitats are not allowed to disappear altogether. A pond can play a part, albeit a small one, in ensuring this does not happen by providing an opportunity for a pond ecosystem to develop and by raising general awareness of the importance and value of ponds.

Size

Ponds can come in all sizes. In general, although very small ones can be interesting, if the pond is to support a full and diverse plant and animal community the rule to adopt is, the bigger the pond, the better! Ideally, a pond should have a minimum surface area of 4–5 m^2. Ponds less than this size are still worthwhile as long as their limitations are remembered and accommodated by concentrating on establishing a few plant and animal species only. It is all too easy to overstock small ponds which leads to overcrowding and results, in the end, with only a few species dominating anyway. This can be avoided by greatly increasing care and maintenance but the effort is seldom satisfactory.

Pond size will be determined by a number of factors: size of the space available; the characteristics of the site (topography and soil conditions in particular will dictate the amount and type of excavation work possible); the intended use of the pond; materials used; money; and labour available to install the pond. All these factors need to be thought through thoroughly at the planning stages so that everyone is aware of what the pond can and will be used for – and unrealistic expectations are avoided!

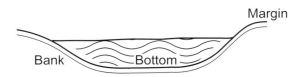

SAUCER SHAPED POND

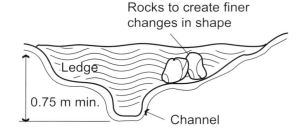

UNDULATING POND BOTTOM

POND BANK

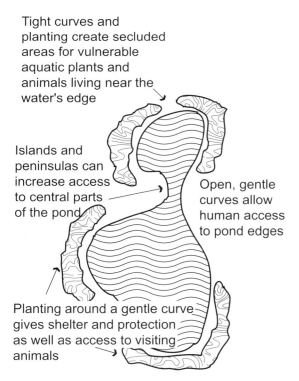

Tight curves and planting create secluded areas for vulnerable aquatic plants and animals living near the water's edge

Islands and peninsulas can increase access to central parts of the pond

Open, gentle curves allow human access to pond edges

Planting around a gentle curve gives shelter and protection as well as access to visiting animals

POND MARGINS

Shape

The shape of a natural pond is very important. There are three basic areas: bottom, banks and margins. The best overall shape is that of a saucer with undulations in all three of these areas to create a range of habitats and territories that will encourage the maximum number and variety of plants and animals living in and near the pond.

The aim is to create a range of depths – forming ledges and channels using both surface contouring and added features such as rocks. In order to stop the pond freezing solid in winter, some parts must reach 0.75 m or deeper. These areas need to be connected by channels at the same depth so that animals can move about easily between the unfrozen parts. Ideally, a natural pond should reach a depth of 1–1.5 m.

There should be at least one bank that is very gently sloping (up to a 1:20 gradient) so that amphibians can easily crawl in and out, and other land animals can wash and drink in safety. This also creates a marshy environment which extends the range of plant and animal species that can be supported. Likewise, some steep banks (1:3 gradient) are needed to support and protect aquatic life. Steep banks can be a safety hazard for children so should be blocked off from direct access via dense and/or thorny planting and even fencing. Free access should be concentrated in the shallower regions.

The shape affects the range and type of plants and animals supported. Changes in the relative 'openness' of the water will also be created by an undulating margin (wide expanses, channels, islands, side pools, etc.), which will affect the aquatic species present. Also the marginal shape influences access to the water both for visiting animals and humans. Generally, gentle curves increase access to the edge, whilst decreasing access to more central regions; whereas tight curves have the opposite effect. This can be reinforced by strategic planting of dense and/or thorny vegetation to create a range of secluded and exposed areas.

On the whole, if space permits a complex marginal shape is best for wildlife.

MATERIALS

For most gardens, a pond habitat will have to be created artificially using some form of waterproof lining to retain the water. There are many different types of lining available and these will play a large role in determining the eventual characteristics of the pond.

There are four main categories of materials available for construction of a natural garden pond. These are:

- flexible liners, e.g. PVC, rubber, polythene
- concrete
- rigid, preformed in plastic or fibreglass clay-lined, 'puddled'.

Factors which will influence the design (and the construction process later) are as follows:

Flexible liners. All flexible liners are prone to puncturing so the bottom and sides of the pond must be well prepared – ensuring all sharp objects (stones, glass, wire, etc.) are removed. Once damaged, flexible linings are also quite difficult to repair. The damaged section must be exposed, dried off, and special adhesive tape applied. Rubber linings may need to be specially rubber-welded.

These are relatively thin waterproof sheeting materials that cover the bottom and sides of the pond. They are the cheapest and most convenient lining material available. With flexible liners, ponds can be made easily and quickly to any size and shape by 'non-experts'. For these reasons, flexible lined pools are the most common in gardens.

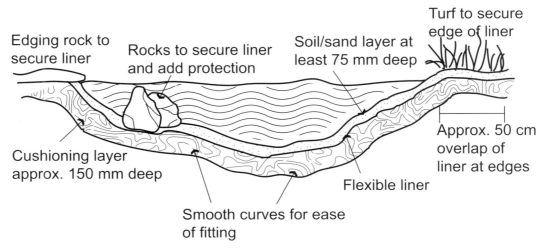

CONSTRUCTION OF A FLEXIBLE LINED POND

Concrete. A well-made concrete pond will last many decades. For years it was the most popular pond construction method as it is extremely strong – the nearest you can get to vandal-proof. It is also possible to create more complex shapes with concrete (compared to flexible and clay-lined ponds) as angles and curves can be built in. However, although concrete is very strong under compression, it is weak under tension which makes it prone to cracking and crumbling. For this reason, good design and construction is very important. Non-experts can create their own concrete pond, but it should not really exceed 3 m^2 and the 'rules' for design and construction should be carefully followed.

Factors to consider

A poorly designed and/or constructed concrete pond prone to cracking will cause endless maintenance problems as it is extremely difficult to repair satisfactorily. Often, there will be no alternative but to drain the pond and completely rebuild it. Concrete ponds are also very expensive relative to flexible lined and rigid plastic ponds, and require a lot more effort to install and prepare them for use. On the other hand, a well-constructed concrete pond has the lowest structural maintenance requirements of them all – plus it has the benefits of being longer lasting, the most vandal-proof and the most wear-and-tear-proof. The suitability of concrete ponds can only really be judged by individual gardeners against their own set of needs and requirements.

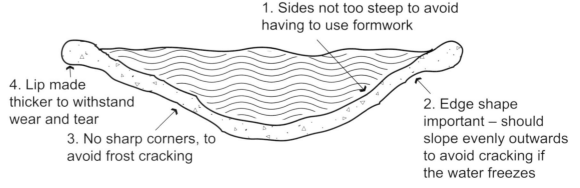

1. Sides not too steep to avoid having to use formwork

4. Lip made thicker to withstand wear and tear

3. No sharp corners, to avoid frost cracking

2. Edge shape important – should slope evenly outwards to avoid cracking if the water freezes

TIPS FOR CONCRETE POND CONSTRUCTION

Rigid, preformed PVC/fibreglass. These are solid pond shapes made out of either PVC or fibreglass. They come in a variety of shapes and sizes (though mostly at the smaller end of the size range) and are readily available in garden centres and specialist stores. As they are relatively foolproof to install and set up, they are very popular. They are also quite durable and resilient to damage once installed. Should repairs be needed, they can easily be done using fibreglass boat repair kits.

Preformed pools, size for size, are probably the most expensive of all the pool construction types. (The PVC versions, though, are slightly cheaper than the fibreglass ones.) They are also the most limited in terms of shape and size choice – it is almost impossible to find one that suits requirements exactly. Their composition and colour (usually grey, green or blue) also makes it difficult to create a natural looking effect. A big problem of using preformed pools for wildlife ponds is that they usually have steep sides and high lips which makes it hard for animals to crawl in to drink and bathe without falling in too deep. These steep sides, combined with their smoothness, also makes it impossible to get a permanent cover of soil over them which causes problems with planting and creating a natural effect. To some extent, this problem can be reduced by piling rocks and stones up in the pond to even out the contours and by placing plants in raised containers.

Clay-lined ponds. Clay-lined ponds are the ideal way to make a wildlife pond as they are the most natural of them all. They are also very reliable and efficient – if maintained well, they can last over 100 years. In addition, the construction process itself has a lot of historic and social interest, stemming from the canal-making days before road transport. Most of Britain's earliest artificial ponds, reservoirs and lakes are also based on this process.

There are drawbacks to using clay-lined ponds:

- If the clay can be obtained on site or locally, the method can be quite cheap. Otherwise it will often work out to be the most expensive of them all. There should be a low silt content in the clay.

- The water level of the pond must never be allowed to drop. If the clay dries out and cracks it will leak and the only way to repair this is to repuddle – which will mean draining the pond and starting again.

- The puddling process is time and labour consuming.

- Despite its apparent simplicity, puddling is an exacting technique and expert advice should really be sought to avoid maintenance problems later.

- The process is really only suited for larger ponds where trampling can be used to puddle the clay. In smaller ponds, puddling would have to be done by hand – much more time consuming and laborious.

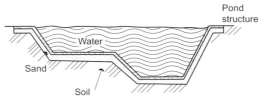

INSTALLATION OF A PREFORMED POND

CONSTRUCTION

Having selected the appropriate material the method of constructing the pond is given as follows:

Flexible liner

There are three basic types of flexible liners to choose from:

Butyl rubber – This is the strongest (especially with respect to tearing, though less so for puncturing) and longest lasting. If installed well it should last 50 years or more. The rubber sheeting is supplied to size, which means the pond must be carefully planned before installation. For these reasons it is the most expensive.

PVC – This is easier to fit than rubber and not as expensive. It is resistant to tearing, but prone to punctures and will not last as long as rubber (maximum of 15 years). It can be purchased in lengths, which will need to be joined together with special adhesive tape, or supplied to size.

Polythene – This can be obtained in rolls and joined with special tape. It is the cheapest and most readily available flexible lining material. It is also the easiest to fit as it is lighter weight and the most pliable. However, it is not nearly as tough or long lasting and is prone to sunlight damage if exposed. A layer of sand, soil and stones must completely cover its surface. For ponds, black, 1000 gauge polythene only should be used.

Construction of flexible lined ponds

- Dig the pond to approximately 150 mm deeper than required all over.
- Try and avoid very sharp angles and changes in shape as it is hard to get the liner to fit properly.
- Once dug, go over site and remove all sharp objects.
- Compact edges and bottom well to give a firm base.
- Line the bottom and sides with soft materials to act as a cushioning layer

This can include newspaper, old carpets, sand, or special pond matting purchased in specialist stores. This will help avoid puncturing damage.

- Lay the liner over the excavated pond and ease it into the shape. If necessary, make one or two deep folds in the lining rather than lots of wrinkles to fit the lining around curves.
- Allow at least a 50 cm overlap at the edge of the pond to anchor the lining. This should be covered in turves, stones, or paving units.
- Cover the bottom and sides with a layer of soil/sand/pea gravel (at least 75 mm deep) and add a few stones and rocks to help secure the liner and add extra protection where needed.
- Gently fill the pond with water so as not to disturb the soil layer.

Concrete

Construction

- Dig the pond hole 150 mm deeper all round than final required size.
- Compact bottom and sides well. There should be no loose, crumbly soil and the base should be solid. A good soil foundation is very important in order to avoid cracking due to the uneven settling of soil around the pond.
- Line the bottom and sides with heavy gauge builders' polythene.
- Cover hole with a 100 mm depth of concrete made from: 1 part cement; 4 parts gravel; and 1 part sand. This can be made on site or purchased ready made. The mix shouldn't be too wet or it will have air bubbles, be prone to cracking as it dries, and won't stick to the sides of the pond well.
- Spread over this a layer of wire netting to act as reinforcing.

- Spread a second layer of concrete (50 mm thick) over this. Ensure this completely encases the wire or rusting will cause cracking later. Do these last two steps as quickly as possible (must be on the same day) so that there will be good bonding between the two layers of concrete.
- Finish the surface of the pond with a trowel.
- Cover with wet sacks and leave 1 week to cure.
- Construction is best done when the weather is dry and not too hot or cold to ensure good curing.
- At the concrete mixing stage, pigments can be added to give the pond a more natural look – brick red, green, blue and black are the most common.

Note: Concrete pools should be kept small unless the 'Gunnite' process (sprayed concrete) is used.

Preparing for wildlife

All concrete ponds will release toxic materials into the water (lime especially) directly after they have been built. They must, therefore, be prepared carefully for wildlife. This can be done in a number of ways:

- leave the pond empty for 6 months
- do not remove algae
- fill and empty the pond several times before stocking
- coat the bottom and sides with special neutralising agent
- fill with a mixture of vinegar and water (1:10 ratio) and leave several days. Drain and repeat.

After these treatments, it is best if the bottom and sides are then painted in a rubber/plastic compound to seal the pond and act as extra waterproofing. The pond should then be filled and left for a month before planting.

Rigid, preformed ponds

Installation above ground

One major advantage of preformed ponds is that they can be installed either in the ground, or raised to waist height above. Reasons for having a raised pond may include:

- the soil surface cannot be dug easily due to hard soil, rockiness, or it is concreted/tarmacked
- where safety concerns with young children prevent a ground-level pond being built
- where the pond may have to be moved or taken away in the near future.

For any of these problems, preformed ponds can provide a solution. A frame to hold the pond up at the required height can be built using timber, concrete blocks, or bricks. The sides and bottom can then be supported with sand bags packed closely around the pond. The pond is then filled with water and the whole structure left to settle before it is planted up. Once filled, the pond will be very heavy so the frame must be well made. Building such a frame is within the bounds of non-experts, but specialist publications should be consulted for information about foundation, joints, and materials of suitable strength.

Installation in the ground

There are a variety of ways preformed ponds can be installed in the ground. A simple method is as follows:

- invert pond in position required. Mark out a rectangle (or oval) to roughly fit
- dig out the rectangle to a depth equivalent to the deepest part of the pool plus approximately 50 mm
- place pool in position and support with bricks, concrete blocks or stones so that the pond edge is only just below the soil line (no more than 10 mm).

Adjust supports until the pond is perfectly level.

- gradually infill the excavated area using the dug soil (which has had all stones removed). This should be compacted well as the filling is added – a piece of timber will do this job well.
- continually check the levels and adjust as necessary.
- once completed, the pond can then be lined with a layer (75 mm deep minimum) of soil/sand/pea gravel and gently filled with water. The weight of the water will help settle the pond into its final position.
- once settled, the edges can be finished with turves, stones or paving and planting can begin.

Clay-lined ponds

The construction is based on the process of 'puddling':

- dig out the pond to the shape and depth required
- cover both the bottom and sides with at least 200 mm of pure clay (no stones).
- moisten the clay well with a hose, and puddle it to give a smooth surface with all the clay smeared together in an even layer. This is ideally done with lots of people wearing Wellingtons trampling the clay (which is a lot of fun!).
- once the clay is smooth, even and sticky the pond should be filled with water straight away before the clay gets a chance to dry out.

PONDS/SWIMMING POOLS

Many informal ponds and pools, if properly constructed, can be used by people for swimming and recreation purposes. These types of pools are much healthier as they contain no chemicals. Conventional pools, especially when seen from the air or a high vantage point, resemble 'a virulent aquamarine rash' in urban and even rural areas, according to Bill Mollison in his book *Permaculture*.

"The colour is artificial and the chemicals used to purify the water are biocides. Chlorine, which is used extensively, is being dumped into our drinking, bathing and swimming waters where it forms carcinogenic chloroform".

Designers can now filter natural pool water below a base pebble bed using the pebbles as algal/bacteria cleaners. The water is then cleansed in a plant bed, usually of reeds and other suitable aquatics, to remove excess nutrients, and a leaf skimmer removes leaves and other surface debris. After this the water is pumped to a waterfall or 'Flowform' where it cascades back into the pool freshly oxygenated. Slow flow through plant bed is essential, as are tests for the presence of E.Coli bacteria.

Water can be warmed by the use of solar panels on any nearby building roof or even the ground, and the pump can even be operated by photovoltaic cells or a small wind turbine.

The siting of such pools calls for the designers' skills in ensuring the correct position for wind protection and solar gain as well as all the other usual elements to ensure successful use.

THE FORMAL ORNAMENTAL POND

Ornamental ponds and pools are usually located inside or adjacent to buildings, as features in their own right. They should be treated with a purifying chemical to keep them clean and sparkling.

Decorative use of water usually falls within one of four basic classifications:

- *Calm water* as in ponds and pools, is appreciated in terms of its overall form and reflective qualities. Water reflections are effective as a complement to buildings and sculptural works. The reflective quality of a pool is attained by keeping the top of water smooth at the surface and the sides and the bottom of the pool dark so these planes do not read through the light on the water surface.
- *Free-falling water* includes waterfalls or the vertical water in a smooth sheet. Considerable volume of water is required to produce a solid sheet for a vertical distance greater than 1 metre, thereby requiring higher initial cost and ongoing energy cost. However, the masking sound produced by a higher volume of water can be effectively used to isolate an area from urban noise.
- *Flowing water* used in streams and channels can produce a variety of visual effects. The shape, size and slope of the channel is an important design consideration. Surface tension retards the rate of fall, keeping more water in motion for any given unit volume. For a 3.60 m change in elevation a free-falling sheet of water requires a flow of about 150 gpm per lineal foot while water directed over a surface requires only 25–35 gpm.
- *Jets* occur when water is being forced upwards. Height of jets depends on orifice size and water pressure. A man-made jet can be either a solid stream of water employed in a formal setting or an air entraining jet such as a bubbler employed for greater visual interest.

The third type of jet produces a water shape such as a dome or a flower form. Contact manufacturers for a variety or available formed jets.

DESIGN

The design depends upon the function of the pond or pool such as paddling or wading pools for children, a reflecting pool in a courtyard, a lily pool in a garden or even a pond for amusement. Each one will also be unique to its location with the surroundings requiring sensitive design considerations.

The size of the water feature will be determined by its use and its surroundings. Its depth may vary – 525 mm (21 inches) for non-paddling pools in public places; 200–400 mm (8–16 inches) for a lily pond, while a reflecting pool can be as shallow as is practicable, taking into account any loss of water through evaporation. Ponds/pools seldom need to be more than 700 mm deep. It is an axiom in ornamental pond or pool water design that the water level be as close to the rim as possible for the most pleasing effects, but obviously wind disturbance has to be allowed for in the design.

As so many ornamental ponds are seen from a building, a bridge, or any other above-ground structure, a person's eyes will penetrate the surface and see the bottom of the pond/pool. For this reason the design should include the bottom surface as it will give added interest when seen through the water and more so as the view will be confused by light refraction.

Pebble mosaics are one of the leading materials for a designer, as they have such a wide range of sizes, shapes and colours. A wide variety of patterns and motifs can be achieved.

Painting the inside of the pool in very dark colours with cement or rubber-based paint will make the pool look deeper, improve surface reflections, and show less dirt. Black tile will give the pool a mirror like quality, thus keeping the equipment from becoming too obvious. Tile or a like smooth surface is necessary for a pool if it is to be maintained with ease.

Drainage

The water has to be skimmed and filtered, especially for a reflecting pool; it will need to have a pH near 7.0 and be treated with a chemical to eliminate algae.

The skimmer should be placed down wind. Rounded corners of the pool will allow surface debris to move into the skimmer more easily and not collect in the corners. Ensure that any splash or overflow water is drained away without damaging any surrounding plants or grass by installing a metal grill or paved strip.

Drains are essential for cleaning all fountains except small simple fountains that can be bailed or siphoned out with a garden hose. Drain lines can lead to a sewer dry well or sump. If water is unchlorinated, drain lines may lead to lawn or garden areas. A check valve should be employed to avoid the basin from draining out each time the pump is shut off; when the pump is at a lower elevation than the source pipe in a basin and when a filter system in a fountain has basins at a higher elevation than the main pool.

Mechanical plant space

Mechanical plant space is essential for all fountains that employ pumps except for a simple fountain using a submersible pump. When equipment is large, a room with normal head height and ventilation is needed. Equipment rooms may be located in an underground vault or an adjacent building, and should be inconspicuous.

Pumps and controls

- **Submersible pump:** for a small fountain or pool, available from 1/50 hp upwards.

- **Isolated manual pump:** used for small or medium pool or fountains, activated by on-off switches.

- **Fully automatic pump:** for large pool or fountain, operated by time clock or electrical switches; reduce maintenance costs for large pool or fountain.

Medium to large fountains have a recirculating system and a filtration system. Recirculating system components include: (1) pump, (2) piping, (3) electrical and mechanical controls, and (4) display fittings.

A recirculating system is the heart of decorative fountains. Calculate total flow rate and pressure requirement to select pump.

Filtration system removes sediment, leaves, papers. Heating and chemical systems, if used, are incorporated into the filtration system.

Underwater lights

Use corrosion resistant materials (brass, bronze, stainless steel, or monel) and ground fault circuit interrupters to prevent shocks.

Economical lamp types are 2000 hr PAR incandescent, 4000 hr tungsten-halogen, and, 8000 hr locomotive or traffic signal incandescent.

MATERIALS

Concrete and masonry

Foundations

These must be constructed on well-compacted ground as in the case of flexible construction. In some cases, such as with concrete, a granular sub-base of hardcore, crushed stone or DoT 'type one' may be required. This is even more important with rigid construction as this has no inherent 'give' should settlement resulting from consolidation occur. The beds of all pools should be constructed with falls to a drainage outlet.

Concrete

Concrete liners are cheaper than Bentonite clays and easier to construct than puddled clay. They are very durable assuming that no cracking occurs; however, the construction is more difficult and requires more specialist knowledge. Where larger waterbodies are required reinforcement is necessary.

Construction of concrete pool linings is similar in principle to rigid pavement construction. The thickness of concrete for small garden pools (up to say 3×3 m^2 and 600 mm deep) should not be less than 150 mm on well-compacted granular soils and around 225 mm on cohesive soils which are likely to settle (where the settlement risk is high then reinforcement should be used). A slip membrane should be included beneath the concrete to allow for differential movement if the edge detailing of the membrane is suitable. It will double in function to provide waterproofing for the concrete.

Proper compaction and an appropriate mix are essential to ensure the concrete will be watertight. Joints between slabs poured at one go should be sealed with a cast-in water bar.

Reinforced concrete structures

'Structural concrete which is designed to resist cracking and is made from dense concrete cast in thick enough sections will be virtually impermeable to the flow of water, even under pressure' (Shirley, 1980). Nevertheless concrete-lined pools and lakes often have a polyethylene liner beneath the slab to prevent outward seepage through the base and sides, as well as the possible ingress of groundwater. Some concrete pools are waterproofed with a 'tanking' membrane).

For all but the most modest of reinforced concrete structures the advice of a structural engineer should be sought (see also BS 5337: 1976). The thickness of bed and walls will depend on the size of the structure and the ground conditions, which will in turn determine the amount of reinforcement required. As a rule of thumb the minimum thickness of the base is likely to be 150 mm while 200 mm is generally an adequate wall thickness. The base of the structure will be cast separately from the walls and in order to ensure the joint between the two is waterproof, a flexible 'water bar' is cast into the base to seal the gap.

Sprayed concrete liners

This technique allows irregularly shaped pools to be created without the use of expensive formwork. Excavation is carried out to the desired formation and the sub-base is compacted. A 30 to 40 mm layer of concrete is placed on this and then steel reinforcing mesh is laid on top. Concrete containing a waterproofing additive is then sprayed onto the mesh.

Masonry structures

For small garden-sized pools, especially where curved plan forms are required, the walls can be constructed as masonry retaining walls, while the base can be either a concrete slab or some kind of flexible liner (see 'Hybrid construction'). As in the case of earth-retaining walls, it is necessary to provide a waterproof coating at the back to prevent groundwater pressure building up from outside the pool.

'Waterproof' render – 1:3 cement render with waterproofing additive – can be used for small 'garden' scale pools constructed of masonry; however, hairline cracks developing in the render will let water leak out. Water-repelling admixtures are sometimes used where a thin cross-section of cement-based material is required to provide a water-repellant layer. (The usual chemical used is calcium stearate, a metallic soap, supplied in powder form.)

Hybrids of rigid and flexible construction

The two forms of construction of informal pools using flexible liners and ornamental pools using rigid construction are by no means mutually exclusive. They can be freely combined, either within the 'cross-section' of one pool, e.g. the combination of a flexible liner with a concrete or masonry edge wall – and/or in 'plan' – where a change of edge detail between 'soft-informal' and 'hard-formal' can take place around the perimeter of one pool/pond.

Tanking

Tanking involves the complete bonding of

rolls of waterproofing membrane to the surface of a concrete slab using a hot bituminous or similar adhesive. This is a technique used for the waterproofing of flat roofs and is sometimes found in small ornamental pools. This is a relatively expensive technique requiring specialist skilled labour, and special attention must be paid to detailing construction and expansion joints. The exposed horizontal surface of the membrane on the bed of the pool is often protected against mechanical damage with a concrete screed; however, there are problems in applying this to the vertical walls of pools. Base and walls should be waterproofed from the outside to prevent a build-up of water under pressure between the tanking and the structure of the pool.

Preformed rigid pool liners

Preformed glassfibre pools

These are the most commonly used in garden situations, but are only available in small sizes and predetermined shapes. They are relatively robust and resistant to the effect of frost and ice, although expensive compared to flexible liners. Pools should be bedded evenly on 25–50 mm of sand blinding on well-compacted ground from which all sharp stones and objects have been removed. It is important that pools are installed level! Attention must be paid to ensuring that the sides and any shelves are evenly supported by backfilling with care. On permeable soils the best way to achieve this may be by watering-in sand or other suitable backfill material. The edges will need to be covered with paving or turf.

Fibreglass construction can also be used for building irregularly shaped pools in situ.

CONSTRUCTION

Liner

One of the great difficulties of using a liner for a formal pond or pool is the difficult task of ensuring a clean and precise excavation.

Also using the liner alone could involve a considerable number of folds and pleats into the corners so that none are visible. It is not impossible but considerable care is required to ensure the liner is not punctured. After excavation, make the base and sides of firmly compacted soil or sand; the ground must be smooth. Place old carpet or underlay to protect the liner and form a ridge of mortar around the rim. Put the liner in place, smooth the bottom and sides, fold in the corners and bring it up over the rim and fix with further mortar. Bed a capping of stone or precast concrete slab on top to form a surround.

Alternatively the liner can be custom made to fit the excavated area precisely.

Liner inside the surrounding walls

If a retaining wall is built around the perimeter of the pond then liners can be used inside the wall. Fill the gap between the wall and the ground with concrete. Ensure that the base is well compacted, covered with sand, followed by an underlay. Lay the liner on top and bring both the underlay and the liner up smoothly over the walls. Fold the corners carefully to ensure a neat fit, then bed the capping securely in a good mortar bed.

Liner behind surrounding walls

This method requires the liner to be laid after the wall footing has been constructed. Bring the liner, sandwiched between layers of underlay, up the sides of the excavated ground and have it held in place temporarily. Build the retaining walls of the chosen material (within the liner) on top of the footing. When the wall has become firm bring the lining materials up over the top of the wall, backfill with concrete and complete the construction with a capping block bedded in mortar.

Semi-raised ponds

There are several advantages of having a pond raised above the ground. They entail less excavation, it is safer for children, easier to keep clean as leaves do not blow in, and also easier to empty. For disabled people they will be able to have better access and contact with the water feature. In fact a raised pond can provide an ideal focal point for people to gather around and sit on the sides of the pond.

One disadvantage is that a raised pond is subject to greater temperature fluctuations – warmer in summer and colder in winter.

The construction method using a liner is the same as given previously, ensuring that the retaining wall is built up from the base to the finished level for strength. Bring the water level up to the underneath of the capping block or stone. The thickness of the wall should not be less than 225 mm (9 inches) and in certain climates where severe frost is experienced it will need to be thicker or reinforced. The outer exposed part of the wall could be constructed of a more aesthetically pleasing material such as natural stone or brick.

'Hard' edge detailing for ornamental pools

Formal pools usually have vertical walls finished with a coping or capping of some sort. The main constructional consideration is the detailing of the edge of the waterproofing membrane, finishing the tanking or the waterproof render. Precautions must also be taken to prevent possible damage to the waterproofing from ice forming on the pool in winter.

The detailing of such 'hybrid' waterbodies is slightly more complicated to the extent that thought needs to be given to the junction of the two forms of construction to ensure that it will be both watertight as well as able to accommodate any movement which may occur due to settlement.

Junctions between puddled clay and a concrete or masonry edge wall are likely to prove particularly difficult as only a small crack between the two will be enough to allow leakage to take place.

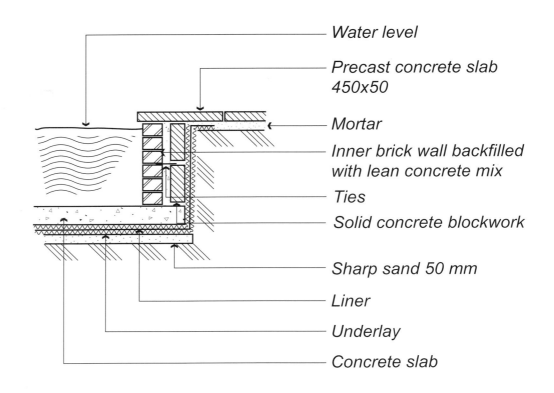

Water level

Precast concrete slab
450x50

Mortar

Inner brick wall backfilled
with lean concrete mix

Ties

Solid concrete blockwork

Sharp sand 50 mm

Liner

Underlay

Concrete slab

SECTION

Scale 1:20

POND CONSTRUCTION
Liner/bricks

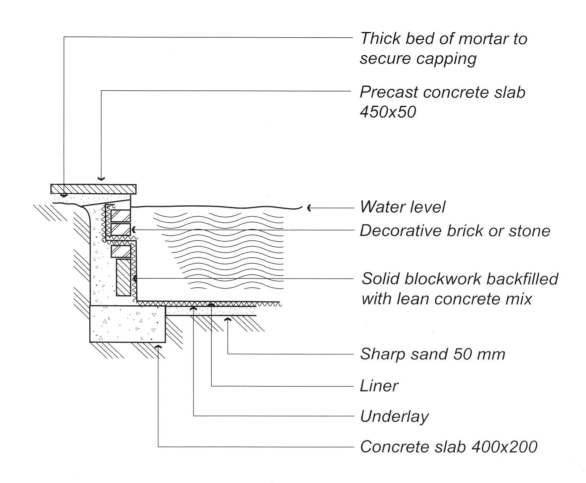

Thick bed of mortar to
secure capping

Precast concrete slab
450x50

Water level

Decorative brick or stone

Solid blockwork backfilled
with lean concrete mix

Sharp sand 50 mm

Liner

Underlay

Concrete slab 400x200

SECTION   **Scale 1:20**

POND CONSTRUCTION
Liner/block/brick

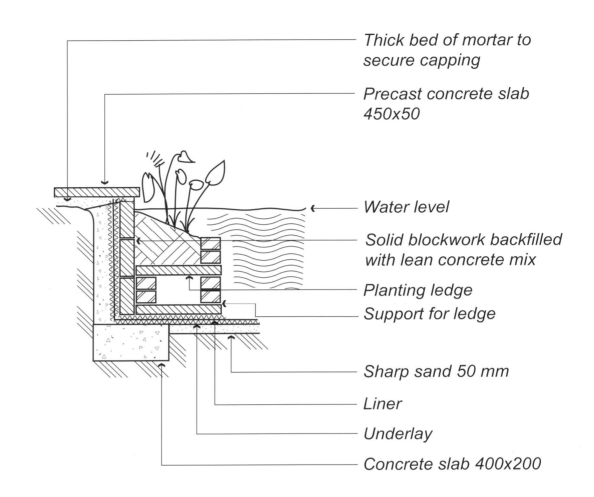

Thick bed of mortar to secure capping

Precast concrete slab 450x50

Water level

Solid blockwork backfilled with lean concrete mix

Planting ledge

Support for ledge

Sharp sand 50 mm

Liner

Underlay

Concrete slab 400x200

SECTION

Scale 1:20

POND CONSTRUCTION
Liner/block

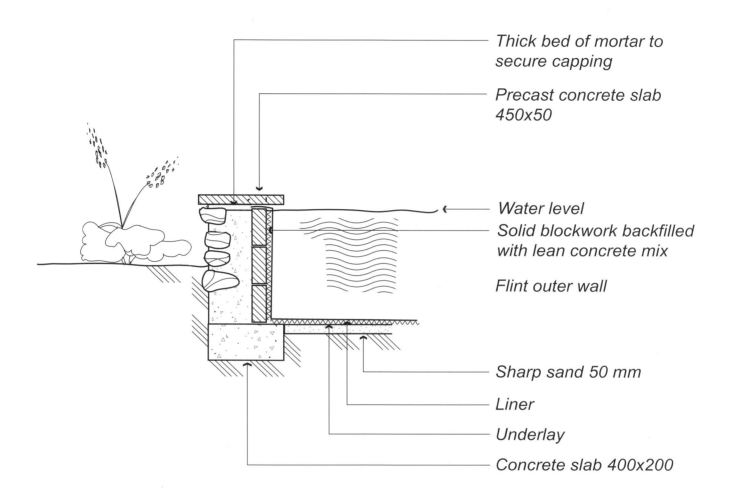

Thick bed of mortar to
secure capping

Precast concrete slab
450x50

Water level

Solid blockwork backfilled
with lean concrete mix

Flint outer wall

Sharp sand 50 mm

Liner

Underlay

Concrete slab 400x200

SECTION

Scale 1:20

POND CONSTRUCTION
Liner/semi-raised block

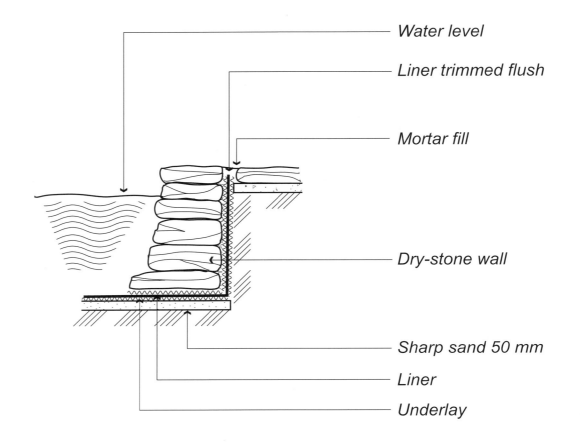

Water level

Liner trimmed flush

Mortar fill

Dry-stone wall

Sharp sand 50 mm

Liner

Underlay

SECTION

Scale 1:20

POND CONSTRUCTION
Liner/stone

40

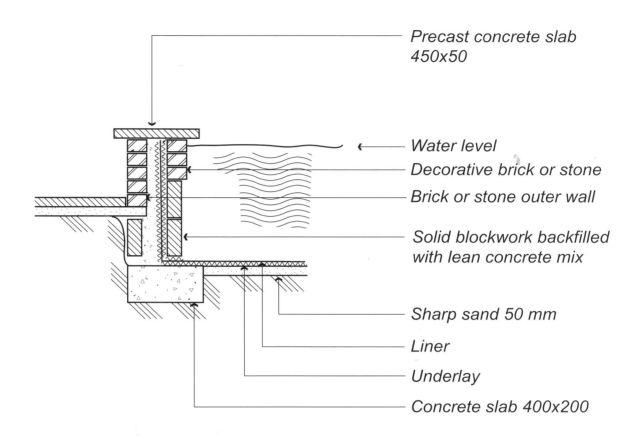

Precast concrete slab 450x50

Water level

Decorative brick or stone

Brick or stone outer wall

Solid blockwork backfilled with lean concrete mix

Sharp sand 50 mm

Liner

Underlay

Concrete slab 400x200

SECTION

Scale 1:20

POND CONSTRUCTION
Liner/semi-raised brick

41

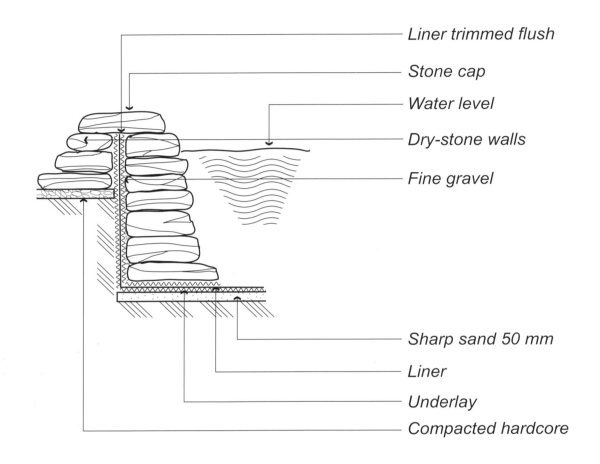

Liner trimmed flush

Stone cap

Water level

Dry-stone walls

Fine gravel

Sharp sand 50 mm

Liner

Underlay

Compacted hardcore

SECTION

Scale 1:20

POND CONSTRUCTION
Liner/semi-raised stone

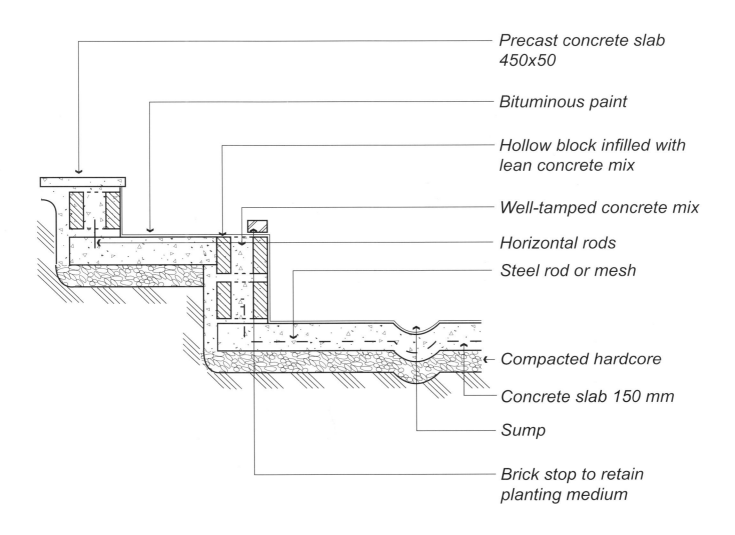

Precast concrete slab 450x50

Bituminous paint

Hollow block infilled with lean concrete mix

Well-tamped concrete mix

Horizontal rods

Steel rod or mesh

Compacted hardcore

Concrete slab 150 mm

Sump

Brick stop to retain planting medium

SECTION   **Scale 1:20**

POND CONSTRUCTION
Concrete/hollow blocks

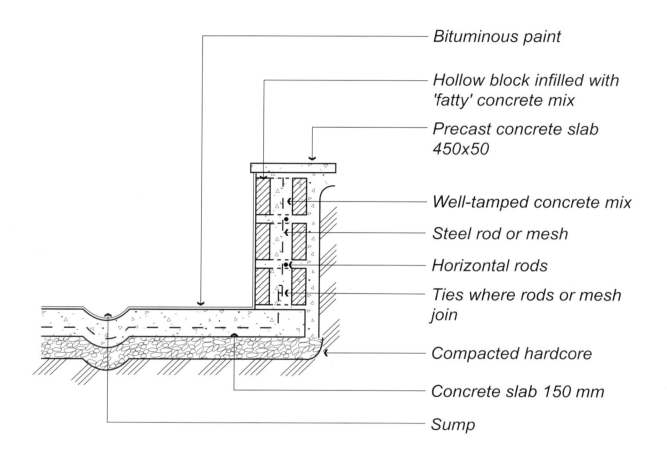

Bituminous paint

Hollow block infilled with 'fatty' concrete mix

Precast concrete slab 450x50

Well-tamped concrete mix

Steel rod or mesh

Horizontal rods

Ties where rods or mesh join

Compacted hardcore

Concrete slab 150 mm

Sump

SECTION

Scale 1:20

POND CONSTRUCTION
Concrete/hollow blocks

44

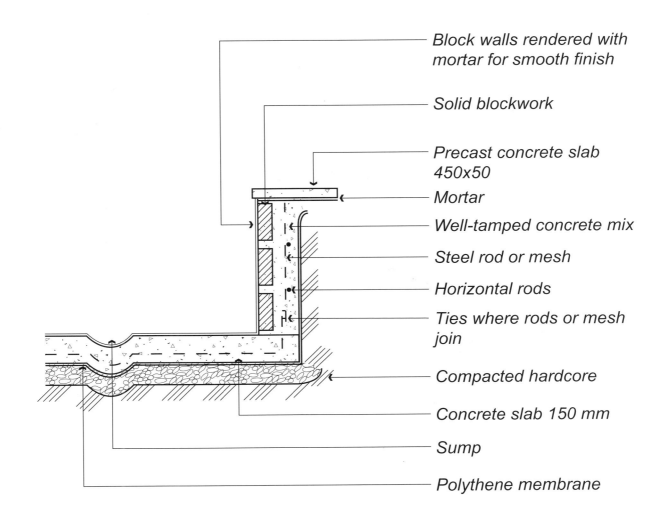

Block walls rendered with mortar for smooth finish

Solid blockwork

Precast concrete slab 450x50

Mortar

Well-tamped concrete mix

Steel rod or mesh

Horizontal rods

Ties where rods or mesh join

Compacted hardcore

Concrete slab 150 mm

Sump

Polythene membrane

SECTION

Scale 1:20

POND CONSTRUCTION
Concrete/block/reinforced

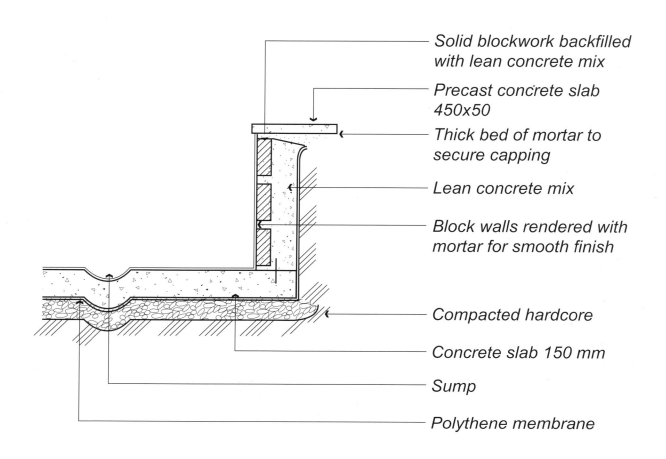

Solid blockwork backfilled with lean concrete mix

Precast concrete slab 450x50

Thick bed of mortar to secure capping

Lean concrete mix

Block walls rendered with mortar for smooth finish

Compacted hardcore

Concrete slab 150 mm

Sump

Polythene membrane

SECTION

Scale 1:20

POND CONSTRUCTION
Concrete/solid block

46

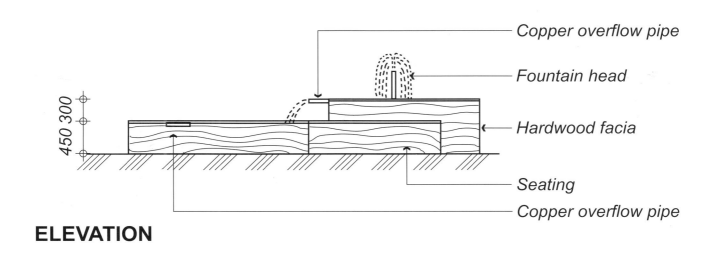

ELEVATION

Copper overflow pipe

Fountain head

Hardwood facia

Seating

Copper overflow pipe

450 300

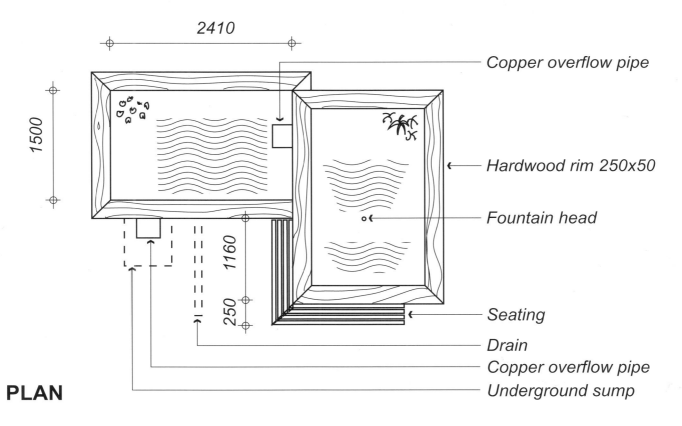

2410

1500

1160

250

Copper overflow pipe

Hardwood rim 250x50

Fountain head

Seating

Drain

Copper overflow pipe

Underground sump

PLAN

Scale 1:20

POND CONSTRUCTION
Concrete – raised (1)

47

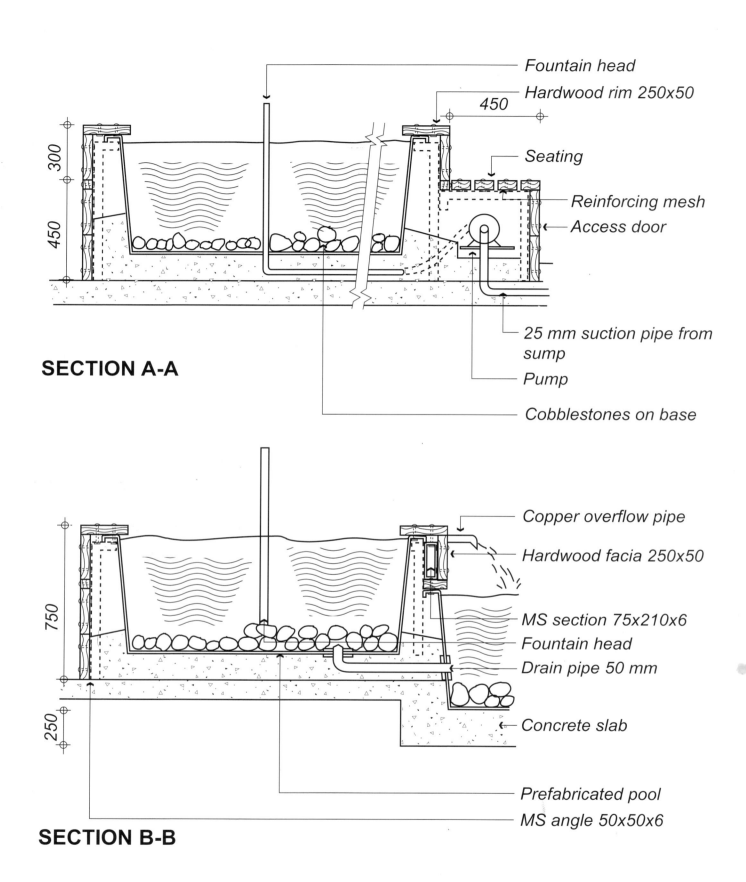

SECTION A-A

Fountain head

Hardwood rim 250x50

450

Seating

Reinforcing mesh

Access door

300

450

25 mm suction pipe from sump

Pump

Cobblestones on base

SECTION B-B

Copper overflow pipe

Hardwood facia 250x50

MS section 75x210x6

Fountain head

Drain pipe 50 mm

Concrete slab

750

250

Prefabricated pool

MS angle 50x50x6

Scale 1:20

POND CONSTRUCTION
Concrete – raised (2)

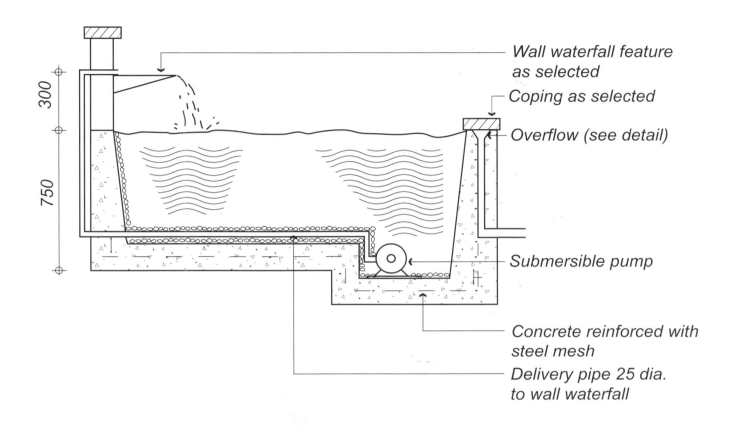

300

750

Wall waterfall feature
as selected

Coping as selected

Overflow (see detail)

Submersible pump

Concrete reinforced with
steel mesh

Delivery pipe 25 dia.
to wall waterfall

SECTION

Scale 1:20

POND CONSTRUCTION
Concrete – rectangular

49

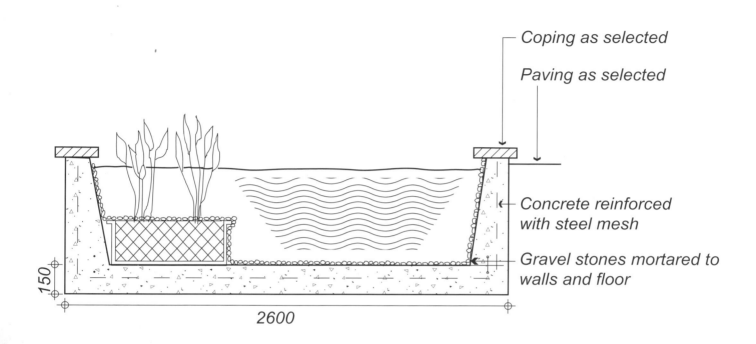

Coping as selected

Paving as selected

Concrete reinforced with steel mesh

Gravel stones mortared to walls and floor

150

2600

SECTION

Scale 1:20

POND CONSTRUCTION
Concrete

50

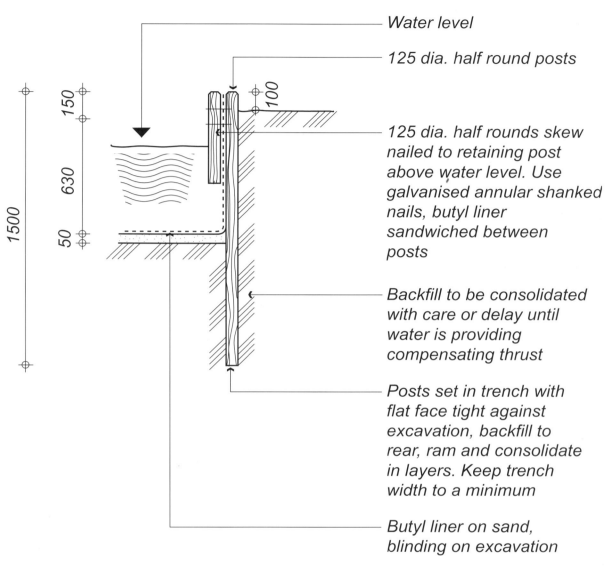

Water level

125 dia. half round posts

125 dia. half rounds skew nailed to retaining post above water level. Use galvanised annular shanked nails, butyl liner sandwiched between posts

Backfill to be consolidated with care or delay until water is providing compensating thrust

Posts set in trench with flat face tight against excavation, backfill to rear, ram and consolidate in layers. Keep trench width to a minimum

Butyl liner on sand, blinding on excavation

150

630

50

1500

100

SECTION

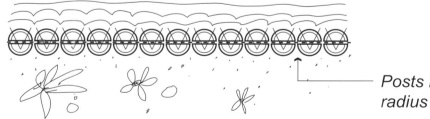

Posts laid to line or to radius

PLAN

Scale 1:20

POND CONSTRUCTION
Formal – timber

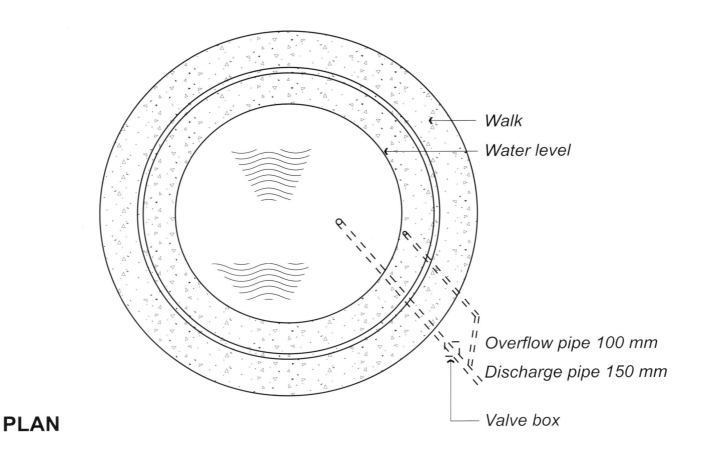

PLAN

Walk

Water level

Overflow pipe 100 mm

Discharge pipe 150 mm

Valve box

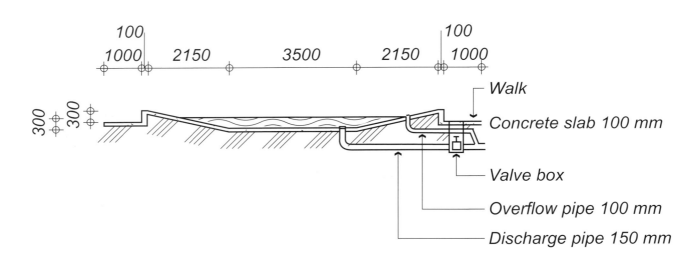

100
1000   2150   3500   2150   100
1000

300   300

Walk

Concrete slab 100 mm

Valve box

Overflow pipe 100 mm

Discharge pipe 150 mm

SECTION   **Scale 1:100**

POND CONSTRUCTION
Wading – circular

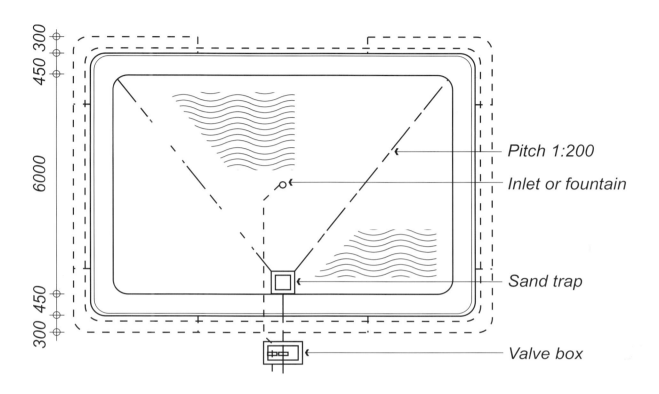

450 300

6000

300 450

Pitch 1:200

Inlet or fountain

Sand trap

Valve box

PLAN

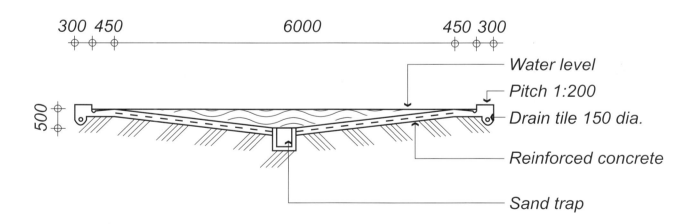

| 300 450 | 6000 | 450 300 |

Water level

Pitch 1:200

Drain tile 150 dia.

Reinforced concrete

Sand trap

500

SECTION   **Scale 1:100**

POND CONSTRUCTION
Wading – rectangular

53

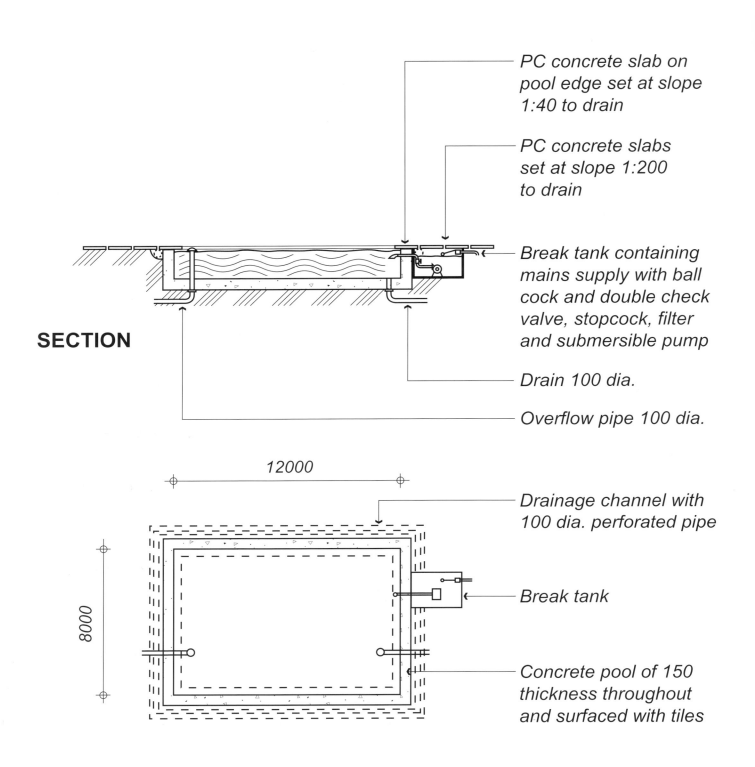

SECTION

PC concrete slab on pool edge set at slope 1:40 to drain

PC concrete slabs set at slope 1:200 to drain

Break tank containing mains supply with ball cock and double check valve, stopcock, filter and submersible pump

Drain 100 dia.

Overflow pipe 100 dia.

12000

8000

Drainage channel with 100 dia. perforated pipe

Break tank

Concrete pool of 150 thickness throughout and surfaced with tiles

PLAN

Scale 1:50

POND CONSTRUCTION
Reflecting

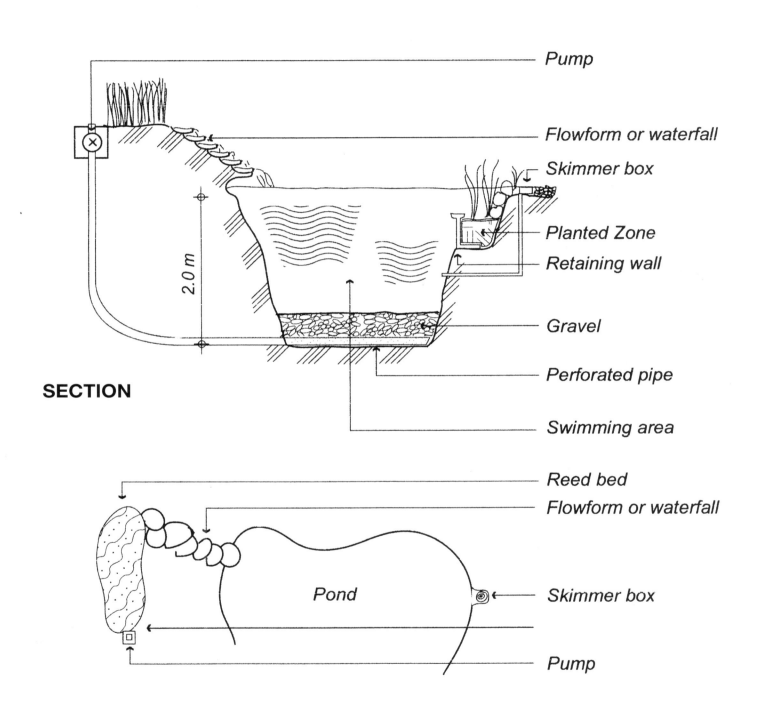

Pump

Flowform or waterfall

Skimmer box

Planted Zone

Retaining wall

Gravel

Perforated pipe

Swimming area

2.0 m

SECTION

Reed bed

Flowform or waterfall

Pond

Skimmer box

Pump

PLAN

Scale 1:50

POND CONSTRUCTION
Natural Swimming

55

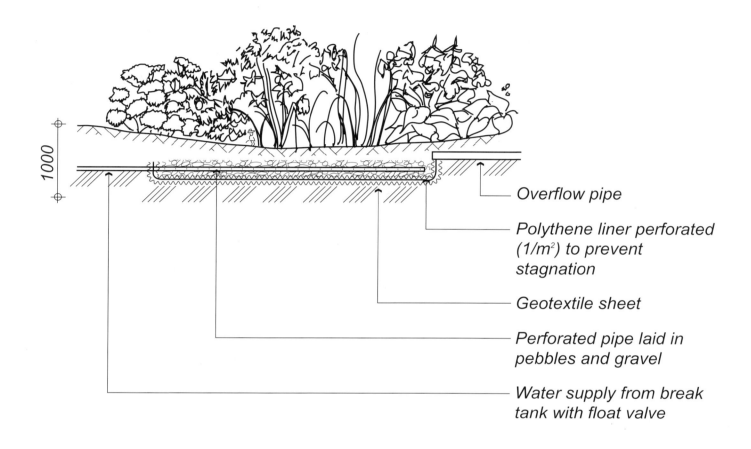

1000

Overflow pipe

Polythene liner perforated ($1/m^2$) to prevent stagnation

Geotextile sheet

Perforated pipe laid in pebbles and gravel

Water supply from break tank with float valve

SECTION

Scale 1:50

POND CONSTRUCTION
Bog area

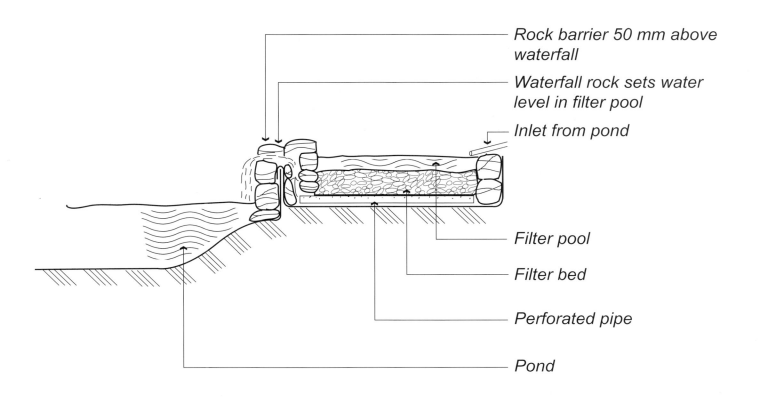

Rock barrier 50 mm above
waterfall

Waterfall rock sets water
level in filter pool

Inlet from pond

Filter pool

Filter bed

Perforated pipe

Pond

SECTION   **Scale 1:50**

POND
Rock filter

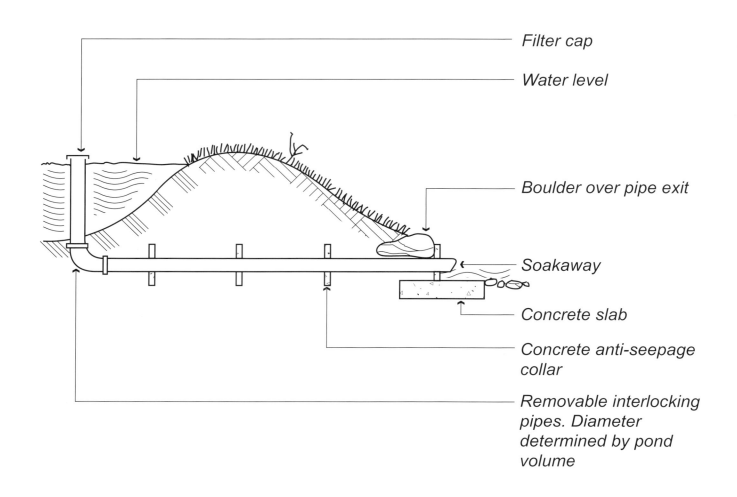

Filter cap

Water level

Boulder over pipe exit

Soakaway

Concrete slab

Concrete anti-seepage collar

Removable interlocking pipes. Diameter determined by pond volume

SECTION   **Scale 1:50**

POND
Overflow

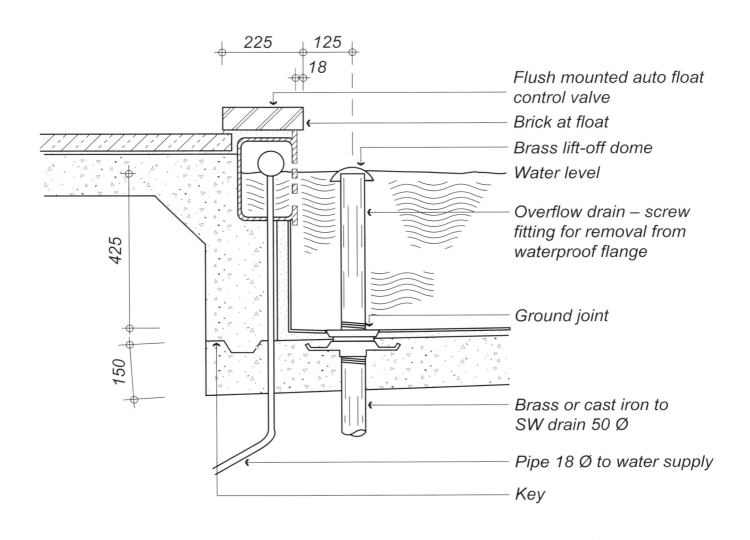

225   125

18

Flush mounted auto float
control valve

Brick at float

Brass lift-off dome

Water level

Overflow drain – screw
fitting for removal from
waterproof flange

Ground joint

425

150

Brass or cast iron to
SW drain 50 Ø

Pipe 18 Ø to water supply

Key

SECTION   **Scale 1:10**

POND
Overflow

59

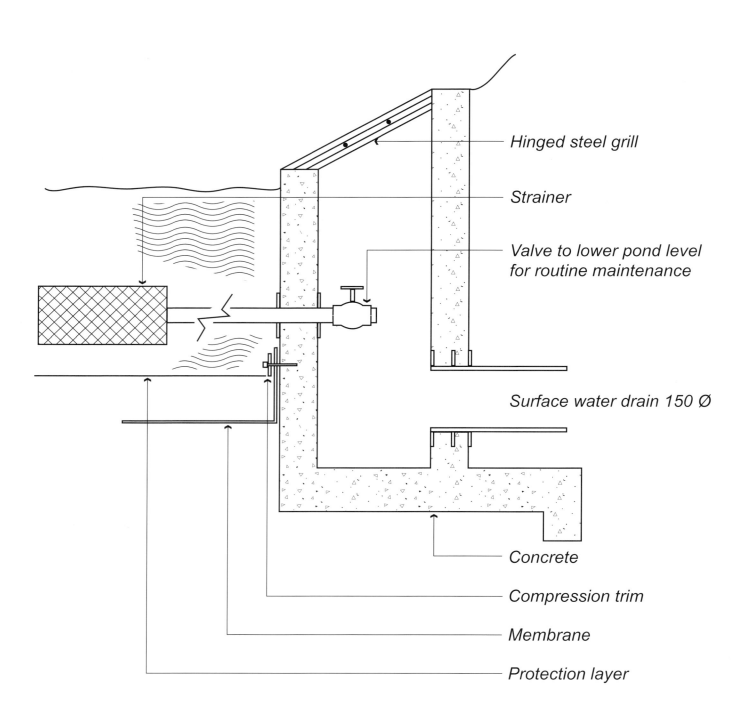

Hinged steel grill

Strainer

Valve to lower pond level
for routine maintenance

Surface water drain 150 Ø

Concrete

Compression trim

Membrane

Protection layer

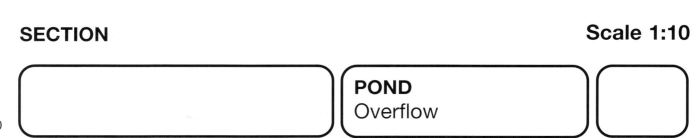

SECTION   **Scale 1:10**

POND
Overflow

60

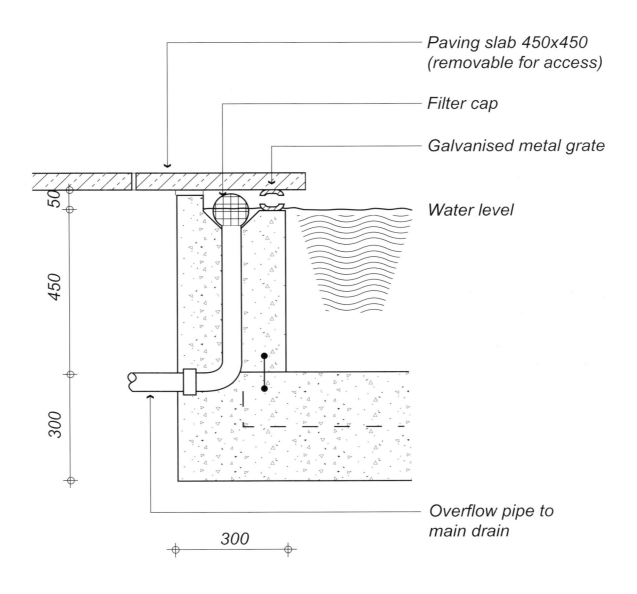

Paving slab 450x450
(removable for access)

Filter cap

Galvanised metal grate

Water level

50

450

300

Overflow pipe to
main drain

300

SECTION

Scale 1:10

POND
Overflow – concealed (1)

61

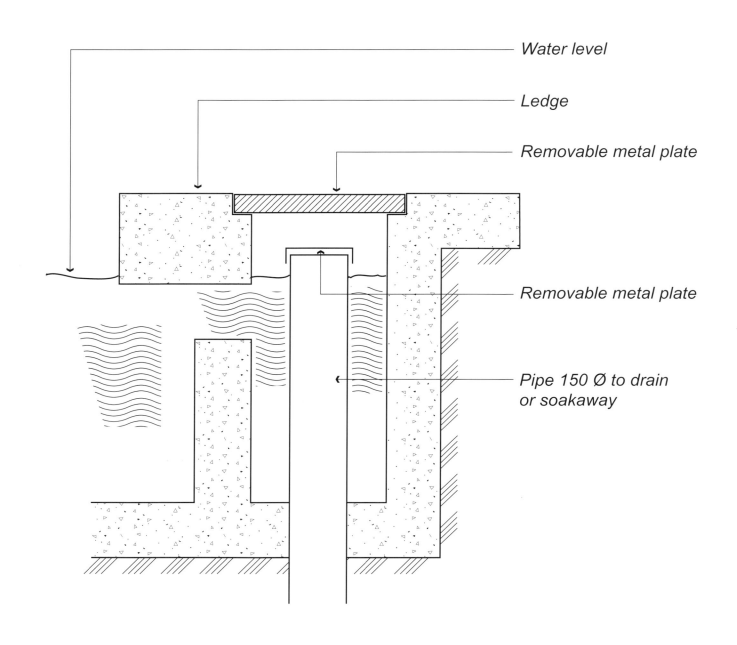

Water level

Ledge

Removable metal plate

Removable metal plate

Pipe 150 Ø to drain or soakaway

SECTION
Scale 1:10

POND
Overflow – concealed (2)

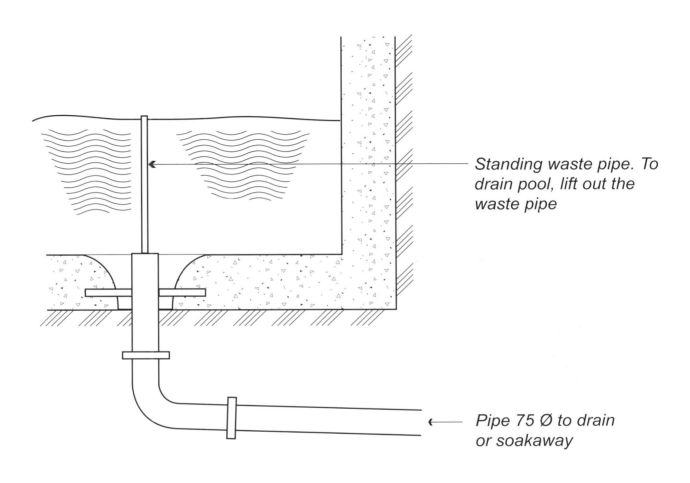

Standing waste pipe. To drain pool, lift out the waste pipe

Pipe 75 Ø to drain or soakaway

SECTION

Scale 1:10

POND
Overflow – concealed (3)

63

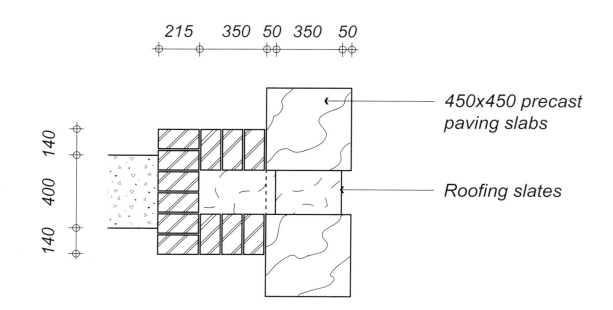

215　350　50　350　50

140　140
400
140

450x450 precast
paving slabs

Roofing slates

PLAN

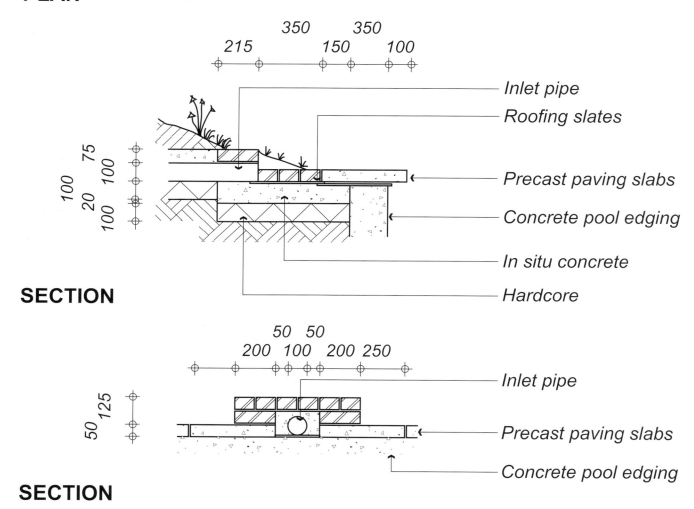

350　350
215　150　100

100　75
20　100
100

Inlet pipe

Roofing slates

Precast paving slabs

Concrete pool edging

In situ concrete

Hardcore

SECTION

50　50
200　100　200　250

50　125

Inlet pipe

Precast paving slabs

Concrete pool edging

SECTION

Scale 1:20

POOL
Inlet detail

64

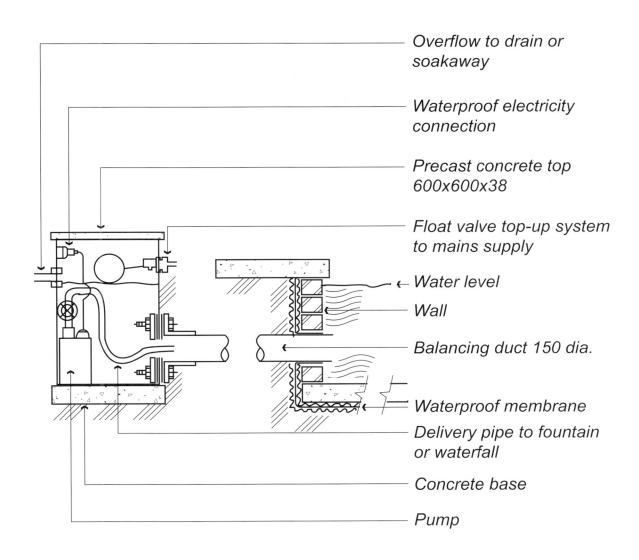

Overflow to drain or soakaway

Waterproof electricity connection

Precast concrete top 600x600x38

Float valve top-up system to mains supply

← Water level

Wall

Balancing duct 150 dia.

Waterproof membrane

Delivery pipe to fountain or waterfall

Concrete base

Pump

SECTION

Scale 1:20

POND
External pump chamber

65

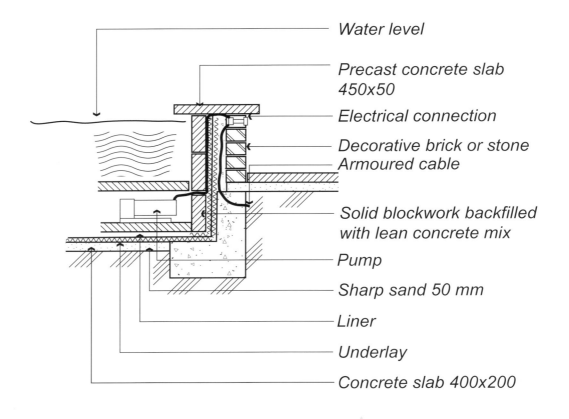

Water level

Precast concrete slab
450x50

Electrical connection

Decorative brick or stone
Armoured cable

Solid blockwork backfilled
with lean concrete mix

Pump

Sharp sand 50 mm

Liner

Underlay

Concrete slab 400x200

SECTION   **Scale 1:20**

POOL
Pump – concealed

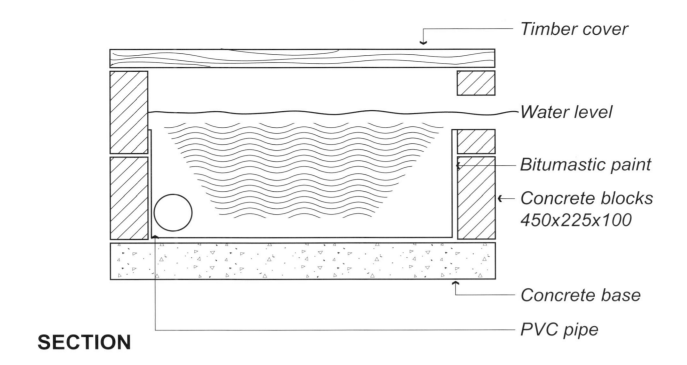

Timber cover

Water level

Bitumastic paint

Concrete blocks
450x225x100

Concrete base

PVC pipe

SECTION

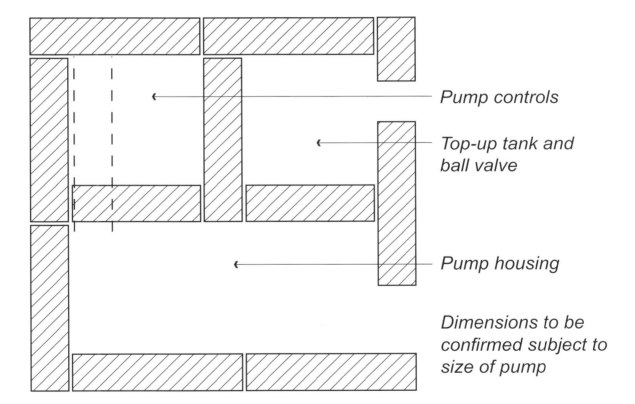

Pump controls

Top-up tank and
ball valve

Pump housing

Dimensions to be
confirmed subject to
size of pump

PLAN

Scale 1:10

POND
Pump chamber

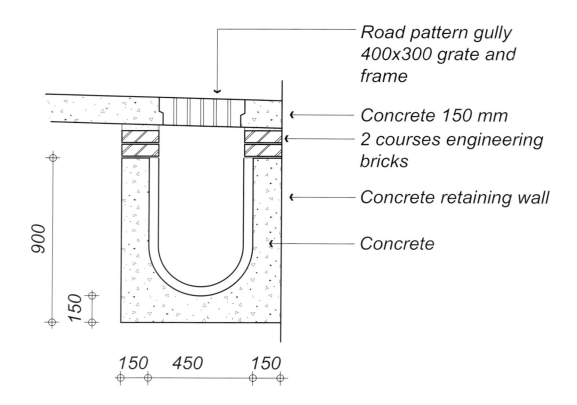

Road pattern gully
400x300 grate and
frame

Concrete 150 mm

2 courses engineering
bricks

Concrete retaining wall

Concrete

900

150

150   450   150

SECTION

Scale 1:20

POND
Cleaning channel

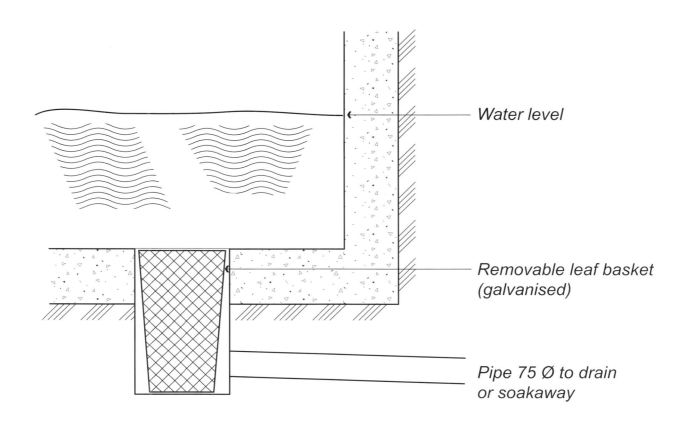

Water level

Removable leaf basket
(galvanised)

Pipe 75 Ø to drain
or soakaway

SECTION **Scale 1:10**

POND
Leaf removal

69

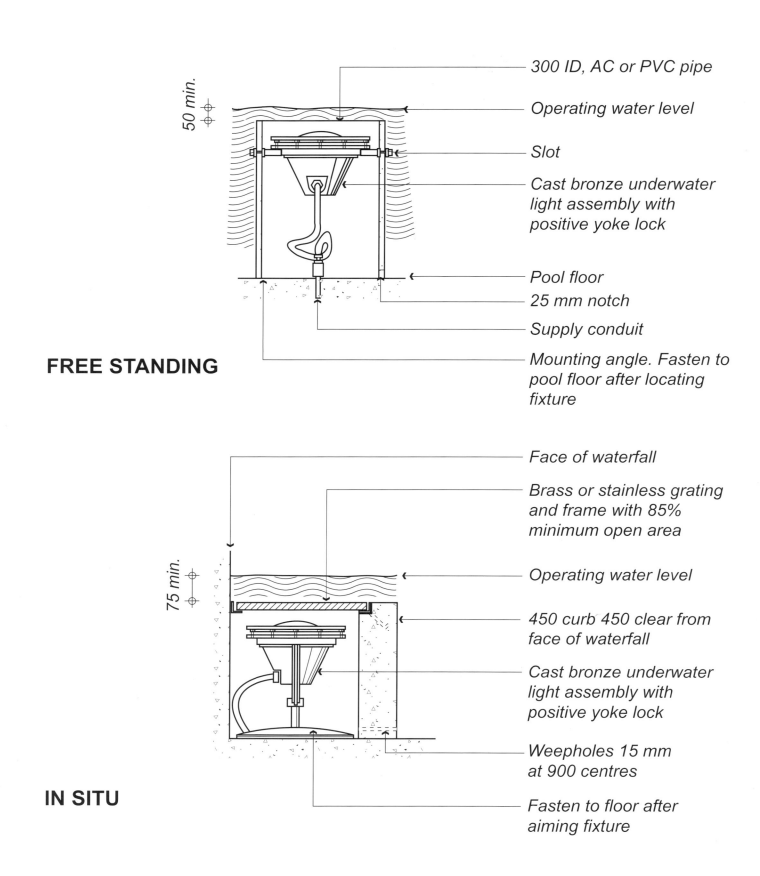

FREE STANDING

- 300 ID, AC or PVC pipe
- Operating water level
- Slot
- Cast bronze underwater light assembly with positive yoke lock
- Pool floor
- 25 mm notch
- Supply conduit
- Mounting angle. Fasten to pool floor after locating fixture

50 min.

IN SITU

- Face of waterfall
- Brass or stainless grating and frame with 85% minimum open area
- Operating water level
- 450 curb 450 clear from face of waterfall
- Cast bronze underwater light assembly with positive yoke lock
- Weepholes 15 mm at 900 centres
- Fasten to floor after aiming fixture

75 min.

Scale 1:10

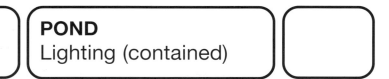

POND
Lighting (contained)

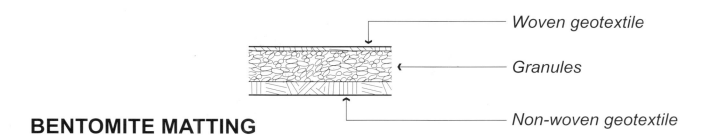

BENTOMITE MATTING

Woven geotextile

Granules

Non-woven geotextile

JOINING LAYERS

JOINING BENTOMAT
Overlap layers of
Bentomat and spread
granules of Bentomite
between the layers and
press layers firmly
together. Granules will
swell when wet providing
a watertight seal

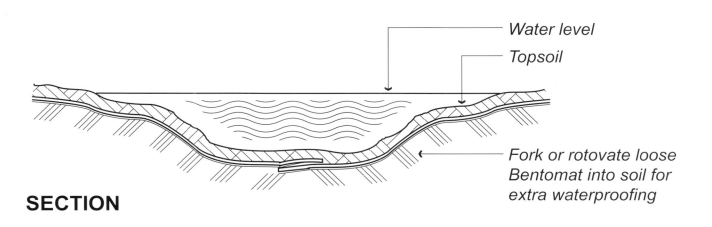

SECTION

Water level

Topsoil

Fork or rotovate loose
Bentomat into soil for
extra waterproofing

LAYING PROCEDURE

LAYING BENTOMAT
Spread the Bentomat
over the surface of the
pond and up the sides.
Firm down and cover
with a layer of topsoil

POND CONSTRUCTION
Bentomite

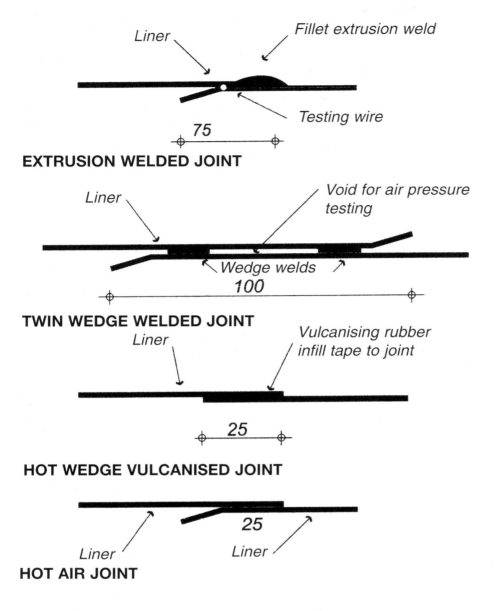

EXTRUSION WELDED JOINT

Liner

Fillet extrusion weld

Testing wire

75

TWIN WEDGE WELDED JOINT

Liner

Void for air pressure testing

Wedge welds

100

HOT WEDGE VULCANISED JOINT

Liner

Vulcanising rubber infill tape to joint

25

HOT AIR JOINT

Liner

Liner

25

The principal types of welding for flexible liners

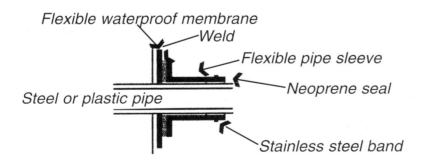

Flexible waterproof membrane

Weld

Flexible pipe sleeve

Neoprene seal

Steel or plastic pipe

Stainless steel band

Detail of a membrane and pipe connection, where the pipe passes through the connection

Panel joining
For plastic liners, the 'heated split wedge open channel' process or 'extrusion welding' is used. For rubber lining, the 'hot wedge vulanising system' is employed.

Testing
The non-detructive test of each weld should be carried out by trained operators. The test procedures are:

- *split wedge open channel joint should be air-pressure tested;*
- *extrusion joints are tested by the copper wire/spark test method;*
- *vulcanised joints are air lanced or vaccum box tested*

Climatic conditions
No welding of panel joints should be carried out where temperatures are below 4°C or above 30°C, or in damp conditions of any kind. Sheet laying can become dangerous when wind speeds exceed 10 kmp.

Scale N/A

FLEXIBLE LINERS
Jronting...

FLEXIBLE LINERS
Jointing

STREAMS AND WATERFALLS

Informal/Formal structures

Water moves in various ways – even a pond that has no perceived outlet or inlet has movement, caused by rainfall and wind, overflowing at some low point around the edge. Rivers and streams in the landscape have their own natural movement and although there is, at times, a need for changes to be made for various purposes, it is better to leave well alone if at all possible. If not then the work should be executed with sensitivity to nature and the local character.

Likewise, with man-made watercourses which are intended to be informal and natural. It is important to ensure that they are correct both in their appearance as well as in their formation, for the selected location. Too often features are added which are unnecessary. The character of a stream depends upon the setting through which it will flow and its creation will be a matter of trial and error. Water will always take the line of least resistance, going round or over solid objects, with falls and weirs making the flow change its speed and sound.

A study of the large Japanese landscaped gardens will reveal the sensitivity with which their schemes have been treated to ensure that they do not look contrived will reward the designer.

Many landscape and garden projects involving the use of moving water and associated elements have failed due to the unconsidered scale and proportion. Water features in a business park should be quite different from those in a garden through the use of these two main design principles. The alignment of the stream watercourse and the inclusion of elements such as boulders, rocks, etc. should follow the same design principles of scale and proportion.

The design of a stream should be planned out roughly on paper and there should always be some different aspects included. There could be the variation in height and number of waterfalls, broken or jagged water flows, or a widening of the stream at certain locations with gravel/cobble areas or even an island if the stream was wide enough.

A stream must have a fall and the amount is determined by the topography of the site (original or created). Normally a stream is constructed on a slope as a series of level sections and the fall in ground level is taken up with waterfalls or weirs. These will control the water levels, reducing sudden fluctuations in natural streams and ensuring, in artificial streams, that the water level is constant after the recirculating system has been stopped.

A stream can be built that meanders through a level garden or landscape, depending upon the volume of water (whether natural or recirculated by a pump), its flow rate and the fall of the stream bed.

Natural streams usually flow in valleys. For the creation of an artificial stream it will be very important to ensure that any ground shaping is executed with this in mind. Soil used from excavations should be graded well back from the stream edge so that a gentle slope runs down towards the water. Other elements, such as trees, rocks and boulders, should be taken into consideration for the overall design. They can assist in making the route of the stream far more forceful and meaningful. It is also important to vary the width, as this will ensure greater interest and diversity.

Waterfalls

Where the stream narrows, waterfalls or weirs can be built and it can then widen into small pools between the falls.

Waterfalls or weirs can be constructed across natural waterways, maybe to impound water for the creation of a lake or a pond, or even to reduce the flow rate and thereby raising the water level. This should provide more scope for diversity in bank treatment and planting.

A waterfall in a garden setting should not be too high as it is difficult to make it look natural – depending on the landform of the site. It will be necessary to circulate a very large volume of water. There are as many types of waterfalls as there are ways of arranging rocks. The height of the fall and the type of rocks used below it will affect the sound. If it is very high it could be too noisy, cause too much splashing and lose water too quickly.

A constant facility for topping up the water supply may be necessary.

The building of a waterfall without mortar being applied to the rocks, except where it is necessary, will ensure that the effect looks as natural as possible.

By varying the shapes of rocks or boulders and the way spillways are formed it is possible to achieve a series of waterfalls of great variety and interest at all times. The artistic flair of the designer will be paramount.

Pumps

It is important to remember that natural streams bring down silt and other materials when in spate and that the force of water going over a fall creates a deeper pool, pushing gravels further downstream, which in time could cause an island or a blockage. An artificial stream will use a pump (surface or submersible) to recirculate the water and in order to do this it will require a large reservoir at the bottom end. This should be in the form of a pond and to prevent a significant drop in level when the pump is switched on, the surface area should be as great as the entire surface of the stream. For example, a stream 70 m long by an average of 700 mm wide would require a pond approximately 49 m^2 or 7 x 7 m (approx. 400 ft^2). Allowance should also be made for loss of water by evaporation, capillary action or leakage. In certain circumstances, e.g. where the bottom pond cannot be as large as described, then the water may have to be topped up. Once the pump is switched off, the stream will continue to flow down until it has reached its static level, with the consequence that the bottom pond could overflow unless allowance has been made for the water in the design.

CONSTRUCTION

As streams need to be on sloping ground they are, in effect, a series of separate, long, narrow ponds and so the excavation and construction is similar to that of informal ponds and pools. The main difference is the change of levels.

Excavation of the ground will require the operator of any machinery to have a clear understanding of the design and the sensitivity to ensure that it is implemented correctly. The shape of the excavation will depend upon the character required for the stream. Allowance must be made for the inclusion of boulders and rocks both on the sides of the stream and where there is a change of levels for the creation of waterfalls.

The majority of informally constructed streams will use butyl liner on an underlay with a concrete base covering both. The concrete is shaped to the profile required and allowance made for rocks and boulders to be set inside the stream profile. Digging out for these should be undertaken prior to their placement and it is essential that the ground is well compacted, not only for these elements but the whole stream. Any hardcore used for filling should be covered with sand to ensure that there are no sharp projections. Begin the lining at the lowest section of the stream bed using the protective liner over the sand. Carefully

construct any waterfalls before positioning the liner and it is important to ensure that the liner sections are securely joined at these junctions in the stream.

A concrete bed will be required for support of any rocks and boulders – its thickness will depend upon their weight. In certain situations the concrete may need to be reinforced.

Grouting of all the waterfall rocks should be undertaken when they are in their final position, using a waterproof mix of sand and cement or self-expanding polyurethane. The grouting could be dusted with powdered rock to make it less obvious ensuring the cracks between the rocks are kept as small as possible. Where there are deep clefts then these can be filled with gravels or clay pushed in and used for plants, such as mosses, etc.

On top of the liner place soil to a shallow depth but deeper where planting is required. To create enclosures for aquatic plants place small boulders or cobblestones towards the centre of the stream, as these will contain the soil and stop it being washed away prior to the plants' establishment. In a man-made stream there is less likelihood of this soil erosion due to the constant flow and because there are no sudden spates as occur in a natural water course.

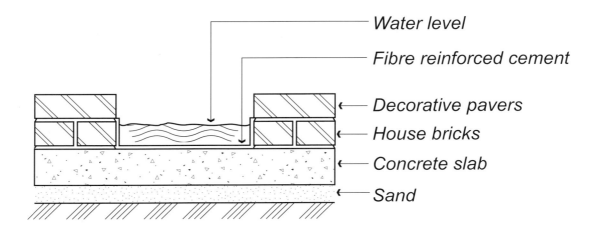

Water level

Fibre reinforced cement

Decorative pavers

House bricks

Concrete slab

Sand

SECTION

Scale 1:10

STREAM
Formal stream

76

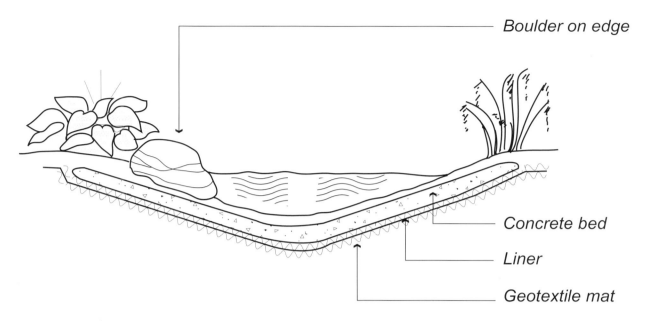

Boulder on edge

Concrete bed

Liner

Geotextile mat

MEADOW STREAM

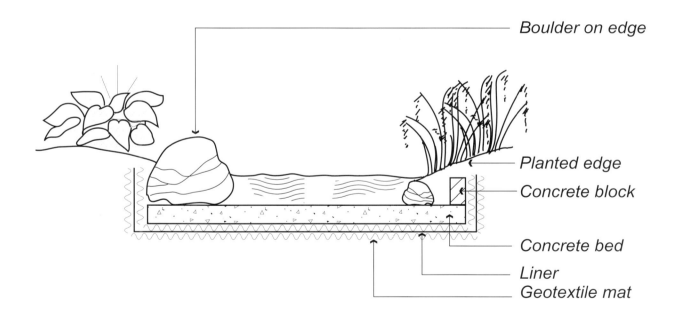

Boulder on edge

Planted edge

Concrete block

Concrete bed

Liner

Geotextile mat

ROCK STREAM

Scale 1:20

STREAM
Profiles

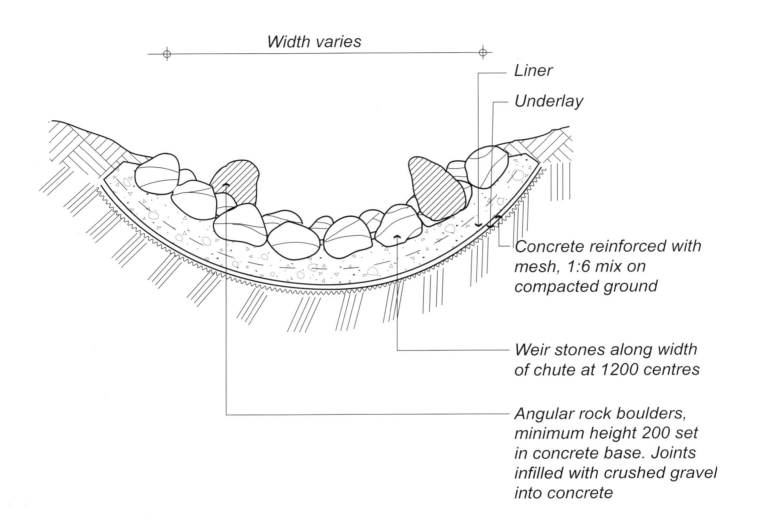

Width varies

Liner

Underlay

Concrete reinforced with mesh, 1:6 mix on compacted ground

Weir stones along width of chute at 1200 centres

Angular rock boulders, minimum height 200 set in concrete base. Joints infilled with crushed gravel into concrete

CROSS SECTION

Scale 1:10

STREAM
Stone bed channel

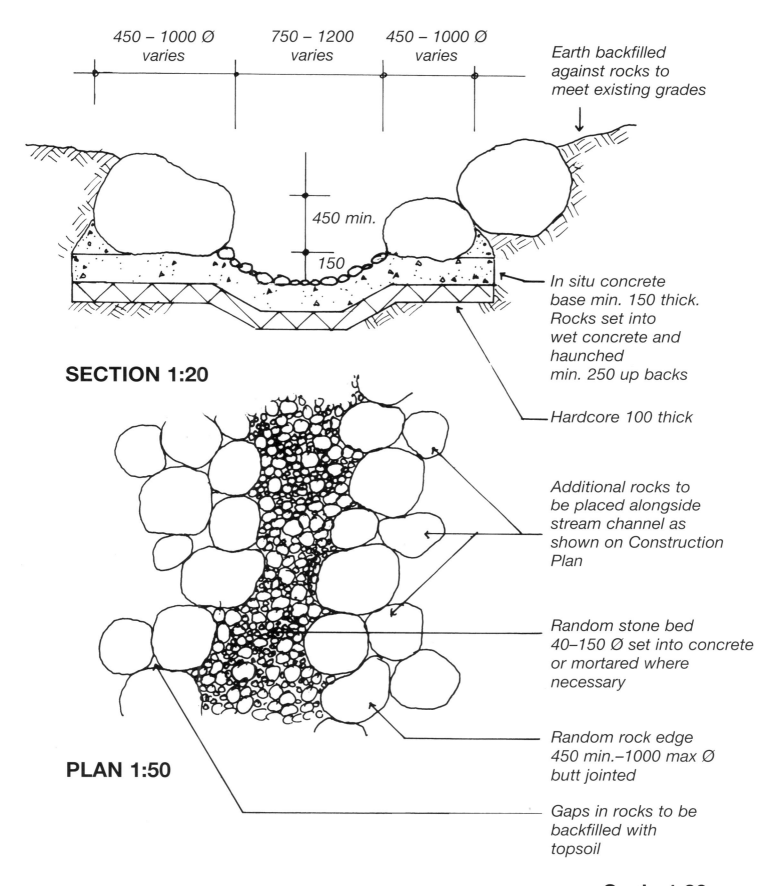

450 – 1000 Ø
varies

750 – 1200
varies

450 – 1000 Ø
varies

*Earth backfilled
against rocks to
meet existing grades*

450 min.

150

SECTION 1:20

*In situ concrete
base min. 150 thick.
Rocks set into
wet concrete and
haunched
min. 250 up backs*

Hardcore 100 thick

*Additional rocks to
be placed alongside
stream channel as
shown on Construction
Plan*

*Random stone bed
40–150 Ø set into concrete
or mortared where
necessary*

*Random rock edge
450 min.–1000 max Ø
butt jointed*

*Gaps in rocks to be
backfilled with
topsoil*

PLAN 1:50

Scale 1:20

STREAM CHANNEL

79

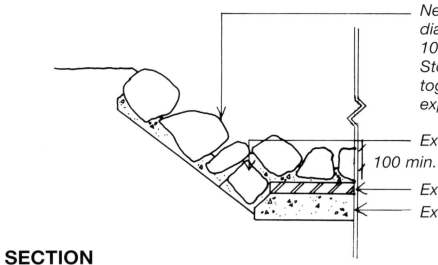

New boulders to be 150 – 250 diameter local stone set into 100 minimum depth concrete. Stones to be fitted tightly together to minimise area of exposed concrete

Existing stone

100 min.

Existing PC slab

Existing concrete slab

SECTION

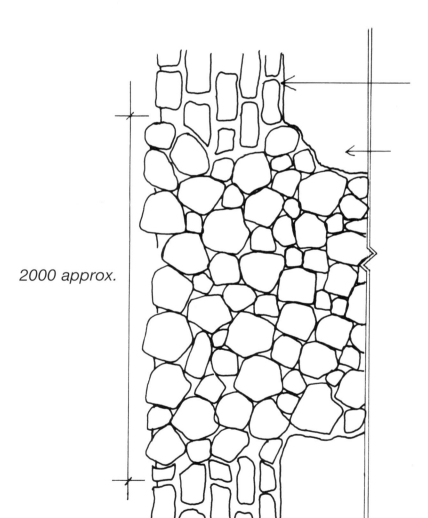

Existing block stone to be removed from area to be modified

Existing PC slab

2000 approx.

PLAN

Scale 1:20

STREAM BANK MODIFICATION

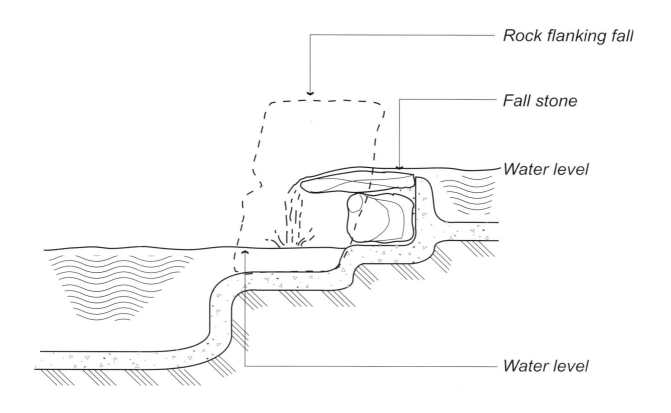

Rock flanking fall

Fall stone

Water level

Water level

SECTION   **Scale 1:20**

WATERFALL
Natural rock

81

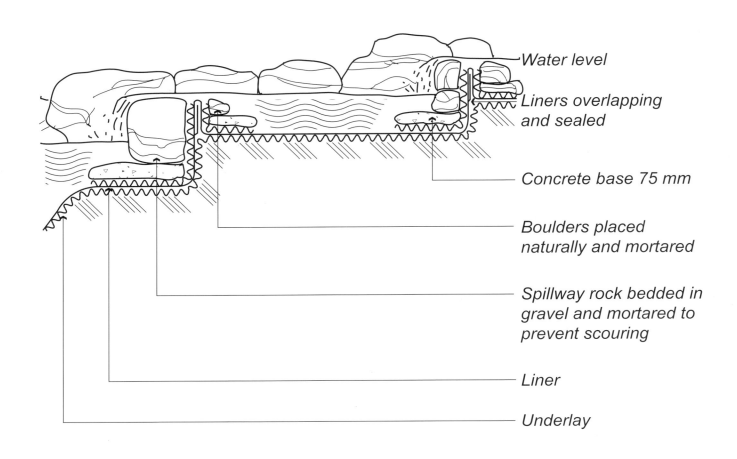

Water level

Liners overlapping
and sealed

Concrete base 75 mm

Boulders placed
naturally and mortared

Spillway rock bedded in
gravel and mortared to
prevent scouring

Liner

Underlay

SECTION

Scale 1:20

WATERFALLS
Natural stone/liner

82

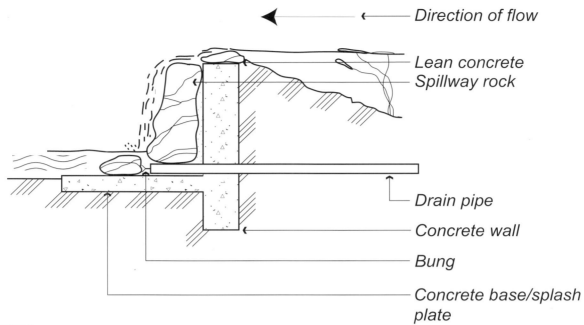

Direction of flow

Lean concrete

Spillway rock

Drain pipe

Concrete wall

Bung

Concrete base/splash plate

SECTION

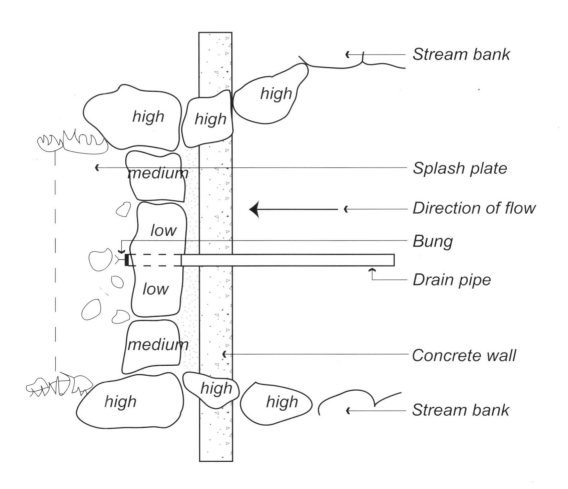

Stream bank

Splash plate

Direction of flow

Bung

Drain pipe

Concrete wall

Stream bank

PLAN

Scale 1:20

	WATERFALLS Rock and concrete	

83

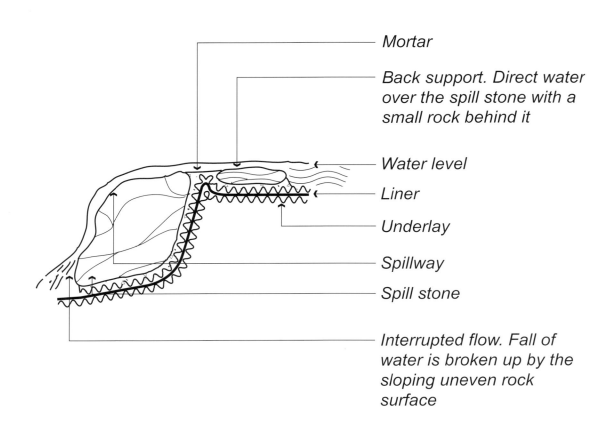

Mortar

Back support. Direct water over the spill stone with a small rock behind it

Water level

Liner

Underlay

Spillway

Spill stone

Interrupted flow. Fall of water is broken up by the sloping uneven rock surface

SECTION

Scale 1:20

WATERFALLS
Interrupted flow

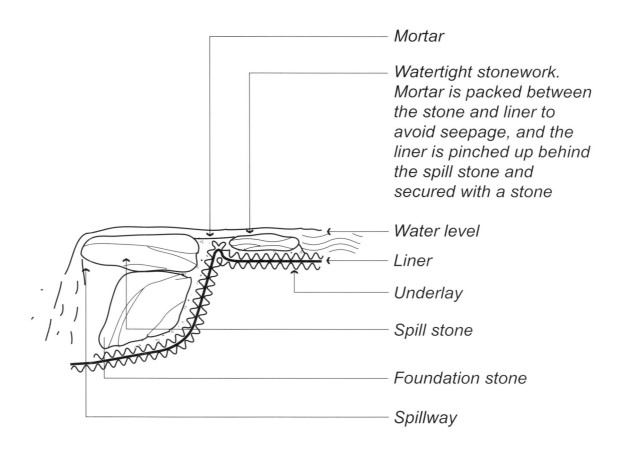

Mortar

Watertight stonework. Mortar is packed between the stone and liner to avoid seepage, and the liner is pinched up behind the spill stone and secured with a stone

Water level

Liner

Underlay

Spill stone

Foundation stone

Spillway

SECTION

Scale 1:20

WATERFALLS
Unbroken flow

FOUNTAINS

Fountains date back to antiquity. From the simple but effective effects of hydraulic technology, especially in the formal landscapes of the eighteenth and nineteenth centuries, to the modern and spectacular designs of the twentieth and twenty-first centuries, each provides constant interest at all times. Today, fountains can be made to order to fit any scheme embellishing all types of water gardens and landscapes, providing movement, sound and dramatic aesthetic effects. Being man-made features, fountains are more suited to the formal and architectural features of a landscape or garden design, rather than a natural setting. However, single jets or high plumes of water in a large natural lake or pond can be effective, provided the scale and setting are equally, if not more, imposing and dramatic.

Location

A fountain should be located in a position to catch the sunlight at the appropriate times of the day for the viewer, especially when seen from a distance through a foreground of deep shade. A jet of water when it appears luminous can look most spectacular.

For climatic reasons fountains should not be located in a small enclosed space. Care should also be exercised in siting fountain jets close to public paths due to wind gusts. The distance should be at least three times the height of the jet. This may be modified if the height can be controlled by valves.

The type of fountain selected by the designer will also influence the sounds being made, such as water falling on a hard surface compared to water falling on water. Both will be governed by the height and number of the jets associated with the fountain. The jets can also have nozzles of varying shapes and sizes selected by the designer that will provide sounds and displays of such variation that many can be compared to a musical overture. Simple adjustments to the valves controlling the flow can also make considerable difference to the sound.

For circular pools and basins a single vertical jet is preferable for the degree of simplicity it can provide, but for a rectangular pool, more than two down the middle would be more suitable for this shape. Depending upon the location jets could be placed at the sides or corners of a rectangular pool and arch into the centre. For square, octagonal or very small rectangular pools the use of jets in each corner would be effective.

Care must be taken that the height of the jet is not out of scale and proportion both with the pool and its immediate setting. Consideration must be given by the designer to the location of the prevailing wind and if there will be adequate protection for the type of jets selected. It may be necessary in certain locations for a more ornamental type of fountain to be used with shorter falls of water.

Pumps, pipes and valves

To ensure the fountain operates efficiently and effectively a pump is necessary. For a small fountain, a jet attached to a submersible pump can be hidden from view (in clear water), by being contained inside a block unit or under a plinth located at the side of the pool. Water can enter the chamber through fine mesh. Control valves should be located for ease of access, preferably near the side of the pool, especially where several jets are operated by the same pump. Each jet must have its own control valve so that its height can be adjusted. However, for a long, narrow pool, containing a line of jets, it would be preferable to have one large pipe down the middle feeding smaller pipes linked to each jet.

Pipes could be placed in a groove along the bottom of the pool or basin and covered with a weak mortar. This would allow for the pipe to be removed easily should any repairs be required.

If a large pool or lake contains a fountain then a larger pump located outside the pool would be preferable to a submersible one. This will allow for easier access to undertake maintenance and any repairs required.

Even with protection from winds, spray will inevitably fall on the surrounding area to the pool. Should this be a hard surface then a drainage channel will need to be incorporated into, or at the edge of, the paved area to collect the surface water along with any rainfall.

There are many different types of nozzles available such as:

- smooth bore or finger
- multiple spray
- aerating, etc.

to create different effects and the designer should obtain technical data from the manufacturer.

Wall fountains

Many wall fountains have provided an enjoyable feature in a garden or courtyard because they occupy such a small amount of space. They are easily installed and can be linked to a submersible pump to enable them to function satisfactorily.

As a rule of thumb the ratio of fountain height to pool radius should not exceed 1:1. For more exposed locations the limit is 1:1.5 or 1:2.

Typically the height above water (freeboard) is 150 mm. In some projects a low level sprayed water curtain can help contain spray from the fountain.

As wind speed rises, fountain height should be reduced by 10 per cent for each 5 mph of wind speed above 10 mph. For critical situations a wind sensor should switch off the fountain.

Pool water depth is typically 400 mm. Beyond 500 mm there is a much increased safety risk. Below 300 mm many water feature components are impractical. The size of all abstraction and delivery fittings should be increased by 10 per cent of every 25 mm below 400 mm depth.

Water availability

Where small nozzles are used, water quality must be controlled, especially if the water source is not fully filtered. Effective nozzle cleaning is very difficult.

Several water effects are water-level dependent. This is particularly a problem for natural settings where winter and summer water levels can be very different, especially for pools in a tiered system. In these the lowest water feature typically does not operate until the pumps have drawn down water from the rest of the system. One solution is floating fountains'. (Scrivens, 1988).

Wall fountains can be obtained ready made in a wide range of materials such as stone, terracotta, lead, bronze, steel or glass. They can also be designed and created specifically for a site with the backdrop of the wall playing a very important aesthetic role.

Likewise the basins for catching the water can range from an old stone sink to an antique lead casket or a purpose-made one in stone, brick or timber with a butyl liner inside.

The height of the spout above the water in the basin is small to ensure the minimum of wastage caused through splashing. Equally the size of the basin will also have an influence, especially if it is large enough to catch all the water.

Sometimes the water from the spout may fall directly into a purpose-made 'stream' or rill in which case the height may be restricted to ensure the minimum loss of water through splashing. In fact the design of the spout itself will play a very significant part in its height above the stream.

Water supply

As the basin is usually small there is a tendency for a loss of water through evaporation and splashing. In summer it may have to be topped up from a mains supply on a regular basis, utilising a float valve.

It is usually helpful if the submersible pump is located in a separate tank out of sight, especially as all the cables and pipework to the pool and wall fountain can be hidden.

The use of aquatic plants in pools and basins can produce extensive biological activity. This can lead to the creating of continual wet surfaces with moss and fine green slime. Whilst this may be acceptable on some materials, such as stone, it would be unacceptable on brightly polished and smooth materials used in modern water features.

Bubble fountains

These are considered as an interpretation of a natural spring and their purpose is to keep surrounding material, such as river washed cobbles and gravels, continuously damp or wet.

Care should be taken to ensure the even distribution of water with a compatible overflow system surrounding the feature.

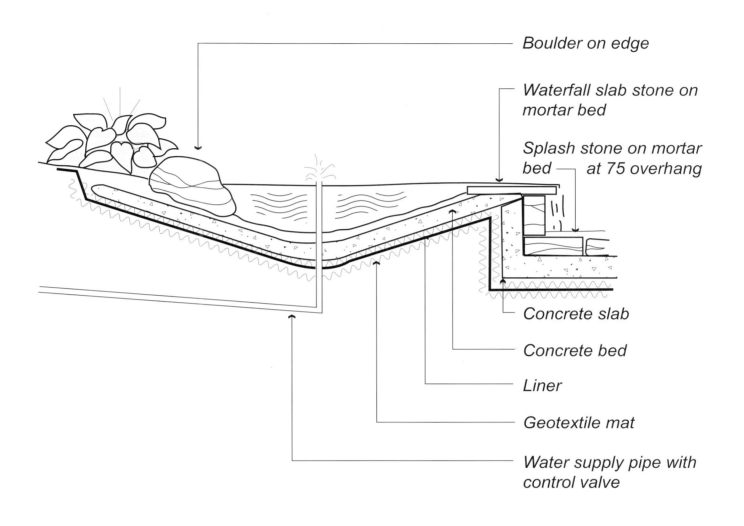

Boulder on edge

Waterfall slab stone on mortar bed

Splash stone on mortar bed — at 75 overhang

Concrete slab

Concrete bed

Liner

Geotextile mat

Water supply pipe with control valve

SECTION   **Scale 1:20**

FOUNTAIN
Bubble

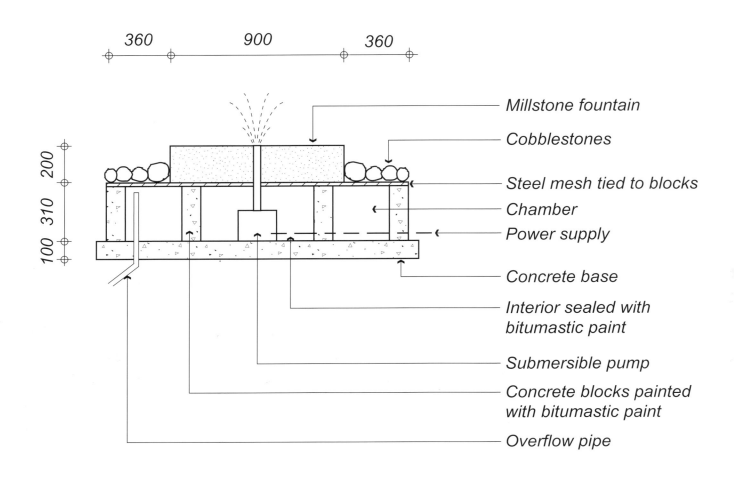

360   900   360

200   100 310

Millstone fountain

Cobblestones

Steel mesh tied to blocks

Chamber

Power supply

Concrete base

Interior sealed with
bitumastic paint

Submersible pump

Concrete blocks painted
with bitumastic paint

Overflow pipe

SECTION   **Scale 1:20**

FOUNTAIN
Millstone

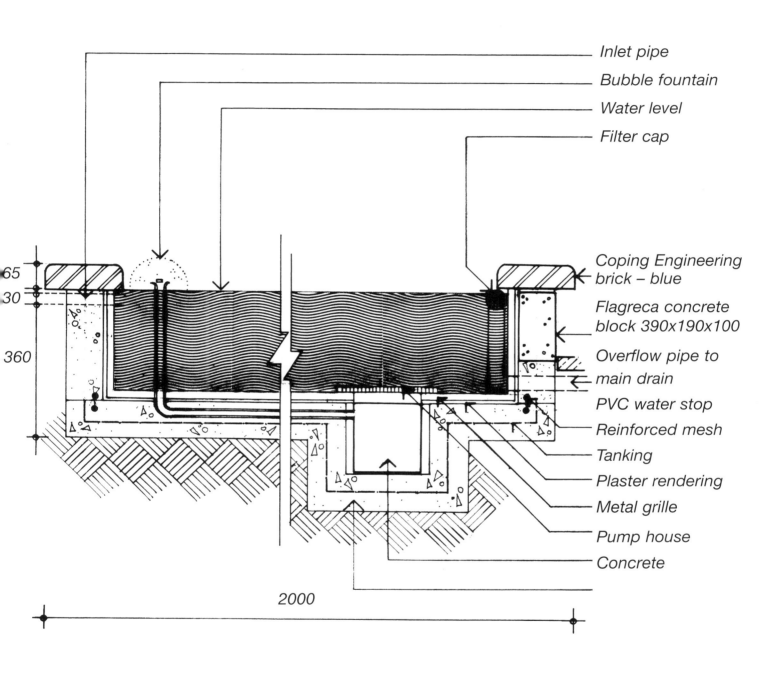

Inlet pipe

Bubble fountain

Water level

Filter cap

Coping Engineering brick – blue

Flagreca concrete block 390x190x100

Overflow pipe to main drain

PVC water stop

Reinforced mesh

Tanking

Plaster rendering

Metal grille

Pump house

Concrete

65

30

360

2000

SECTION

Scale 1:10

FOUNTAIN
Format

91

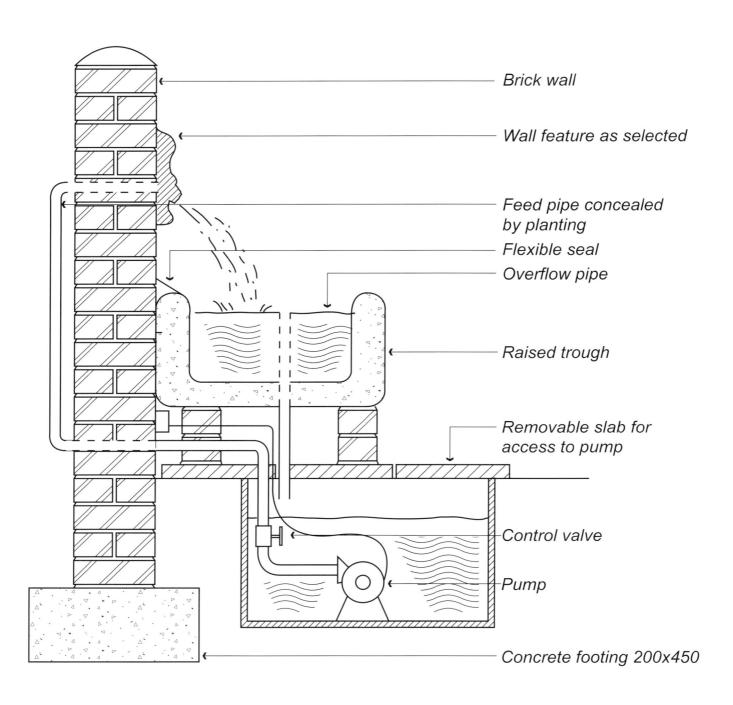

Brick wall

Wall feature as selected

Feed pipe concealed
by planting

Flexible seal

Overflow pipe

Raised trough

Removable slab for
access to pump

Control valve

Pump

Concrete footing 200x450

SECTION

Scale 1:20

FOUNTAIN
Wall feature

92

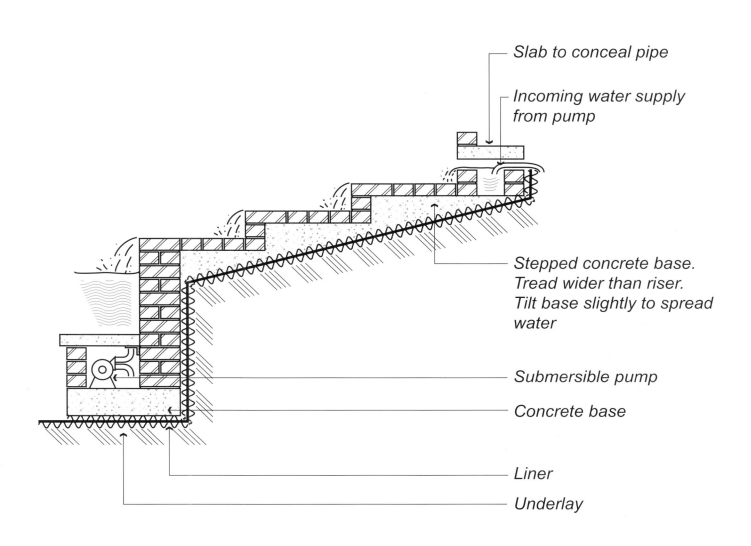

Slab to conceal pipe

Incoming water supply from pump

Stepped concrete base. Tread wider than riser. Tilt base slightly to spread water

Submersible pump

Concrete base

Liner

Underlay

SECTION

Scale 1:20

FOUNTAIN
Step cascade

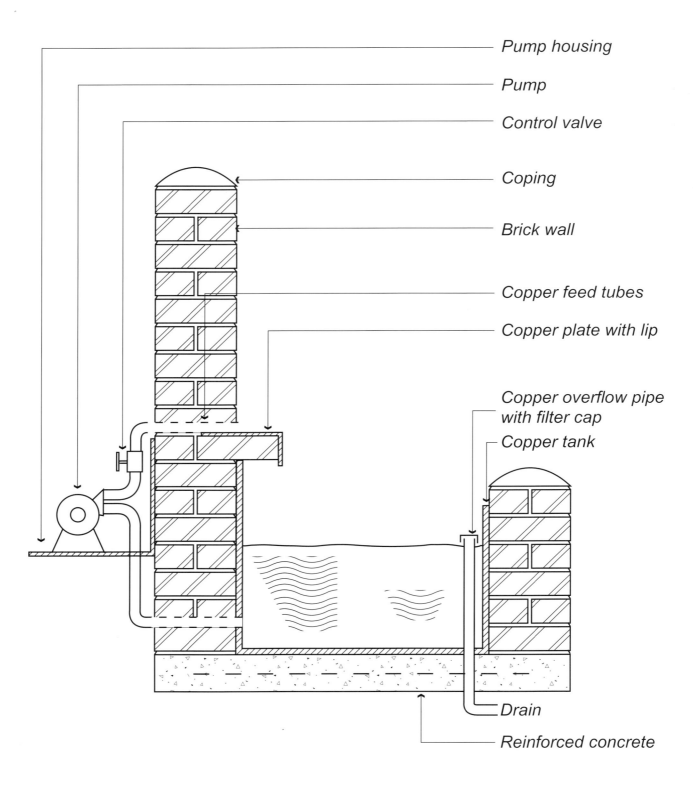

Pump housing

Pump

Control valve

Coping

Brick wall

Copper feed tubes

Copper plate with lip

Copper overflow pipe
with filter cap

Copper tank

Drain

Reinforced concrete

SECTION

Scale 1:10

FOUNTAIN
Wall feature

94

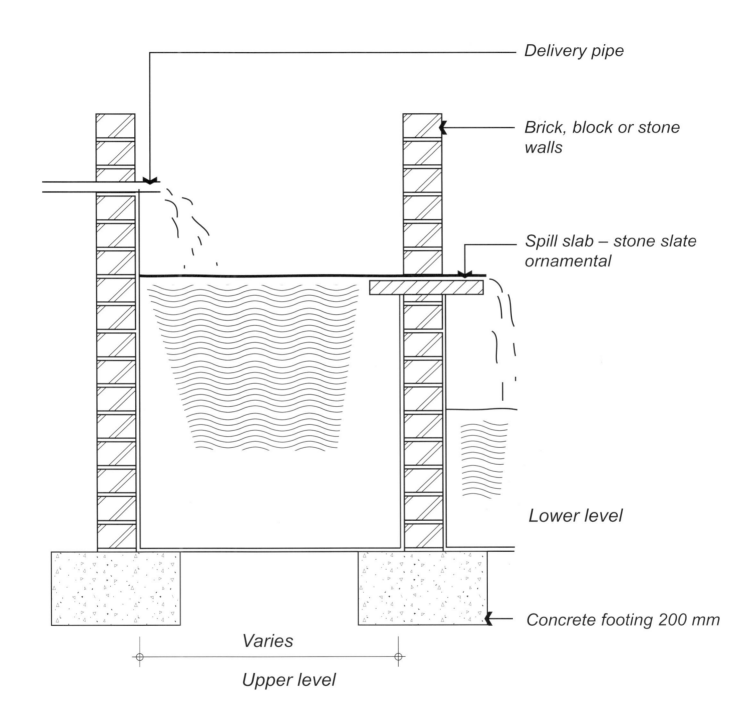

Delivery pipe

Brick, block or stone walls

Spill slab – stone slate ornamental

Lower level

Concrete footing 200 mm

Varies

Upper level

SECTION

Scale 1:10

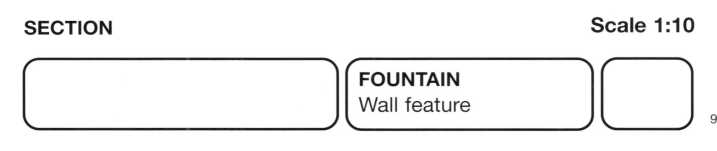

FOUNTAIN
Wall feature

95

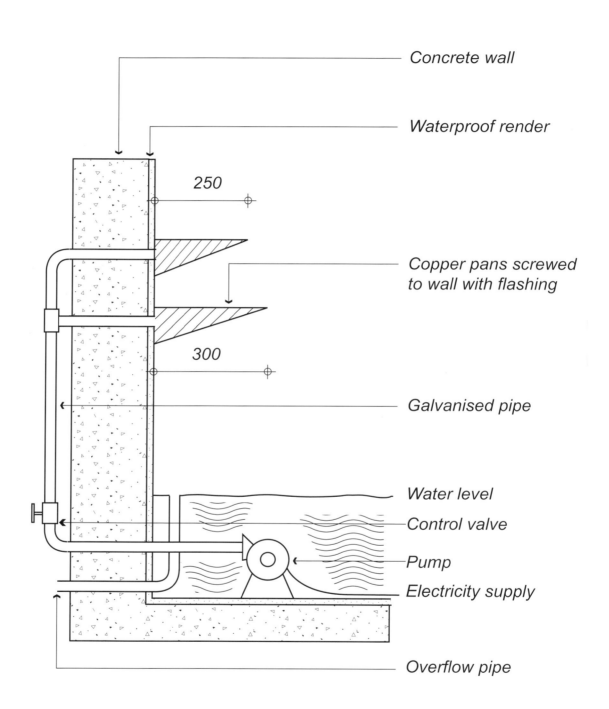

Concrete wall

Waterproof render

250

Copper pans screwed
to wall with flashing

300

Galvanised pipe

Water level

Control valve

Pump

Electricity supply

Overflow pipe

Scale 1:10

FOUNTAIN
Wall/feature

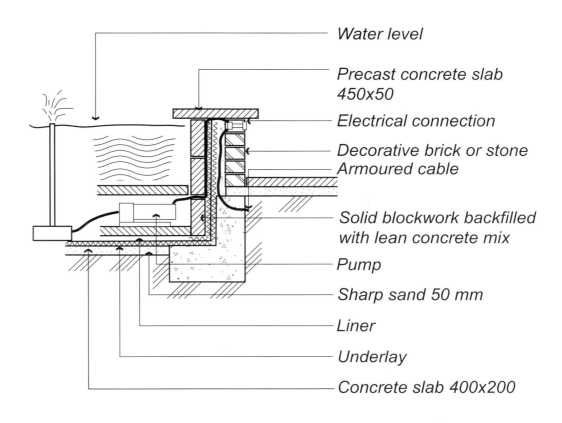

Water level

Precast concrete slab 450x50

Electrical connection

Decorative brick or stone
Armoured cable

Solid blockwork backfilled with lean concrete mix

Pump

Sharp sand 50 mm

Liner

Underlay

Concrete slab 400x200

SECTION

Scale 1:20

POOL
Pump – concealed

97

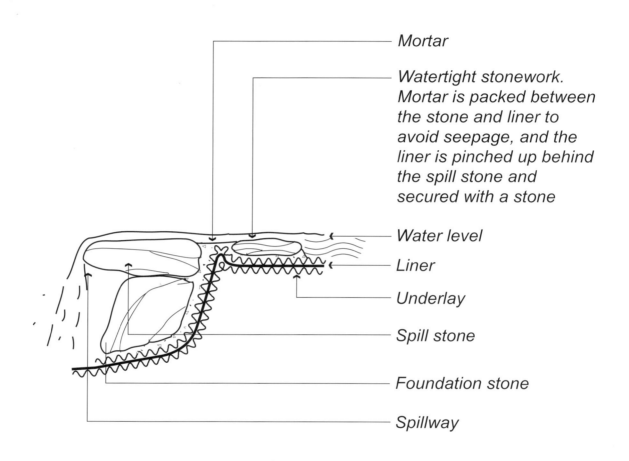

Mortar

Watertight stonework. Mortar is packed between the stone and liner to avoid seepage, and the liner is pinched up behind the spill stone and secured with a stone

Water level

Liner

Underlay

Spill stone

Foundation stone

Spillway

SECTION

Scale 1:20

WATERFALLS
Unbroken flow

98

EDGES

EDGES

Edges cover the surrounds to a pond whether it is formal or informal and usually serve more than one function. Firstly, they can secure the liner and even conceal it from view, depending upon water level. Secondly, the edge can provide a definitive surround to the pond, which will give the finishing touch.

For informal ponds a detailed hard edge may not be required as the rim can be concealed by planting or by cobblestones or a shingle beach.

Formal ponds

The design of the pond, its location and the use of other materials in the landscape or garden will all play a major influence on the selection of the edge material. In formal situations, harmony and stability are necessary and the beholder's eye is inevitably drawn first to the water, then any movement and finally to the overall framework; the point at which the water meets the land.

Formal ponds look best when the water is brimming to the rim and the edging helps to disguise the liner that is taken up directly beneath it.

The capping has to be absolutely level and must follow the shape of the pond. It should be bedded on a thin layer of mortar at the front, where it can be seen, but at the rear it should be thick and strong to give it stability.

The choice of materials for edges is reasonably large – stone slabs, granite setts, cobblestones, large pebbles, bricks, marble, slate and timber in certain situations. Form must always follow function. In practice it is preferable to use a contrasting material for the edge than select a poor match to the surrounding paving. This will not only define the edge aesthetically but will, given the appropriate material, assist in safety. Slate, for example, can become very slippery, especially in high rainfall areas.

Where the pond is set in a large lawn with minimal foot traffic a hard surround to the pond may not be necessary. Grass could be allowed to grow up to the water's edge if the design of the rim allows for it. Care must be taken when mowing that clippings do not fall onto the surface of the pond, as they are difficult and time consuming to remove.

Informal ponds

For wildlife ponds in the landscape or garden there is very often no need for a hard edge, except for a very small area for viewing. Marginal planting or grass around the edge of a lined pond would be a better and cheaper option.

Other than wildlife ponds, support for the top of the liner around the perimeter will be necessary should a mown grass edge or a hard access be required. For larger ponds and lakes, the action of the wind and waves as well as waterfowl may require a suitable edge to prevent erosion.

To ensure the continuity of the water with the landscape, an invisible edge will be far more aesthetically pleasing. There are many examples of various edges available, especially ones where gravel, pebbles and shingle can be used. The slope to ensure their containment has to be shallow and this type of edging offers a textured contrast with the water as well as offering a gradual transition from dry ground to water.

For small children, the cobble beach is a small deterrent for access to the water due to the uneven surface.

There are various materials available for visible edges such as stone, brick, timber and rock. Ideally the selection of a material should be based on what is appropriate for the area or region. Stone should be used cut into rough square or rectangular pieces to ensure the retention of a natural appearance. Fairly large pieces can be used for an edging without the use of mortar on the same principle as a dry stone wall. Where more precise cut stone has been used in the surrounding buildings and landscape, it would be preferable to emulate this if the edge is visible above or below the water line.

The use of bricks and especially where the capping is in the same material can produce a more precise and crisp edge. Engineering bricks or pavers should be used, as they are hard and impervious to frost. They are also available in a wide range of colours, which provide the designer with an excellent choice. Timber, when used externally, should look solid and not weak or fragile. For edgings and capping it is best if it responds to the thickness of a pavior or brick. Although it is less durable than stone or brick, it can produce a finish for both formal and

informal ponds. However, it is difficult to bend for short tight curves but for larger ponds a curved timber edge should be quite feasible.

Rocks or boulders should be set in position to achieve a natural look and for best effects resemble natural outcrops. They need to be placed on a concrete ledge in a pond of the same construction and on a concrete raft on top of a liner.

In both cases the rocks should be placed so that the water level is at least one third to half of their height. They will need to be bedded on soft mortar or on gravel and soil, depending upon their weight and size. Place gravel or mortar behind the boulder where they meet the ground and ensure that, in the case of a liner, it is above the water level and is protected from any damage.

The art of ensuring a natural appearance is to emulate nature and select rocks that are indigenous to the area. To bring rocks from long distances is not only expensive but also damaging to the environment. Many limestone features have been damaged by the removal of rocks and the use of artificial rocks, as seen at the Welsh Garden Festival, may well have to be considered in future.

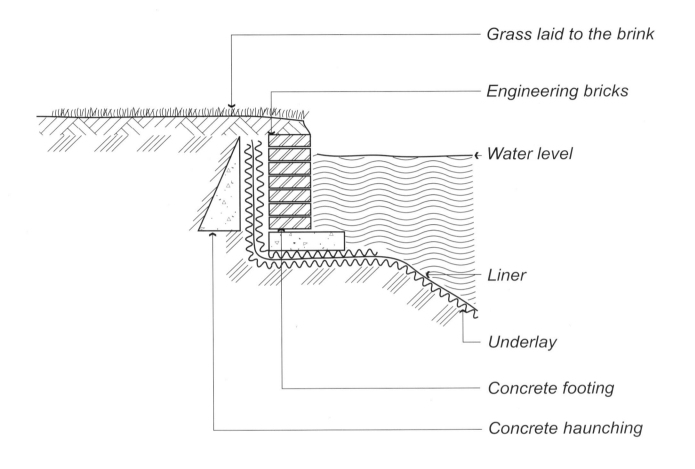

Grass laid to the brink

Engineering bricks

Water level

Liner

Underlay

Concrete footing

Concrete haunching

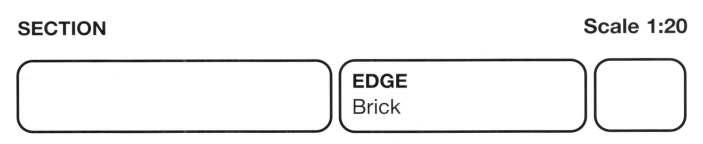

SECTION　　　　　　　　　　　　　　　　　　　　**Scale 1:20**

EDGE
Brick

101

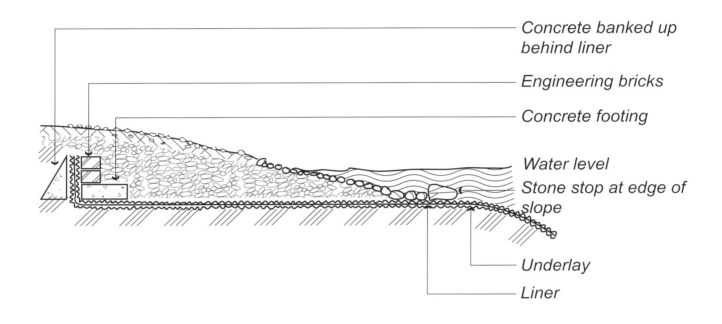

Concrete banked up behind liner

Engineering bricks

Concrete footing

Water level

Stone stop at edge of slope

Underlay

Liner

SECTION　　　　　　　　　　　　　　　　　　**Scale 1:20**

EDGE
Brick

102

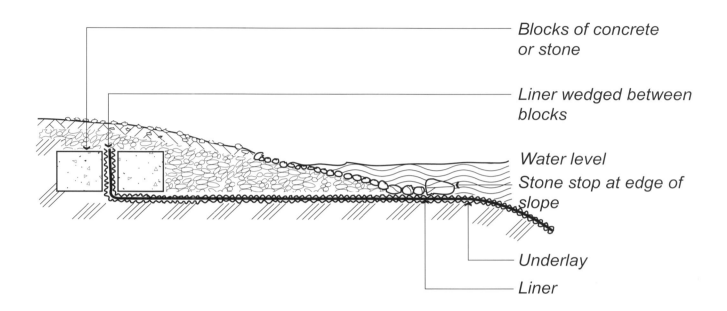

Blocks of concrete
or stone

Liner wedged between
blocks

Water level

Stone stop at edge of
slope

Underlay

Liner

SECTION

Scale 1:20

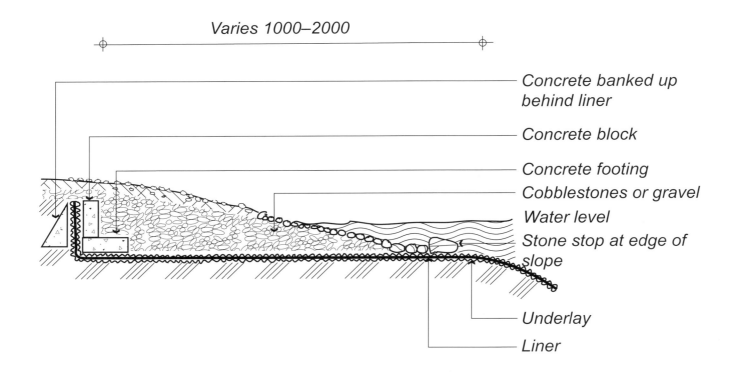

Varies 1000–2000

Concrete banked up behind liner

Concrete block

Concrete footing

Cobblestones or gravel

Water level

Stone stop at edge of slope

Underlay

Liner

SECTION

Scale 1:20

EDGE
Concrete/block

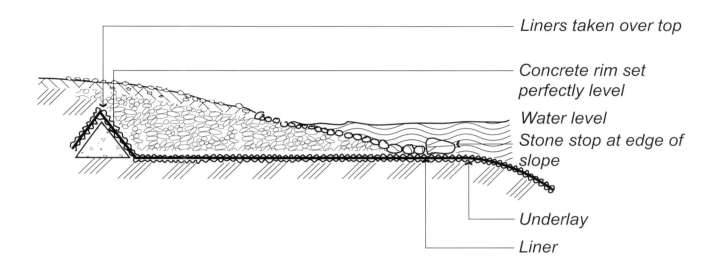

Liners taken over top

Concrete rim set perfectly level

Water level

Stone stop at edge of slope

Underlay

Liner

SECTION   **Scale 1:20**

EDGE
Concrete

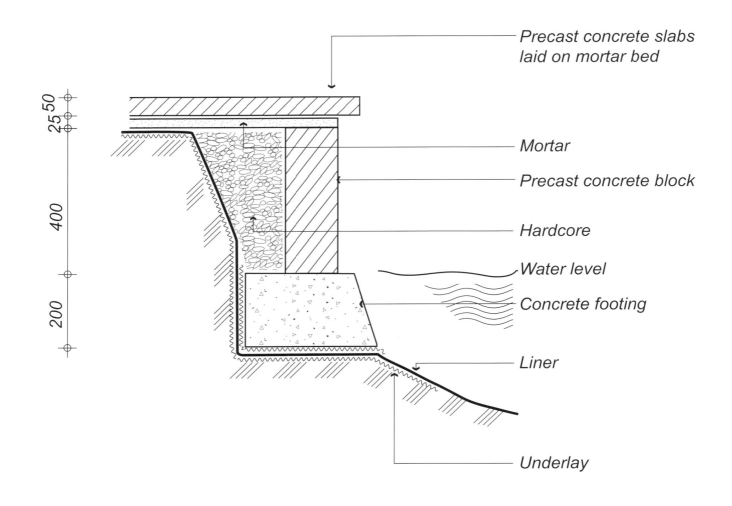

Precast concrete slabs laid on mortar bed

Mortar

Precast concrete block

Hardcore

Water level

Concrete footing

Liner

Underlay

25 50

400

200

SECTION

Scale 1:10

EDGE
Concrete

106

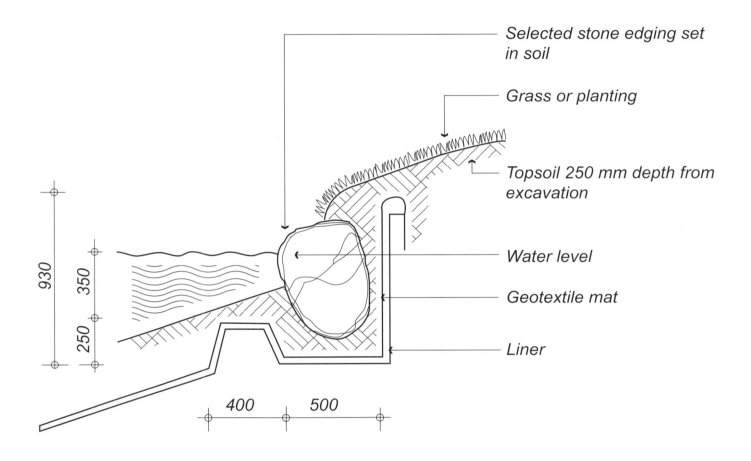

Selected stone edging set in soil

Grass or planting

Topsoil 250 mm depth from excavation

Water level

Geotextile mat

Liner

930

350

250

400

500

SECTION

Scale 1:20

EDGE
Natural stone

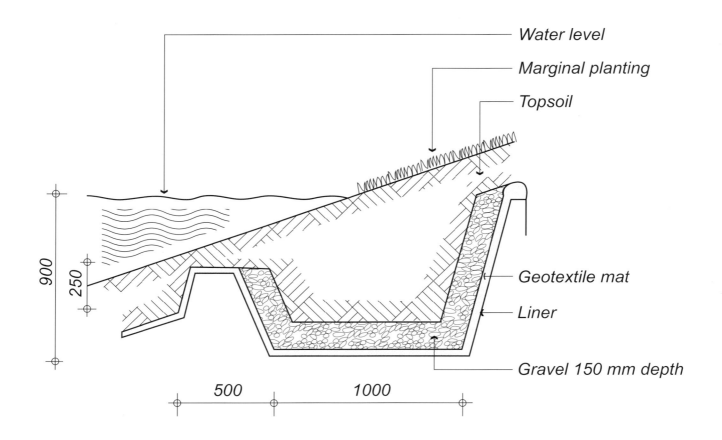

Water level

Marginal planting

Topsoil

Geotextile mat

Liner

Gravel 150 mm depth

900

250

500

1000

Scale 1:20

EDGE
Marginal planting

108

250   200

200

75–150

50

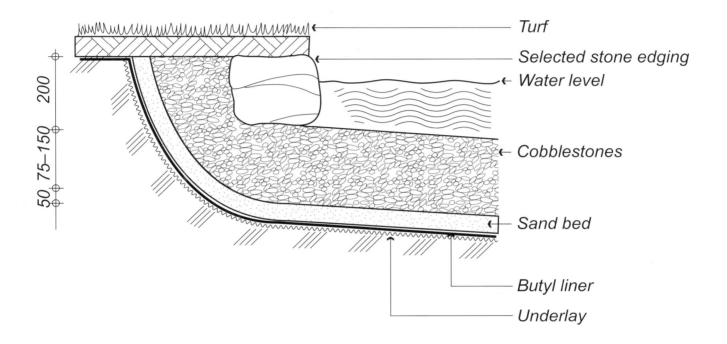

← Turf

← Selected stone edging

← Water level

← Cobblestones

← Sand bed

— Butyl liner

— Underlay

SECTION

Scale 1:20

EDGE
Stone/turf bank

250   200

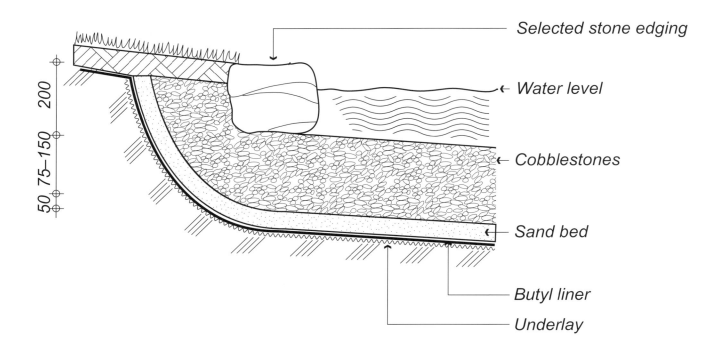

Selected stone edging

Water level

Cobblestones

Sand bed

Butyl liner

Underlay

200

75–150

50

SECTION   **Scale 1:10**

EDGE
Stone (2)

110

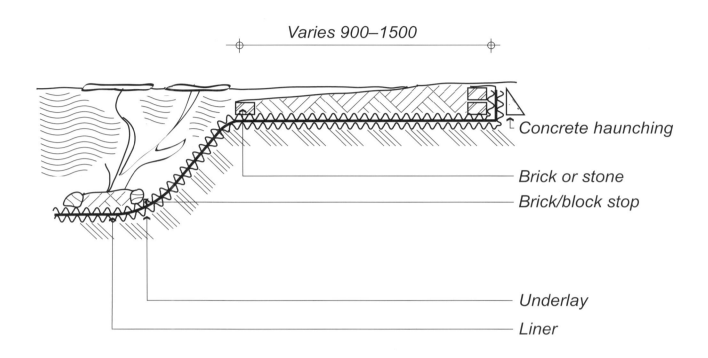

Varies 900–1500

Concrete haunching

Brick or stone

Brick/block stop

Underlay

Liner

SECTION

Scale 1:20

EDGE
Shallow ledge

111

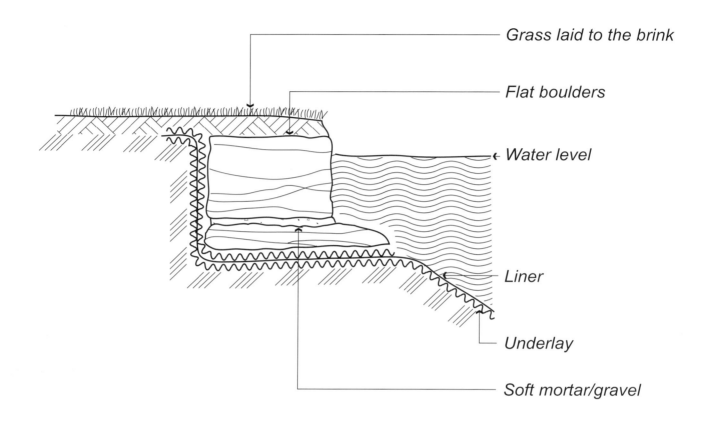

Grass laid to the brink

Flat boulders

Water level

Liner

Underlay

Soft mortar/gravel

SECTION

Scale 1:20

EDGE
Stone

112

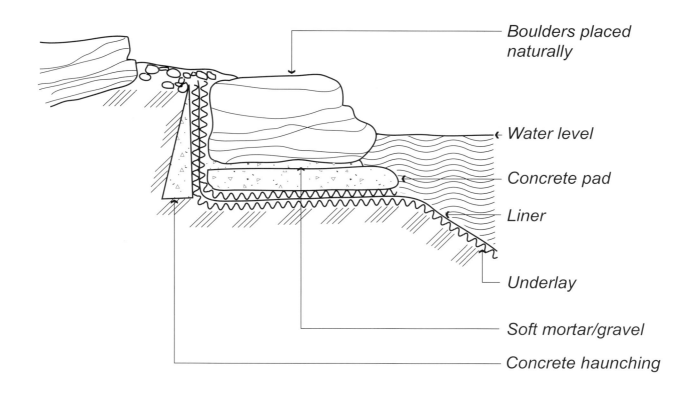

Boulders placed
naturally

Water level

Concrete pad

Liner

Underlay

Soft mortar/gravel

Concrete haunching

SECTION   **Scale 1:20**

EDGE
Rocks on ledges

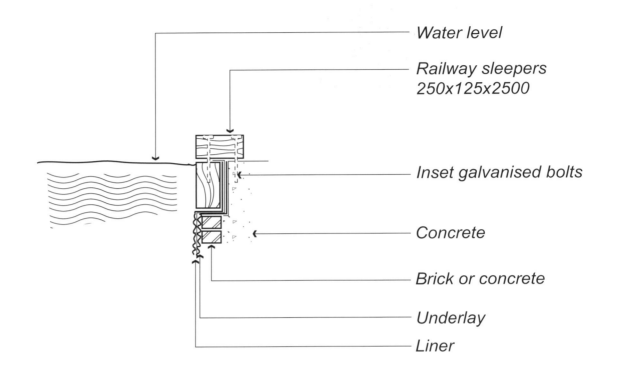

Water level

Railway sleepers
250x125x2500

Inset galvanised bolts

Concrete

Brick or concrete

Underlay

Liner

SECTION

Scale 1:20

EDGE
Timber sleeper (1)

114

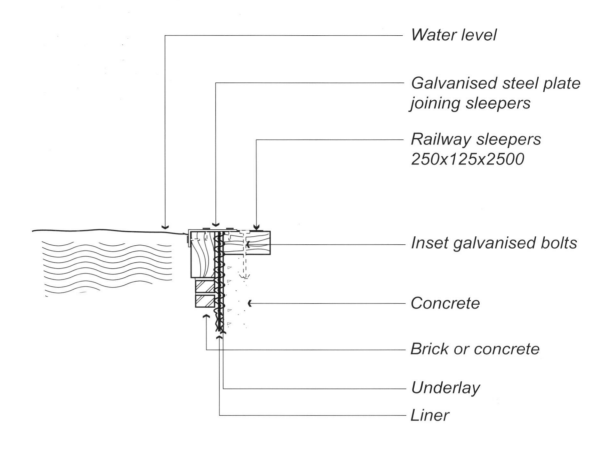

Water level

Galvanised steel plate
joining sleepers

Railway sleepers
250x125x2500

Inset galvanised bolts

Concrete

Brick or concrete

Underlay

Liner

SECTION

Scale 1:20

EDGE
Timber sleeper (2)

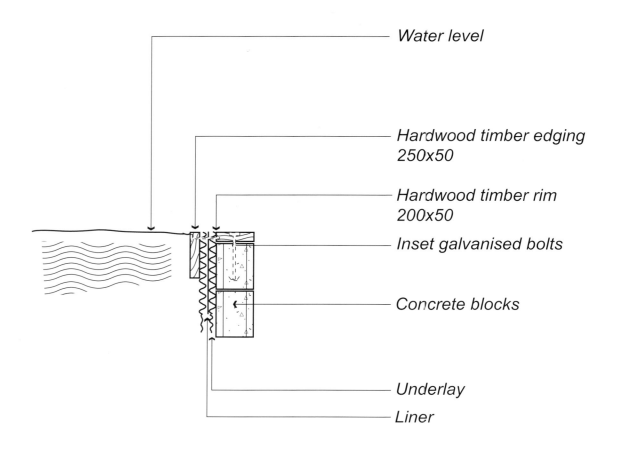

Water level

Hardwood timber edging
250x50

Hardwood timber rim
200x50

Inset galvanised bolts

Concrete blocks

Underlay

Liner

SECTION

Scale 1:20

EDGE
Timber/blocks

116

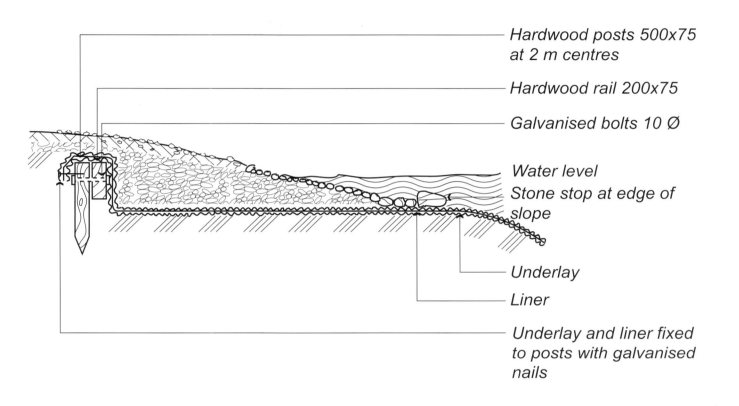

Hardwood posts 500x75
at 2 m centres

Hardwood rail 200x75

Galvanised bolts 10 Ø

Water level
Stone stop at edge of
slope

Underlay

Liner

Underlay and liner fixed
to posts with galvanised
nails

SECTION   **Scale 1:20**

EDGE
Timber

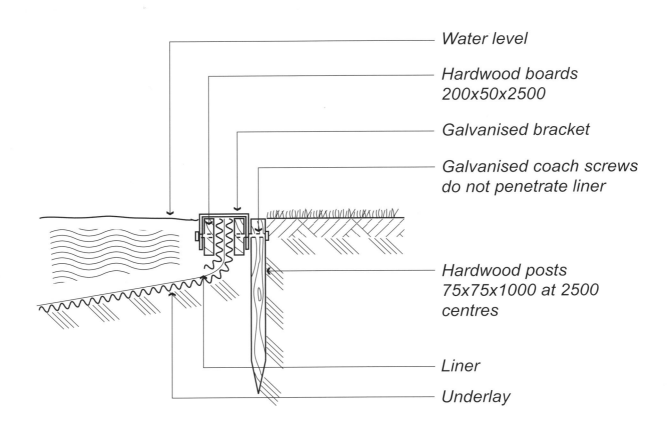

Water level

Hardwood boards
200x50x2500

Galvanised bracket

Galvanised coach screws
do not penetrate liner

Hardwood posts
75x75x1000 at 2500
centres

Liner

Underlay

SECTION   **Scale 1:20**

EDGE
Timber planks

118

BANK PROTECTION

This section does not deal with natural bank protection as this is covered in books on bio-engineering details. Vertical bank protection is discussed including different types of soil retaining walls.

Unprotected steep banks will remain stable only if they are composed of rock or soils with a high resistance to erosion, such as a highly consolidated and cohesive soil.

It is important to note that all forms of vertical protection must be designed to resist not only the erosive forces within the water course but also soil and ground water pressure from the bank.

The design procedure for vertical bank protection is similar to the standard retaining wall design, with allowances being made for the extreme conditions relating to the groundwater level and/or water levels.

Gravity walls

Gravity walls may be monolithic, such as mass concrete construction, or composite, such as brick or masonry walls with mortar joints or stone-filled gabion baskets joined together.

The principal forces acting on a gravity wall are shown diagrammatically below:

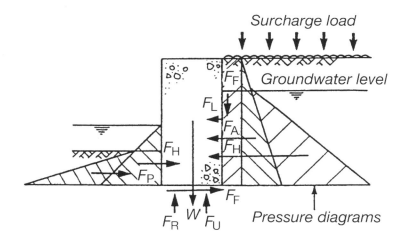

Notes

1. Forces per unit length of wall:
   - Wall self-weight W
   - Friction force F_F
   - Passive soil force F_P
   - Surcharge-related force F_L
   - Active soil force F_A
   - Hydrostatic force F_H
   - Uplift F_U
   - Foundation reaction F_R

2. F_p depends on finite wall movement occurring, otherwise force will be $F_P > F > F_A$.
3. F_F on back wall often ignored in analysis.
4. F_U depends on seepage flow net.

Control of the hydrostatic pressure on the rear of the retaining wall is by the use of free draining material adjacent to the rear face. This material must have adequate thickness and permeability to allow water to move vertically behind the wall without significant head loss, and consequent increase in differential hydrostatic pressure across the wall.

Failure

The design of the wall should be checked against the following possible methods of failure as shown in the diagrams.

Even after this check the design should be inspected by a qualified civil engineer.

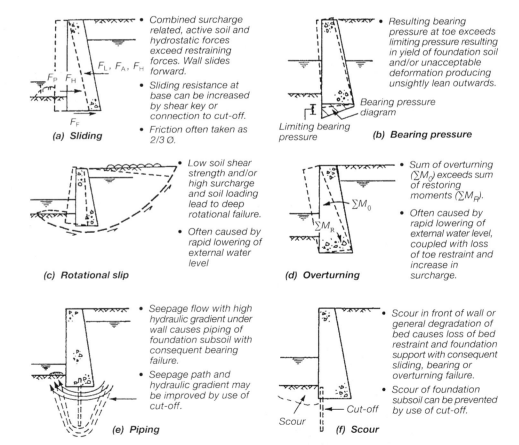

(a) Sliding
- Combined surcharge related, active soil and hydrostatic forces exceed restraining forces. Wall slides forward.
- Sliding resistance at base can be increased by shear key or connection to cut-off.
- Friction often taken as 2/3 Ø.

(b) Bearing pressure
- Resulting bearing pressure at toe exceeds limiting pressure resulting in yield of foundation soil and/or unacceptable deformation producing unsightly lean outwards.

(c) Rotational slip
- Low soil shear strength and/or high surcharge and soil loading lead to deep rotational failure.
- Often caused by rapid lowering of external water level

(d) Overturning
- Sum of overturning ($\sum M_o$) exceeds sum of restoring moments ($\sum M_R$).
- Often caused by rapid lowering of external water level, coupled with loss of toe restraint and increase in surcharge.

(e) Piping
- Seepage flow with high hydraulic gradient under wall causes piping of foundation subsoil with consequent bearing failure.
- Seepage path and hydraulic gradient may be improved by use of cut-off.

(f) Scour
- Scour in front of wall or general degradation of bed causes loss of bed restraint and foundation support with consequent sliding, bearing or overturning failure.
- Scour of foundation subsoil can be prevented by use of cut-off.

With masonry, brickwork and mass concrete walls, it is normal practice to avoid tension in the rear face of the wall, except under extreme loading conditions. This implies that the resultant force in the wall remains within the middle third of the cross-section.

Mass walls

These are usually constructed of concrete and with a batter on the rear face as it is easier and more economic to do. Should the foundation soil be weak then toe and heel extensions are often used to reduce bearing pressure and spread the foundation load over a larger area.

Ensure weepholes are formed of pipe material and that a filter is constructed to ensure that soil, or other fill behind the wall, is not transported into the weepholes by seepage flow. Features of a mass gravity wall are shown in the diagram.

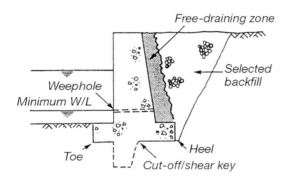

Note:
Weepholes are essential features to reduce differential hydrostatic pressure across the wall. Locate at or below minimum external water level.

Gabion walls

Walls constructed from gabions are more flexible and permeable than those built from masonry brickwork, blockwork or mass concrete. Gabion boxes may also be used as a stacked protective facing tied back into the soil mass as a composite structure. If is flexible therefore it can accommodate settlement or consolidation of the foundation after construction.

Gabion walls should be constructed with the front face at a slight angle (10 in 1) to the vertical, which may be achieved by either sloping the entire foundation, or by stepping back individual units, as illustrated.

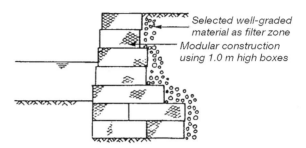

(a) Gabion box structure

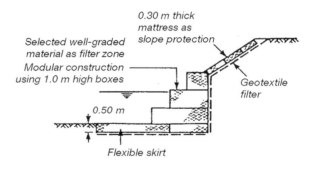

(b) Combined box/mattress structure

Piling

Vertical bank protection by piling is especially appropriate in waterways as there is usually no need to dewater or provide a coffer dam. It can also be undertaken in very restricted areas where other types of retaining walls are not as flexible.

Sheet piled walls are of two types – cantilevered or anchored. Cantilevered walls depend for their stability entirely on the soil in which they are driven, and require minimal lateral space. The bending movement can become excessive as the wall increases in height and it is not advised to exceed 2.50 m.

Heavy reinforced concrete capping beams are generally used to prevent excessive variations in movement of the top of the wall. If carefully designed and detailed they can also enhance the appearance of the wall.

Anchored walls are restrained at the top and bottom by a horizontal walling near the top of the wall. This reduces the maximum bending movement compared to a cantilever wall of similar height.

Anchorages must be located far away from the wall to be outside any potential failure surface.

If space is restricted, a cantilever wall may have to be used.

Notes:

1. Cantilevered walls relatively uneconomical in relation to anchored walls for retained heights in excess of about 3 m.

2. Restricted space for installation of tie rod may necessitate use of cantilevered wall or ground anchor (in drill-hole from water face).

3. Anchorage must lie outside potential zone of failure.

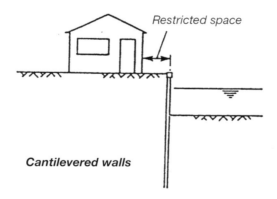

Cantilevered walls

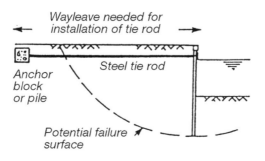

Anchored walls

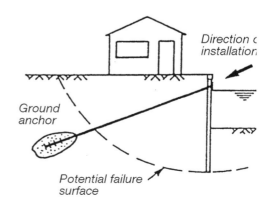

122

Visual effects

Large areas of steel piling may be visually disturbing and although it can be painted, or even clad, it may not prove cost effective. Very often it is only the area above the water line that requires to be painted providing the water level does not fluctuate. Alternatively, vegetation can be allowed to grow from the top of the bank downwards to the water level.

Precast concrete unit walls

These units are a typically inverted Tee design, constructed from reinforced concrete. The restraining mass is provided by the heel of the unit. It is essential to place these units on a prepared, dry foundation.

Rubber tyre walls

Old tyres can be used for a low height wall and the restraint is dependent upon the vertical posts or stakes over which the tyres are placed. Two rows of tyres are essential to ensure continuous protection for the bank.

While it may appear unattractive this method is cheap and if plants are placed among the spaces then the wall can be eventually covered.

Crib walls

These are built in exactly the same way as for retaining walls on land projects.

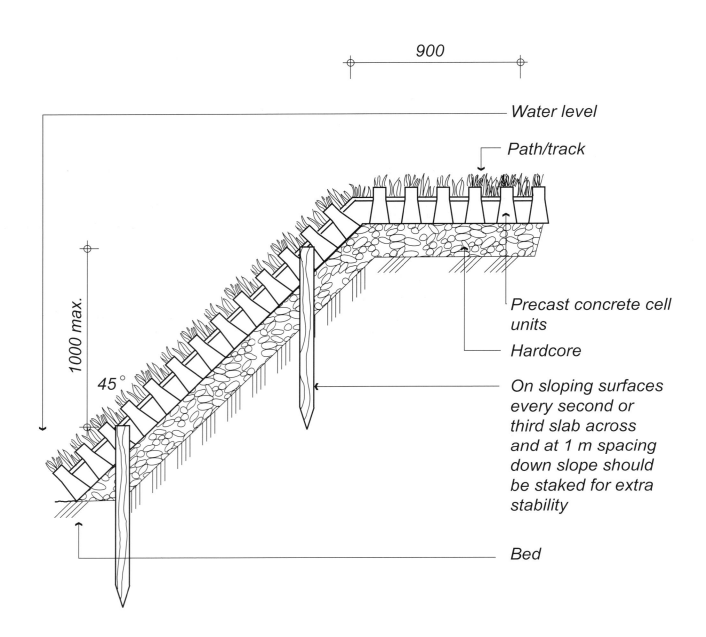

900

Water level

Path/track

1000 max.

45°

Precast concrete cell units

Hardcore

On sloping surfaces every second or third slab across and at 1 m spacing down slope should be staked for extra stability

Bed

SECTION

Scale 1:20

BANK PROTECTION
Precast concrete

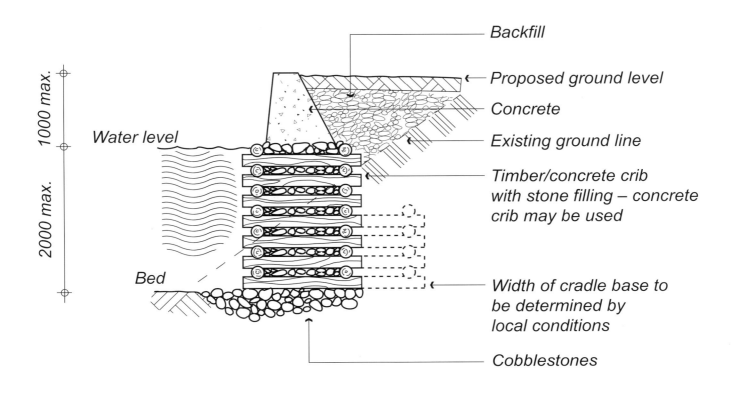

1000 max.

2000 max.

Water level

Bed

Backfill

Proposed ground level

Concrete

Existing ground line

Timber/concrete crib with stone filling – concrete crib may be used

Width of cradle base to be determined by local conditions

Cobblestones

SECTION

Scale 1:50

BANK PROTECTION
Concrete/crib wall

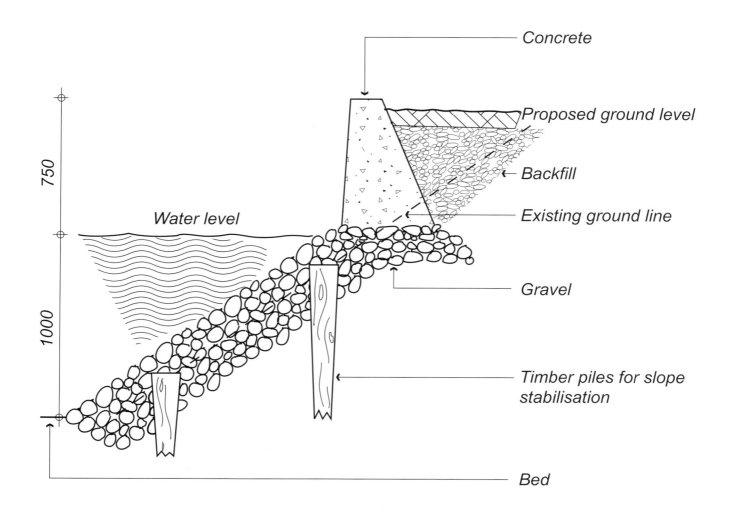

Concrete

Proposed ground level

Backfill

Existing ground line

Gravel

Timber piles for slope stabilisation

Bed

750

1000

Water level

SECTION

Scale 1:20

BANK PROTECTION
Concrete/rip-rap

126

CONCRETE

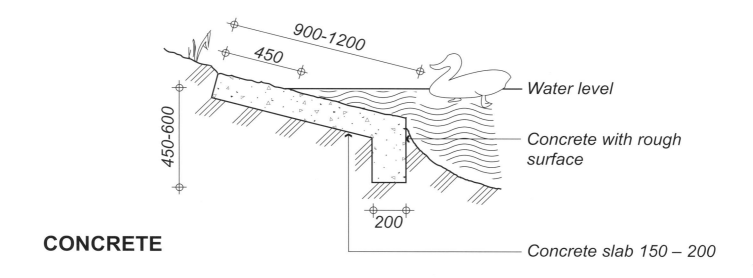

900-1200

450

450-600

200

Water level

Concrete with rough surface

Concrete slab 150 – 200

TIMBER

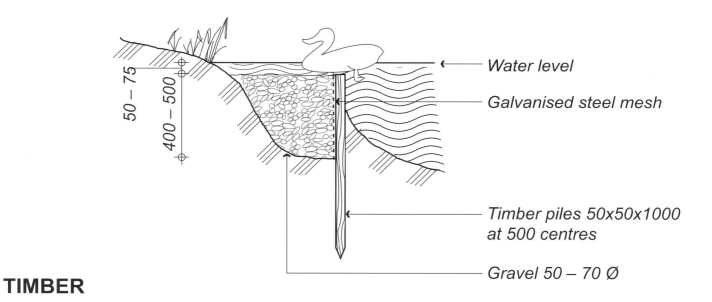

50 – 75

400 – 500

Water level

Galvanised steel mesh

Timber piles 50x50x1000 at 500 centres

Gravel 50 – 70 Ø

SECTION

Scale 1:20

BANK PROTECTION
Timber/concrete

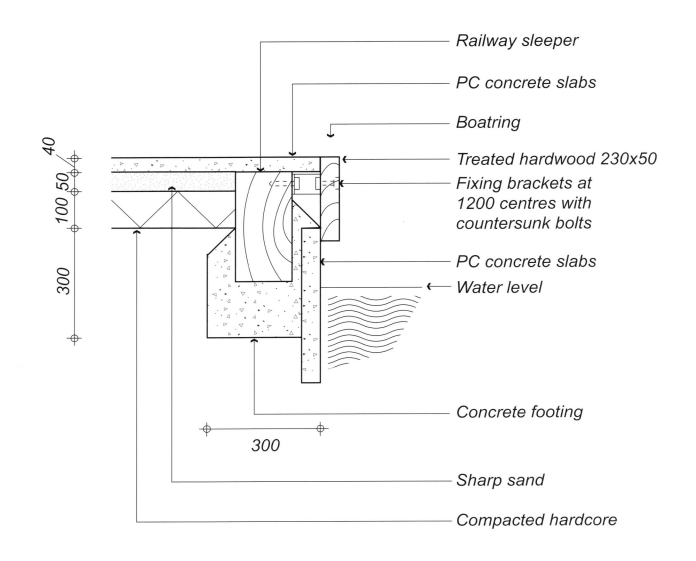

40

100 50

300

300

Railway sleeper

PC concrete slabs

Boatring

Treated hardwood 230x50

Fixing brackets at 1200 centres with countersunk bolts

PC concrete slabs

Water level

Concrete footing

Sharp sand

Compacted hardcore

SECTION

Scale 1:10

BANK PROTECTION
Edge concrete/timber

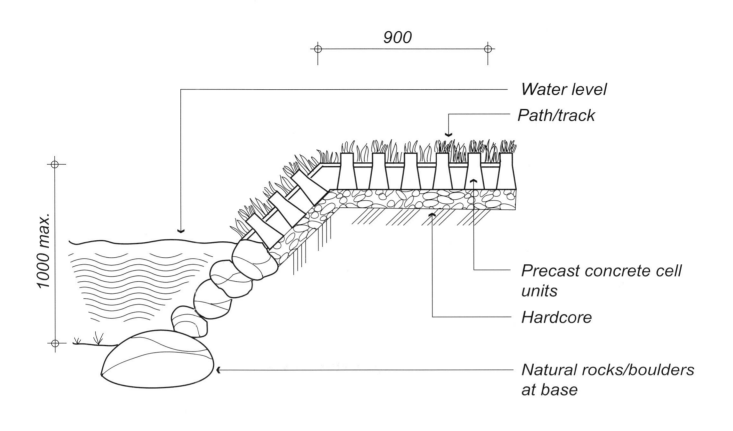

900

Water level

Path/track

1000 max.

Precast concrete cell units

Hardcore

Natural rocks/boulders at base

SECTION

Scale 1:20

BANK PROTECTION
Concrete/stone

129

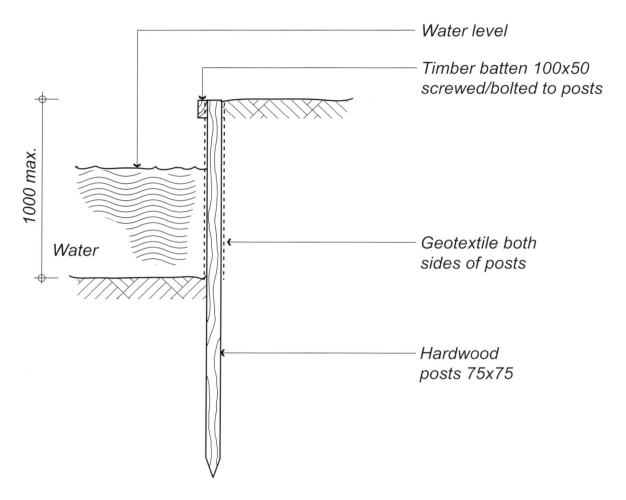

Water level

Timber batten 100x50
screwed/bolted to posts

1000 max.

Water

Geotextile both
sides of posts

Hardwood
posts 75x75

SECTION

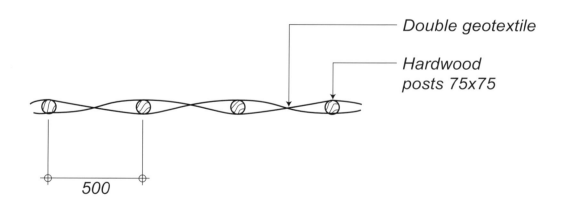

Double geotextile

Hardwood
posts 75x75

500

PLAN

Scale 1:20

BANK PROTECTION
Geotextile

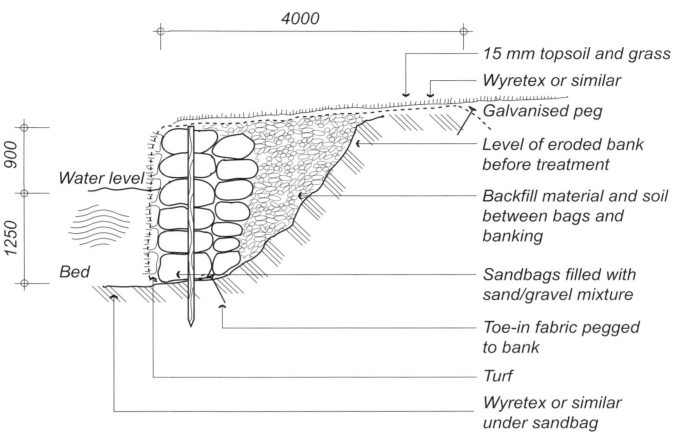

4000

15 mm topsoil and grass

Wyretex or similar

Galvanised peg

Level of eroded bank before treatment

Backfill material and soil between bags and banking

Sandbags filled with sand/gravel mixture

Toe-in fabric pegged to bank

Turf

Wyretex or similar under sandbag

900

1250

Water level

Bed

SECTION

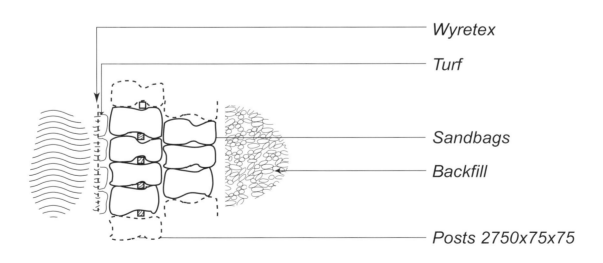

Wyretex

Turf

Sandbags

Backfill

Posts 2750x75x75

PLAN

Scale 1:50

BANK PROTECTION
Sandbags/geotextile

131

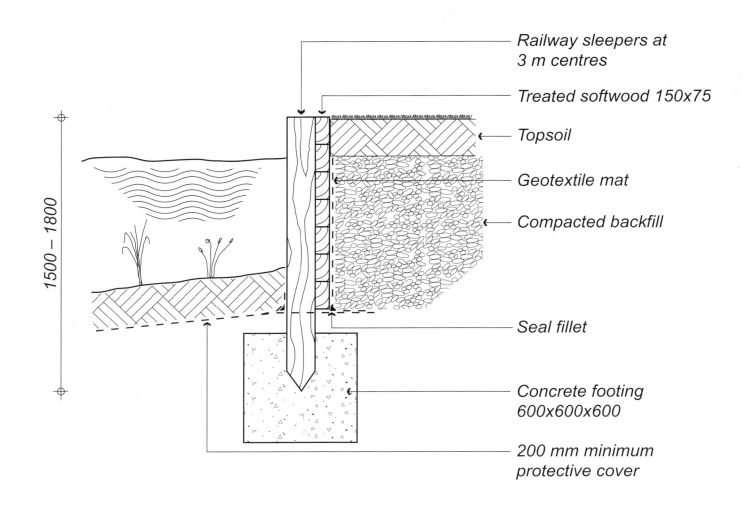

Railway sleepers at 3 m centres

Treated softwood 150x75

Topsoil

Geotextile mat

Compacted backfill

Seal fillet

Concrete footing 600x600x600

200 mm minimum protective cover

1500 – 1800

SECTION

Scale 1:20

BANK PROTECTION
Sleepers and geotextile

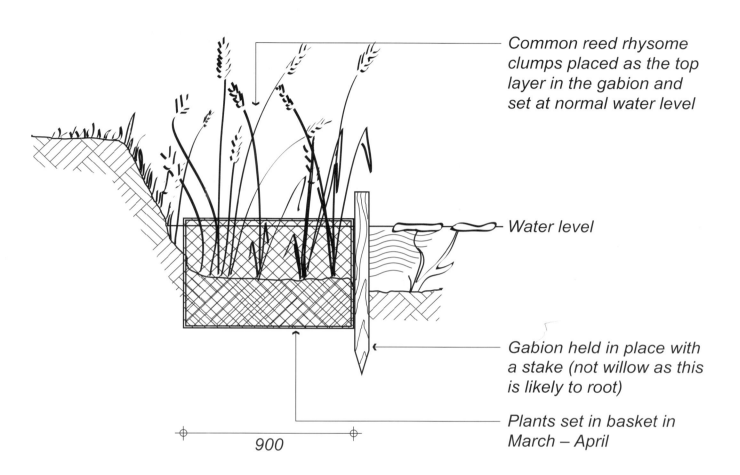

Common reed rhysome clumps placed as the top layer in the gabion and set at normal water level

Water level

Gabion held in place with a stake (not willow as this is likely to root)

Plants set in basket in March – April

900

SECTION

Scale 1:20

BANK PROTECTION
Gabion basket/reed

133

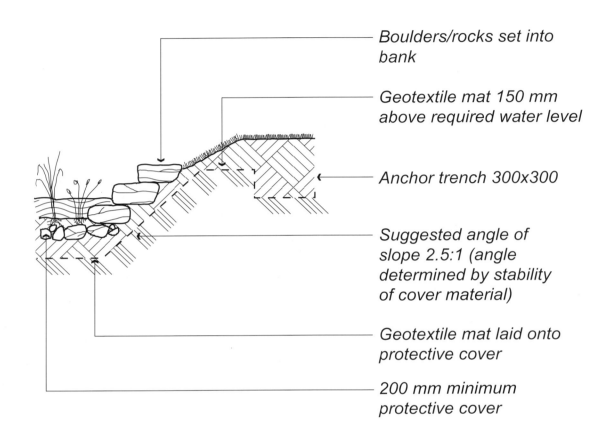

Boulders/rocks set into bank

Geotextile mat 150 mm above required water level

Anchor trench 300x300

Suggested angle of slope 2.5:1 (angle determined by stability of cover material)

Geotextile mat laid onto protective cover

200 mm minimum protective cover

SECTION

Scale 1:20

BANK PROTECTION
Natural boulders/
geotextile

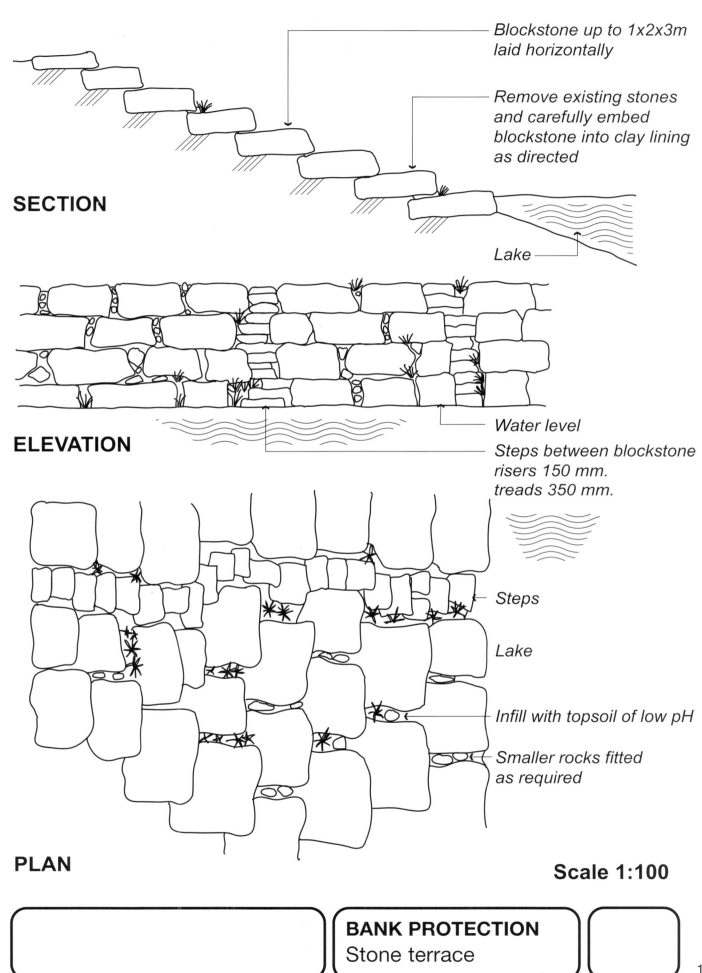

SECTION

Blockstone up to 1x2x3m laid horizontally

Remove existing stones and carefully embed blockstone into clay lining as directed

Lake

ELEVATION

Water level

Steps between blockstone risers 150 mm. treads 350 mm.

PLAN

Steps

Lake

Infill with topsoil of low pH

Smaller rocks fitted as required

Scale 1:100

BANK PROTECTION
Stone terrace

135

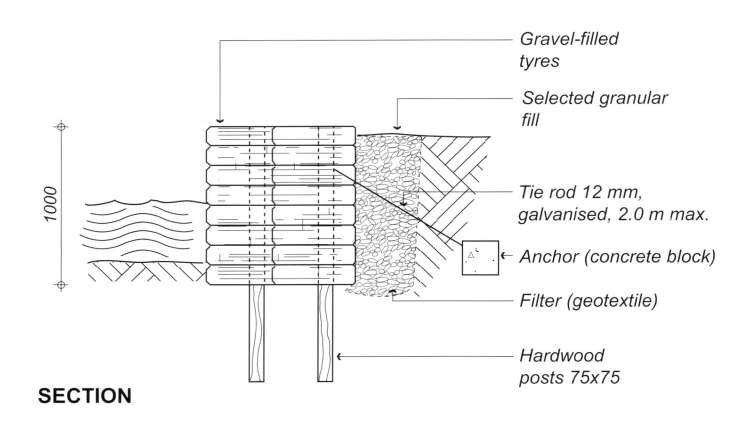

Gravel-filled tyres

Selected granular fill

Tie rod 12 mm, galvanised, 2.0 m max.

Anchor (concrete block)

Filter (geotextile)

Hardwood posts 75x75

1000

SECTION

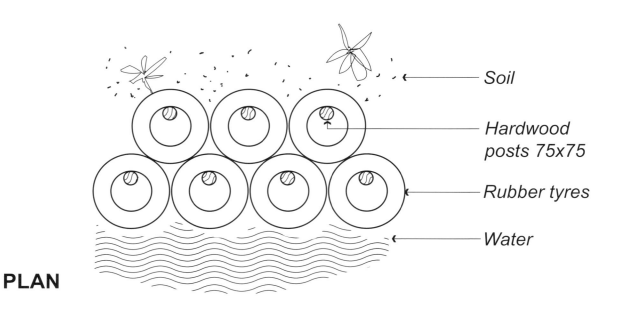

Soil

Hardwood posts 75x75

Rubber tyres

Water

PLAN

Scale 1:20

BANK PROTECTION
Rubber tyre

136

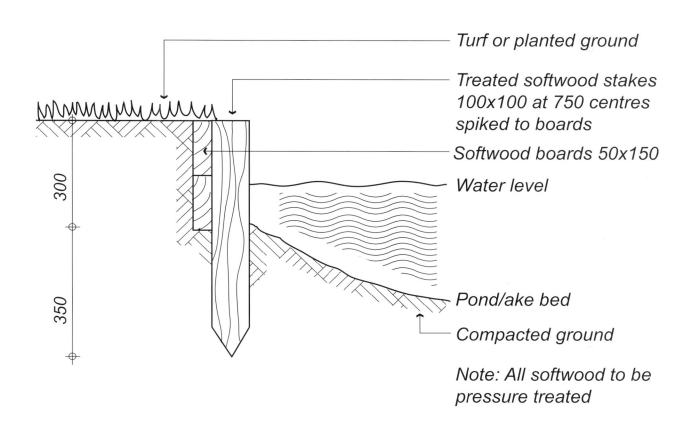

Turf or planted ground

Treated softwood stakes
100x100 at 750 centres
spiked to boards

Softwood boards 50x150

Water level

Pond/ake bed

Compacted ground

Note: All softwood to be
pressure treated

300

350

SECTION

Scale 1:10

BANK PROTECTION
Timber

137

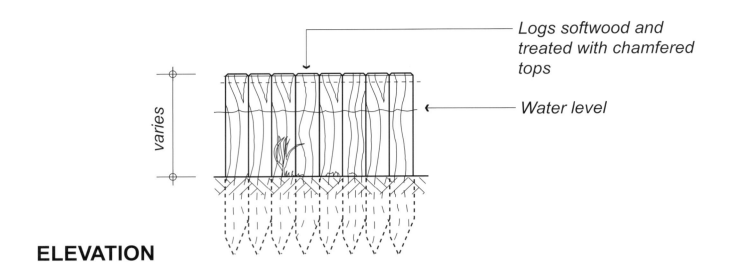

ELEVATION

Logs softwood and treated with chamfered tops

Water level

varies

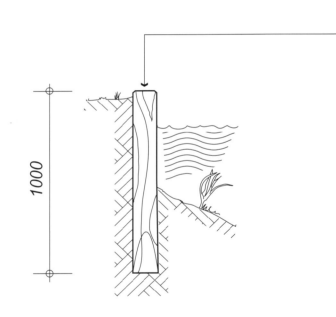

SECTION

1000

Logs driven and backfilled to level. If driven by impact, protect top of log. If driven hydraulically, logs must be guided

Lengths and diameters of logs to be determined by situation

PLAN

Logs set to line or radius

Scale 1:20

BANK PROTECTION
Timber logs

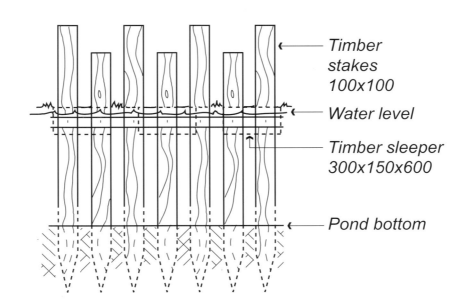

ELEVATION

Timber
stakes
100x100

Water level

Timber sleeper
300x150x600

Pond bottom

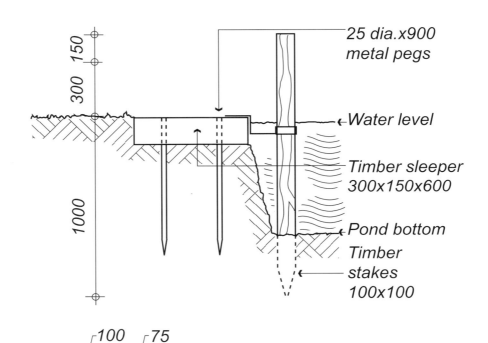

SECTION

25 dia.x900
metal pegs

Water level

Timber sleeper
300x150x600

Pond bottom
Timber
stakes
100x100

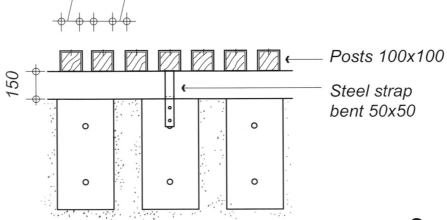

PLAN

Posts 100x100

Steel strap
bent 50x50

Scale 1:20

BANK PROTECTION
Timber stakes

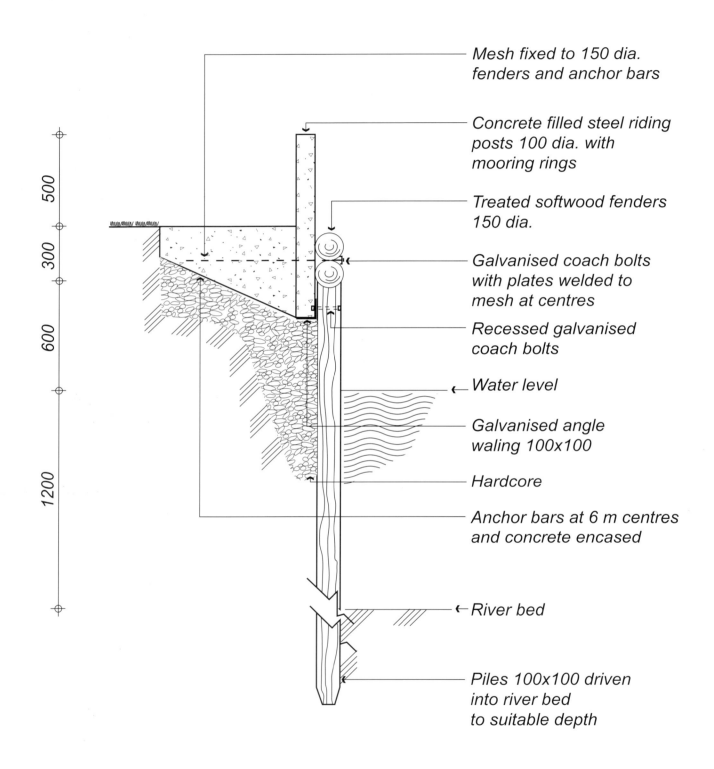

Mesh fixed to 150 dia. fenders and anchor bars

Concrete filled steel riding posts 100 dia. with mooring rings

Treated softwood fenders 150 dia.

Galvanised coach bolts with plates welded to mesh at centres

Recessed galvanised coach bolts

Water level

Galvanised angle waling 100x100

Hardcore

Anchor bars at 6 m centres and concrete encased

River bed

Piles 100x100 driven into river bed to suitable depth

500
300
600
1200

SECTION

Scale 1:20

BANK PROTECTION
Timber with mooring posts (1)

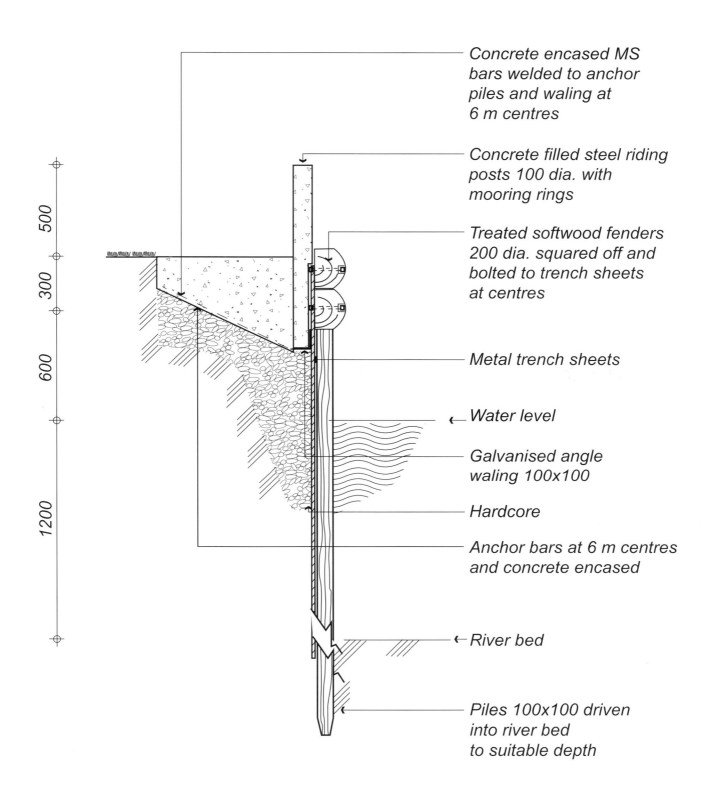

Concrete encased MS bars welded to anchor piles and waling at 6 m centres

Concrete filled steel riding posts 100 dia. with mooring rings

Treated softwood fenders 200 dia. squared off and bolted to trench sheets at centres

Metal trench sheets

Water level

Galvanised angle waling 100x100

Hardcore

Anchor bars at 6 m centres and concrete encased

River bed

Piles 100x100 driven into river bed to suitable depth

500
300
600
1200

SECTION

Scale 1:20

BANK PROTECTION
Timber with mooring posts (2)

141

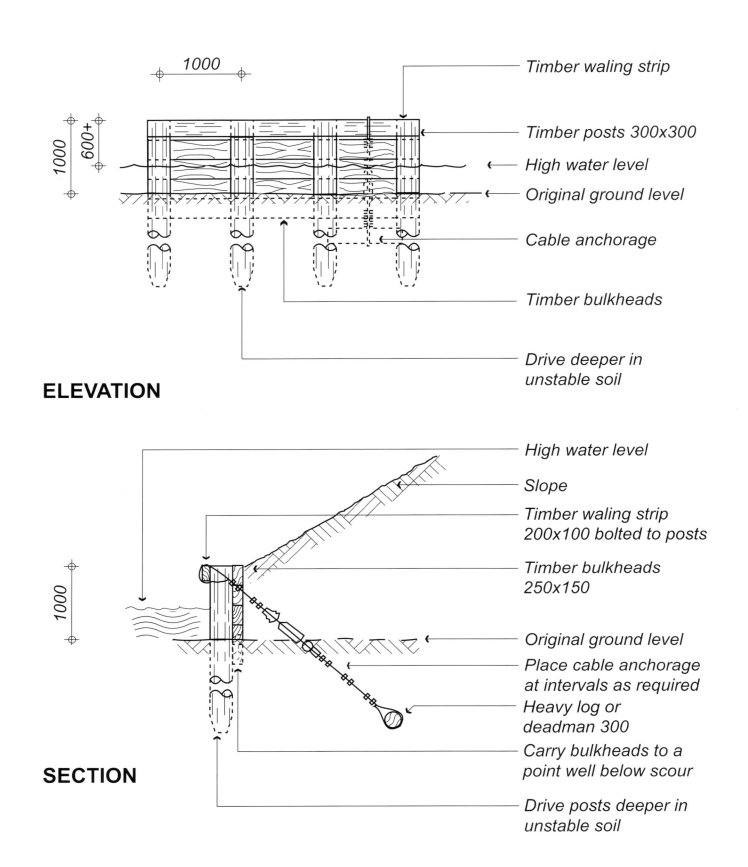

1000

1000

600+

ELEVATION

Timber waling strip

Timber posts 300x300

High water level

Original ground level

Cable anchorage

Timber bulkheads

Drive deeper in unstable soil

1000

SECTION

High water level

Slope

Timber waling strip 200x100 bolted to posts

Timber bulkheads 250x150

Original ground level

Place cable anchorage at intervals as required

Heavy log or deadman 300

Carry bulkheads to a point well below scour

Drive posts deeper in unstable soil

Scale 1:50

BANK PROTECTION
Timber bulkheads

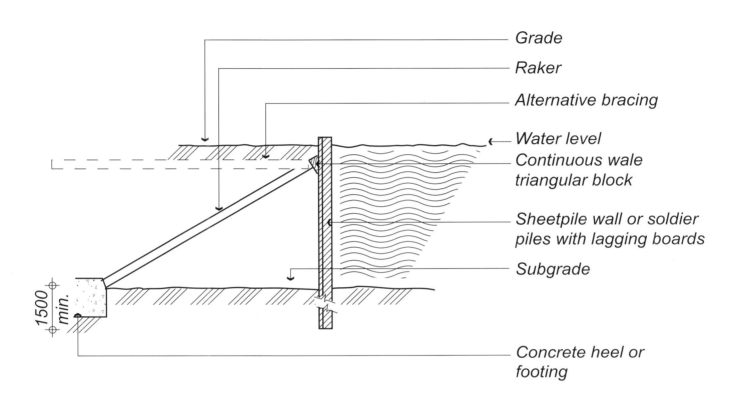

Grade

Raker

Alternative bracing

Water level

Continuous wale
triangular block

Sheetpile wall or soldier
piles with lagging boards

Subgrade

Concrete heel or
footing

1500
min.

SECTION　　　　　　　　　　　　　　　**Scale 1:100**

BANK PROTECTION
Excavation/rakers

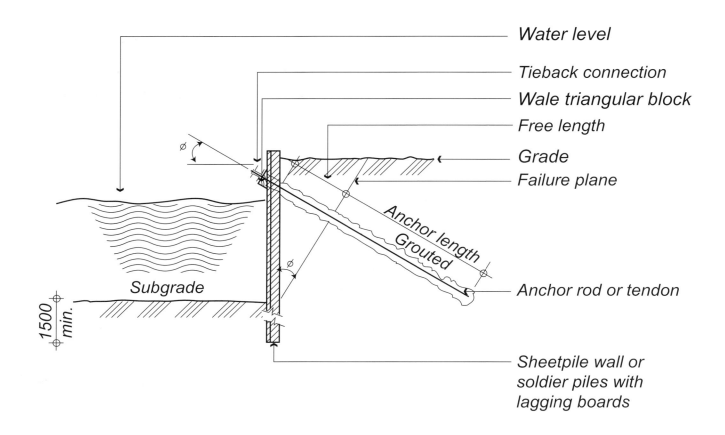

Water level

Tieback connection

Wale triangular block

Free length

Grade

Failure plane

φ

φ

Anchor length

Grouted

Subgrade

Anchor rod or tendon

1500 min.

Sheetpile wall or
soldier piles with
lagging boards

SECTION

Scale 1:100

BANK PROTECTION
Earth anchors

144

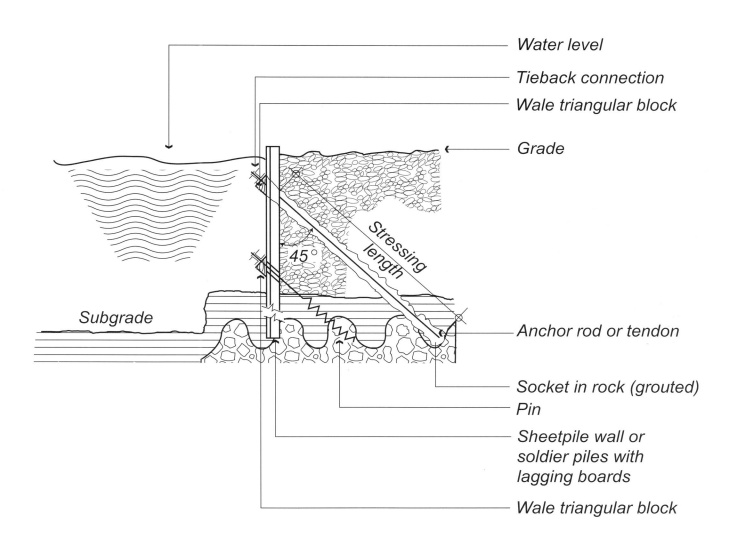

Water level

Tieback connection

Wale triangular block

Grade

Subgrade

45°

Stressing length

Anchor rod or tendon

Socket in rock (grouted)

Pin

Sheetpile wall or soldier piles with lagging boards

Wale triangular block

SECTION

Scale 1:100

BANK PROTECTION
Rock anchors

145

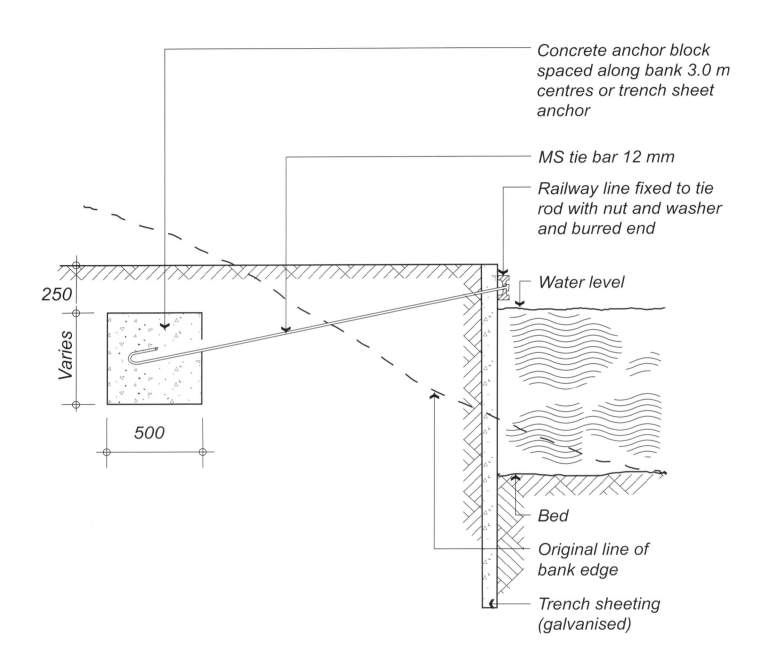

Concrete anchor block spaced along bank 3.0 m centres or trench sheet anchor

MS tie bar 12 mm

Railway line fixed to tie rod with nut and washer and burred end

Water level

250

Varies

500

Bed

Original line of bank edge

Trench sheeting (galvanised)

SECTION

Scale 1:20

BANK PROTECTION
Sheetpiling/rail line

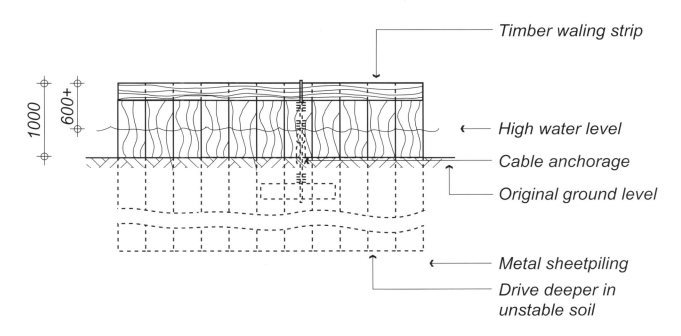

1000
600+

Timber waling strip

High water level

Cable anchorage

Original ground level

Metal sheetpiling

Drive deeper in
unstable soil

ELEVATION

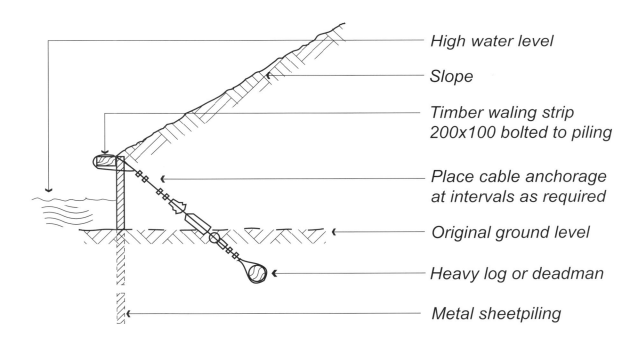

High water level

Slope

Timber waling strip
200x100 bolted to piling

Place cable anchorage
at intervals as required

Original ground level

Heavy log or deadman

Metal sheetpiling

SECTION

Scale 1:50

BANK PROTECTION
Metal sheetpile

147

REVETMENTS

A revetment is a cladding that is constructed on a sloping soil bank to protect and stabilise its surface against erosion by currents and wave action. A revetment usually has to accommodate surface water drainage and groundwater movement or subsoil drainage in the underlying bank. Unless it forms part of a composite structure, a revetment does not improve the mass stability of the underlying bank, which must therefore be stable under static water conditions.

Components

The component parts of a typical revetment are illustrated schematically in cross-section below. The revetment comprises the armour layer and the underlayer. Its performance is strongly dependent on the nature of the subsoil, as well as the effectiveness of the crest, toe and edge construction.

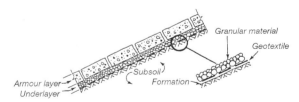

COMPONENTS OF A TYPICAL REVETMENT

Armour layer

The armour layer (or cover layer as it is also called) provides protection against the direct erosive forces of currents, wave action or other external effects.

It also exerts a positive normal stress on the subsoil formation that can enhance its stability against shallow failure.

Two key engineering properties, which affect the performance of the armour layer under current or wave action, are:

1. Permeability – which determines the degree to which external water motion and pressure due to currents or waves is 'felt' by the underlayer and the subsoil.

2. Flexibility – which enables the armour layer to accommodate minor deformation due to settlement, loss or migration of underlying material, and thus maintain the composite integrity of the revetment.

Underlayer

The underlayer is taken to include all material between the armour layer and the subsoil formation. It may be granular material, or a geotextile, or a combination. The component materials are generally selected to perform one or more of the functions listed below. An essential part of the design process is therefore to properly identify the particular functions that the underlayer can be expected to perform.

Revetment failure occurs most frequently due to the failure of the underlayer, generally as a result of the cumulative action of hydraulic forces within it and inadequate design considerations.

The functions that the underlayer can perform are as follows:

1. To act as a **filter** to restrain movement of the formation soil due to water movement into and out of the subsoil.

2. To provide a **drainage** zone parallel to the slope of the revetment to assist drainage of the underlayer and the subsoil.

3. To **protect** the formation **from erosion** by flow over its surface – parallel to the slope of the revetment.

4. To **regulate** an uneven soil surface to provide an even foundation for the revetment.

5. To **separate** the armour layer and other parts of the underlayer from the subsoil.

6. To provide **secondary protection** in case of loss of the armour layer.

7. To **dissipate energy** of internal flow in the underlayer caused by wave or current action (this function is normally utilised only in bank protection applications subject to high current or wave attack).

DESIGN

The design of revetments should generally proceed in the following steps:

- identification of design conditions (design loads; function of protection)

- preliminary selection of revetment type assessment of geotechnical stability of bank

- check on subsoil bearing capacity

- design of armour layer

- design of underlayer(s)

- detailing of crest, toe and edge.

Subsoil

The subsoil of most channel banks in this country is capable of supporting the weight of a revetment so long as it is distributed uniformly. The exceptions are fine silt soils and organic soils, which have a low bearing capacity. If the underlying subsoil is not consolidated then uneven settlement could occur, which could lead to voids beneath the armour unless the armour layer is flexible and deformable.

Design of armour layer

Types of armour

1. Stone

- Rip-rap or rock armour, occasionally grouted.
- Hand-pitched stone.
- Masonry, random or dressed.
- Gabion or wire mesh mattresses.

2. Concrete

- Plain precast blocks, open-jointed or grouted interlocking blocks.
- Cable-tied or geotextile-bonded blocks.
- Cast in situ slabs and monolithic structures.
- Fabric containers.

3. Geotextiles

- Grassed composites – mats, fabrics and meshes.
- Three-dimensional retaining mats and grids.
- Two-dimensional fabrics.

4. Asphalt

- Open stone asphalt-filled geotextile mat.
- Open or dense stone asphalt.

The stability of the armour layer from wave and current action has to be considered in the design, depending upon whether the layer is permeable or impermeable.

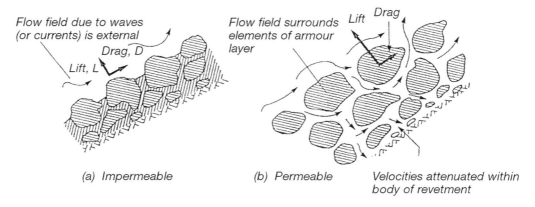

Flow field due to waves (or currents) is external

Drag, D

Lift, L

Flow field surrounds elements of armour layer

Lift Drag

(a) Impermeable

(b) Permeable   Velocities attenuated within body of revetment

EFFECT OF ARMOUR LAYER PERMEABILITY ON HYDRODYNAMIC FORCES ON REVETMENT

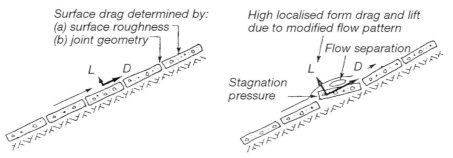

Surface drag determined by:
(a) surface roughness
(b) joint geometry

L   D

High localised form drag and lift due to modified flow pattern

Flow separation

Stagnation pressure

L   D

EFFECT OF ARMOUR LAYER FORM ON HYDRODYNAMIC FORCES ON REVETMENT

Factors affecting the stability

The ability of the armour layer to resist the hydraulic loading due to wave action, currents, subsoil drainage or groundwater movement will depend on some or all of the following factors:

- Weight and/or dimensions of elements of the armour layer; or the weight/unit area of continuous armour.

- Support provided by the underlayer or subsoil.

- Friction between adjacent elements of the armour layer, and between the armour layer and the underlayer or subsoil formation.

- Compressive forces in the plane of the revetment.

- Revetment slope.

- Interlock, grouting or cabling between elements of the armour layer.

- Anchorage and mechanical shear restraint between elements of the armour layer and the subsoil.

Design of the underlayer

Although geotextiles are now widely used for filtration, erosion control and separation functions, granular materials are probably more commonly used for regulating energy dissipation and secondary protection purposes. Different features of geotextile and granular material as underlayers are summarised in the table. In some applications a combination of geotextile and granular material may provide the most effective solution.

It is emphasised that the effectiveness of the composite revetment is dependent on good contact being maintained between the underlayer and the adjacent subsoil and armour layer. The design of the underlayer must take realistic account of construction constraints and likely consolidation of the subsoil following construction. In order to accommodate possible localised subsoil movement, a low-modulus geotextile that stretches and deforms easily may be used. Non-woven fabrics are usually considered more appropriate for this purpose.

FEATURES OF GEOTEXTILE AND GRANULAR MATERIALS AS UNDERLAYERS

Geotextile

Advantages
Cost
In-plane tensile strength
Limited thickness

Disadvantages
Some uncertainty over long-term behaviour
Edges must be carefully protected
Easy to damage; difficult to repair
Careful design and installation needed to accommodate settlement or uneven formation

Granular material

Advantages
Self-healing in some circumstances
Generally very durable
Deformable, retaining good surface contact above and below
Relatively easy to repair

Disadvantages
Careful control needed to achieve specified grading and thickness
Compaction difficult on steep side slopes
Control of construction difficult under water

Filter

The purpose of the filter is to prevent the spread of the base material (generally the subsoil) but still to allow movement of water across the filter bed boundary without causing an unacceptable head loss across it.

Rip-rap

General

Rip-rap is the term given to loose rock armour, usually obtained by quarrying. It is widely used for bank protection in this country. Useful engineering qualities of rip-rap include:

- general ease of placing, can be placed under water
- flexibility
- high hydraulic roughness to attenuate waves and currents
- low maintenance requirements and convenience of repair
- durability.

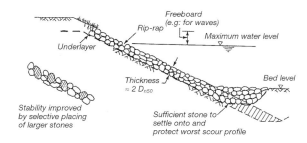

RIP-RAP REVETMENT – AN EXAMPLE

Unlike stone walls, rip-rap covers the banks with a layer of stone at an angle that approximates to the natural slope of the stream banks. If the banks are too steep for this method of protection then they could be regraded to a more stable slope 2:1 or flatter, before the stone is placed.

Rip-rap is applicable in a number of situations such as:

- in shaded areas where it could be difficult to establish woody vegetation
- streams where water levels fluctuate widely
- at locations where water flow could threaten buildings, roads or bridges
- where it is desirable to reduce the force of the water as rip-rap is rough in texture
- where the site requires an indigenous material to blend with the natural environment.

When properly keyed into the stream and bank, rip-rap is very flexible. Any damage that may occur is gradual and minimal. It is also resistant to scour and allows for the percolation of the water. Another advantage of rip-rap is that it is not as difficult to install as building stone walls, although construction skills are required.

However, rip-rap is expensive, especially if stone has to be quarried and hauled long distances. The stone has to be of a large size to resist the force of high water flows. Hand placed stone rip-rap is preferred where the area to be stabilised is small, where machine access may be difficult or where a more natural arrangement of the stone is desired.

Rip-rap can be dumped or placed by hand.

For dumped rip-rap construction, it is better to do this at low water and the stone selected should be heavy enough to resist high water forces.

The stone should be 600 mm thick or more, on the banks, depending on the velocity of the stream. It should be applied over a 150 mm layer of gravel, at a slope not to exceed 2:1. The largest rocks should be placed on the lower levels, and rough rocks should be used on the outside layer.

While some hand labour may be necessary to arrange rock, dumped rip-rap should be keyed into the stream bed to a depth of 1 m to prevent scour, the installation is primarily handled by machine.

Hand placed rip-rap is similar to dumped rip-rap except that the surface layer of stone is placed by hand in a neat, ordered arrangement. The result is similar to a stone wall that is at the same angle as the slope of the stream bank. It should extend at least 300 mm below the low water level, and the entire installation should be keyed at least 1 m into the stream bed to prevent scour.

The hand placed layer of stone is placed over a 150 mm layer of dumped stone and gravel and the total thickness of the stone should be at least 600 mm, while a greater thickness can be used depending on the velocity of the stream.

Certain types of stone, because of the nature of their bedding and structure, are most suitable for this type of revetment; two examples are Kentish ragstone and basalt. The former cleaves naturally to a cubic shape and the latter occurs naturally as octagonal blocks.

Mortar grouted stone

Grouting the stone provides a low cost accessible and visually attractive revetment in urban and suburban areas. As it forms a more rigid revetment it can, for low banks, be constructed on steeper slopes than machine rip-rap or hand placed stone.

It will require a firm toe foundation and if stone cannot be laid in dry conditions then steel piling or sheet steel trenching could be used.

As the whole revetment is sealed, provision for drainage should be with weep holes in places.

There are three methods by which the stones can be grouted. Firstly by brushing dry cement/mortar mix over the surface of the stone so that all the gaps are filled. This is left to harden. The second is by pouring a very wet cement mortar into the gaps until they are all filled. Unfortunately, unless the mortar is wiped off it will adhere to the stone and make it unsightly. The third method is by hand pointing the gaps but it is labour intensive and expensive. However, it provides the best seal and appearance.

Mattresses

Mattresses are a thinner, more flexible, version of the gabion box with a plan size typically 6 m x 2 m, and thicknesses of 150 to 300 mm. They are normally constructed from woven wire, which again may be galvanised and PVC coated.

Mattresses are not used for earth retaining structures but to protect a bed or stable sloping bank against surface erosion. They are especially useful where integrity of the protection must be maintained in the event of major movement, and are commonly used as a protective apron at the toe of a bank or a retaining wall.

The fill material should be a durable stone that will not break down quickly within the mattress by abrasion and weathering. Angular stones are best because they lock together better than rounded stones.

Fill material has a normal size of about 1.5 times the mean mesh dimension, individual stones should be not smaller than the nominal mesh size (varies from 50 mm x 70 mm to 100 mm x 120 mm for commonly available woven boxes), and generally not larger than 200 mm nominal size. The requirements for minimum stone size are sometimes relaxed for filling the core of a gabion structure, distant from the exterior faces.

Machine filling is generally quicker and cheaper. Hand placing will generally produce a better appearance for the finished wall, as well as a denser construction. With either method the fill material must completely fill the box. The fill material must be well packed to minimise voids and achieve good contact between individual rocks, and be packed as tight as possible to reduce the possibility of moving within the box.

Gabion mattresses are normally laid on formal slopes no greater than 1 in 5. The mattresses are assembled and positioned on site with the diaphragms lying perpendicular to the direction in which the stone filling will move, either down the slope or in the directions of the flow. The units are wired together and then filled by machine with any tidying up being done by hand to ensure tight packing before the lids are fixed in place.

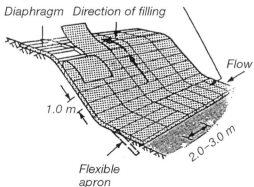

GABION MATTRESS REVETMENT

153

Precast concrete blocks

Blocks have been used for revetments for a long time and have proved very effective.

The types of block that are considered are:

- open joint or grouted blocks
- interlocking blocks
- cable tied or geotextile-bonded blocks
- cellular blocks.

Blocks to be used are usually reinforced with a minimum thickness of 80–100 mm but this is dependent upon the subsoil conditions and properties. These will need to be checked very carefully as they will affect the choice of blocks to withstand the surface loading.

The blocks are normally laid on an underlayer but this can be omitted if the subsoil is impermeable clay. This subsoil would need to be well compacted or consolidated and have a smooth crack-free formation on which the blocks can be firmly bedded. It may be necessary to use a form of toe protection that will withstand scour.

Open jointed or grouted blocks

Blocks can be left with open or grouted joints: the former is relatively flexible and cheaper but it is also susceptible to vandalism unless the individual blocks are too heavy and difficult to be lifted by hand.

Grouting between the blocks increases their stability by wedging them together but it then reduces the flexibility of the revetment. Grouting can be with a granular material, mortar or mastic. Gaps must be left for pressure relief if the bedding is of a granular material, but if the blocks are laid on an impermeable slope then no gaps are necessary.

Blocks should be laid by hand, except for large areas or if they are very heavy then machinery should be used.

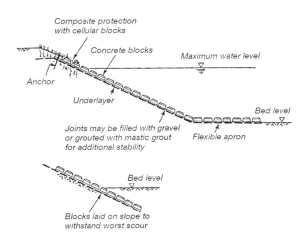

CONCRETE BLOCK REVETMENT

Interlocking blocks

There are various forms of interlocking blocks that provide a far better connection than ordinary blocks. Plain interlocking blocks with various shapes can be used to form a vertically impermeable layer. Many coastal revetments use this system as it offers a better defence against strong wave attacks.

Care must be taken in the design where a significant curvature is required in the plan on the sloping bank without causing problems of poor connection and appearance. Settlement could also cause the same problems.

Stability of concrete blocks

The surface of a block revetment is smooth, unlike rip-rap, and is not subject to large drag forces or wave actions. However, failure will occur if a block or blocks are pushed out as a result of pressure differences between the top and bottom faces. The permeability of the underlayer has a major influence on the stability of the revetment. The designer must ensure that a strict no-damage criterion is applied, as there can be no allowance for even a small degree of damage.

Concrete – in situ

Cast in situ concrete revetments are used in locations where strength, durability or ability to conform to varied surface geometry are important design considerations. These are:

- areas for long service life and minimum maintenance
- access areas
- drainage channels
- transition areas adjacent to structures.

Provision must be made for movement by having joints in appropriate places. As plain cast in situ concrete is impermeable it is essential that weep holes are included to accommodate any groundwater flow.

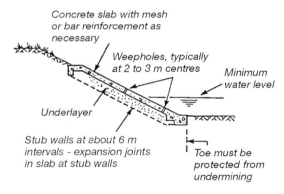

A TYPICAL CONCRETE REVETMENT

A minimum thickness of concrete of between 100 and 150 mm is normal and consideration should be given to the formwork method of placing the concrete and that the slope is satisfactory for the work to be undertaken for long-term durability.

Concrete-filled bags

This method of protection for river and canal banks has been used for a considerably long time. Hessian bags are usually used although synthetic woven bags are also available.

Hessian bags are cheap, biodegradable and the open porous weave allows some cement grout to pass through after they have been filled.

While they are labour intensive, this method of construction is very adaptable, especially for tight curves and corners as well as short runs. They are ideal for repair. The bags are filled with a dry mix concrete with a weak mix being used under normal circumstances. They are usually underfilled to ensure adequate contact between each row of bags. They are laid like bricks, stretcher bond with the open end of the bag facing downstream, folded under and covered with the head of the next bag. To ensure that there is no movement, mild steel bars, approximately 12 mm diameter, are driven through every third bag. They may be built up to ten courses high and can be used to form steep slopes and between vertical and sloping sections.

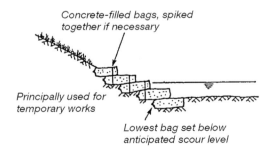

A TYPICAL CONCRETE BAG REVETMENT

SECTION

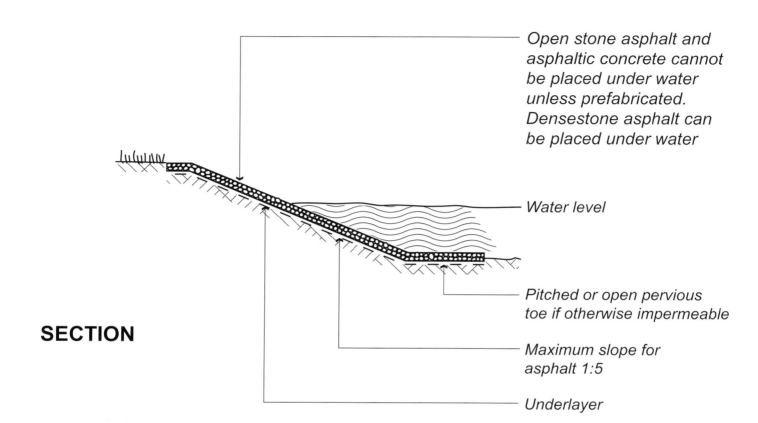

Open stone asphalt and asphaltic concrete cannot be placed under water unless prefabricated. Densestone asphalt can be placed under water

Water level

Pitched or open pervious toe if otherwise impermeable

Maximum slope for asphalt 1:5

Underlayer

Scale 1:50

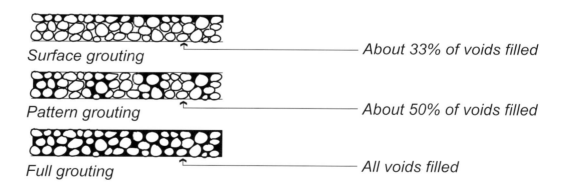

Surface grouting — About 33% of voids filled

Pattern grouting — About 50% of voids filled

Full grouting — All voids filled

TYPES OF GROUTED ROCK

Scale 1:20

REVETMENT
Asphalt

156

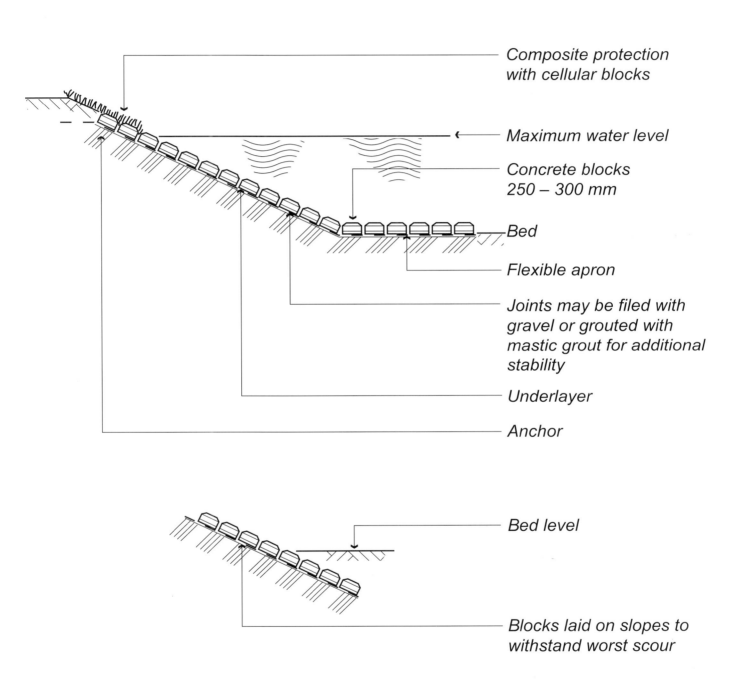

Composite protection
with cellular blocks

Maximum water level

Concrete blocks
250 – 300 mm

Bed

Flexible apron

Joints may be filed with
gravel or grouted with
mastic grout for additional
stability

Underlayer

Anchor

Bed level

Blocks laid on slopes to
withstand worst scour

SECTION   **Scale 1:50**

REVETMENT
Concrete block

157

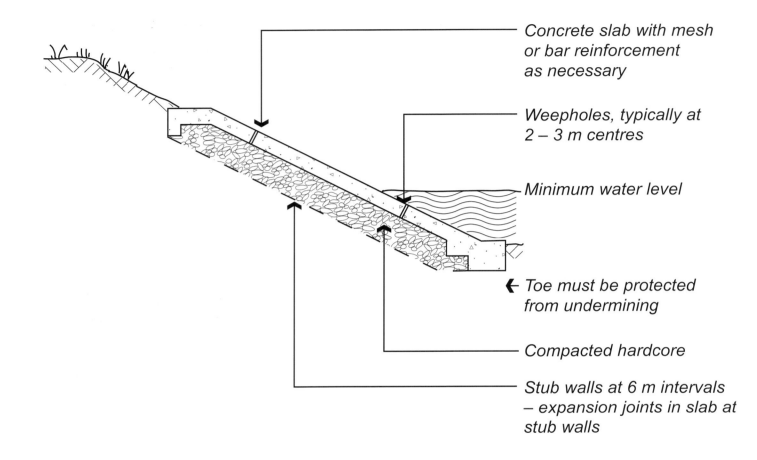

Concrete slab with mesh
or bar reinforcement
as necessary

Weepholes, typically at
2 – 3 m centres

Minimum water level

← Toe must be protected
from undermining

Compacted hardcore

Stub walls at 6 m intervals
– expansion joints in slab at
stub walls

SECTION

Scale 1:50

REVETMENT
Cast *in situ* concrete

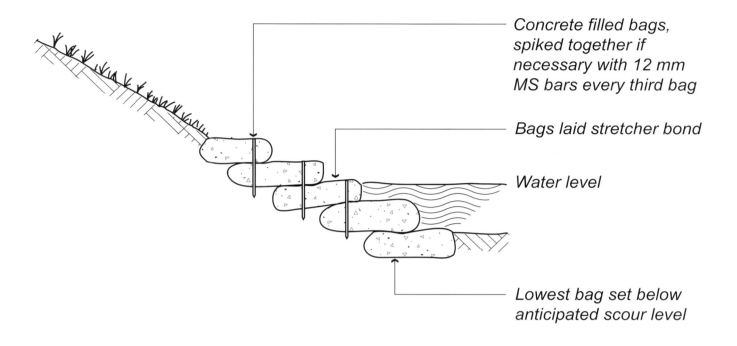

Concrete filled bags, spiked together if necessary with 12 mm MS bars every third bag

Bags laid stretcher bond

Water level

Lowest bag set below anticipated scour level

Note:
Principally used for temporary works

SECTION

Scale 1:50

REVETMENT
Concrete bag

159

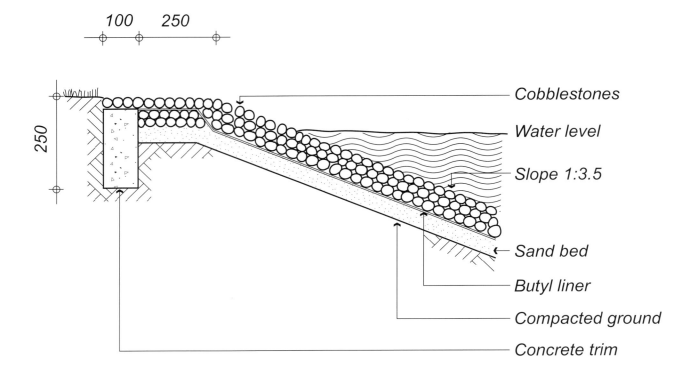

100   250

250

Cobblestones

Water level

Slope 1:3.5

Sand bed

Butyl liner

Compacted ground

Concrete trim

SECTION

Scale 1:10

REVETMENT
Cobblestones on sand

160

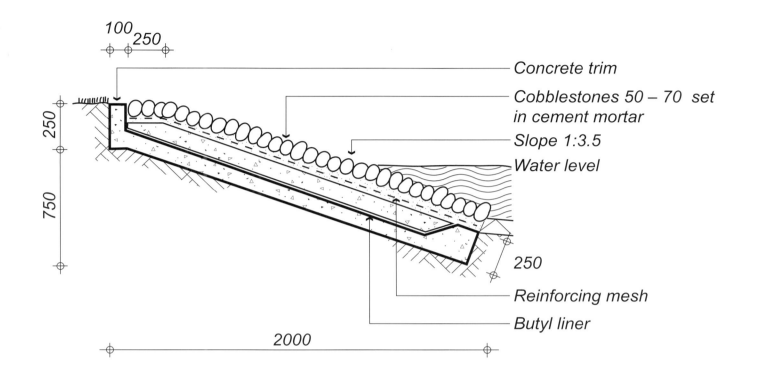

100 250

250

750

2000

Concrete trim

Cobblestones 50 – 70 set in cement mortar

Slope 1:3.5

Water level

250

Reinforcing mesh

Butyl liner

SECTION

Scale 1:20

REVETMENT
Cobblestones/mesh

161

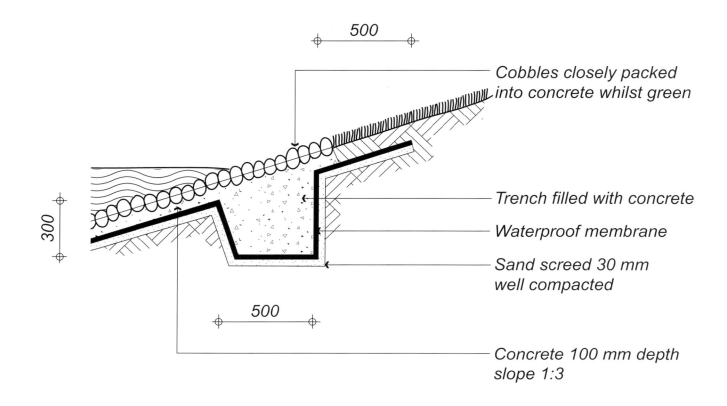

500

300

Cobbles closely packed
into concrete whilst green

Trench filled with concrete

Waterproof membrane

Sand screed 30 mm
well compacted

500

Concrete 100 mm depth
slope 1:3

SECTION

Scale 1:20

REVETMENT
Cobblestones

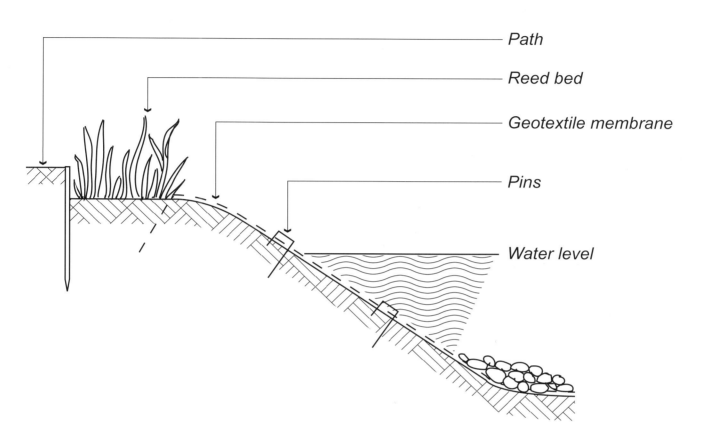

Path

Reed bed

Geotextile membrane

Pins

Water level

Short-term protection only

SECTION

Scale 1:50

REVETMENT
Geotextile fabric protection

163

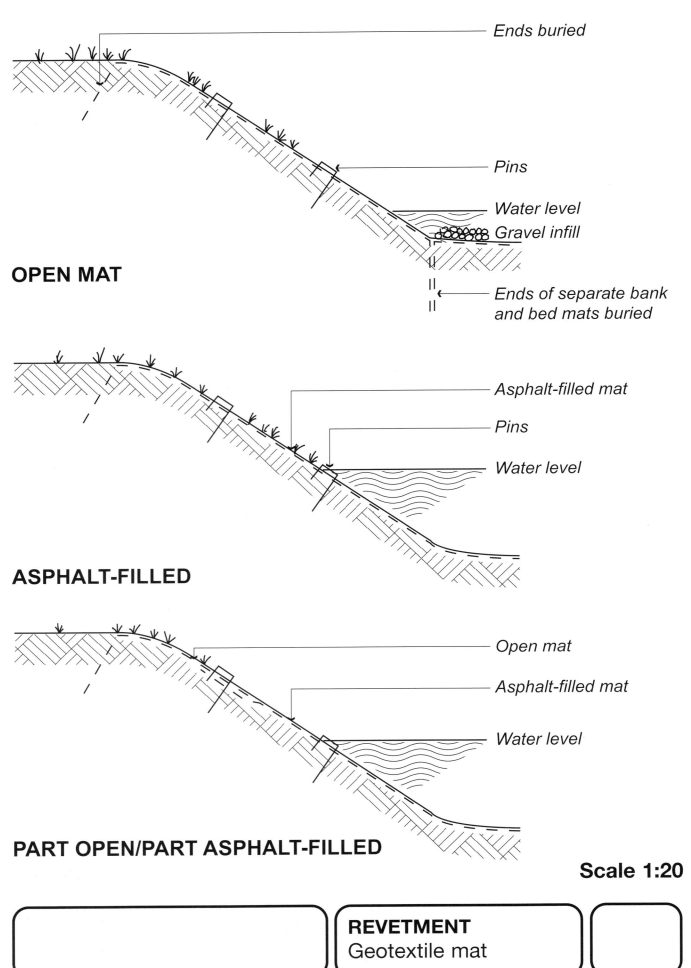

OPEN MAT

Ends buried

Pins

Water level

Gravel infill

Ends of separate bank
and bed mats buried

ASPHALT-FILLED

Asphalt-filled mat

Pins

Water level

PART OPEN/PART ASPHALT-FILLED

Open mat

Asphalt-filled mat

Water level

Scale 1:20

REVETMENT
Geotextile mat

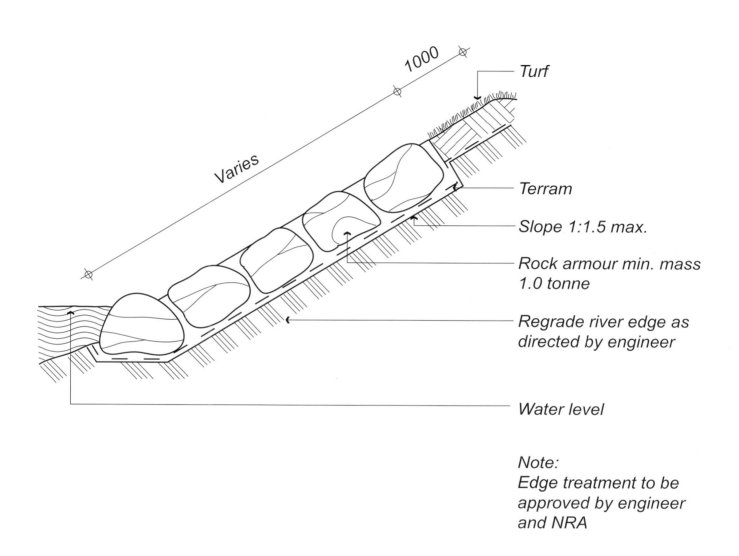

1000

Varies

Turf

Terram

Slope 1:1.5 max.

Rock armour min. mass 1.0 tonne

Regrade river edge as directed by engineer

Water level

Note:
Edge treatment to be approved by engineer and NRA

SECTION

Scale 1:50

REVETMENT
Rock armour

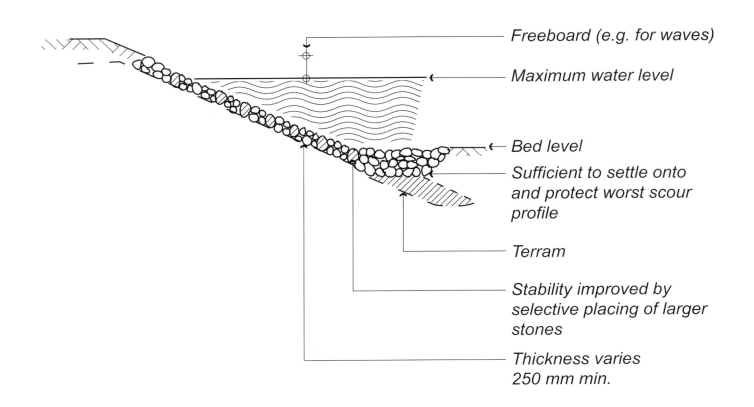

Freeboard (e.g. for waves)

Maximum water level

Bed level

Sufficient to settle onto and protect worst scour profile

Terram

Stability improved by selective placing of larger stones

Thickness varies 250 mm min.

SECTION

Scale 1:50

REVETMENT
Rip-rap

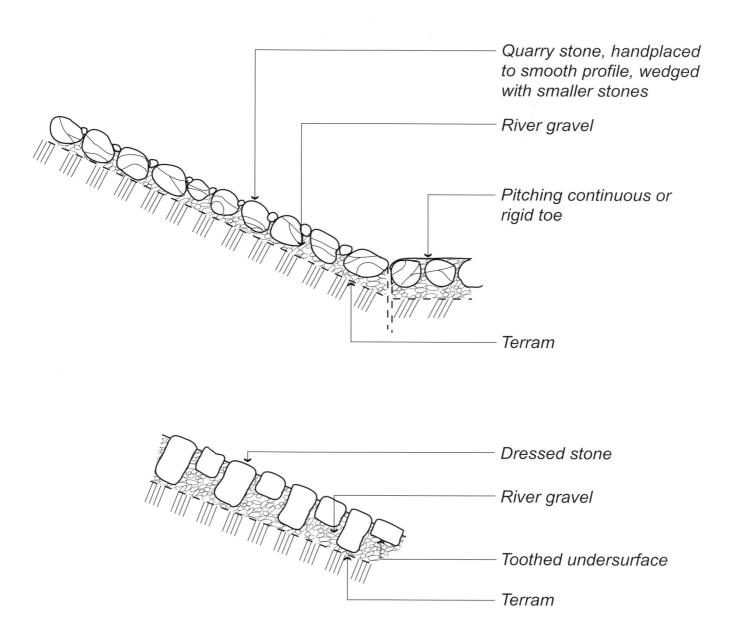

Quarry stone, handplaced to smooth profile, wedged with smaller stones

River gravel

Pitching continuous or rigid toe

Terram

Dressed stone

River gravel

Toothed undersurface

Terram

SECTION

Scale 1:20

REVETMENT
Stone

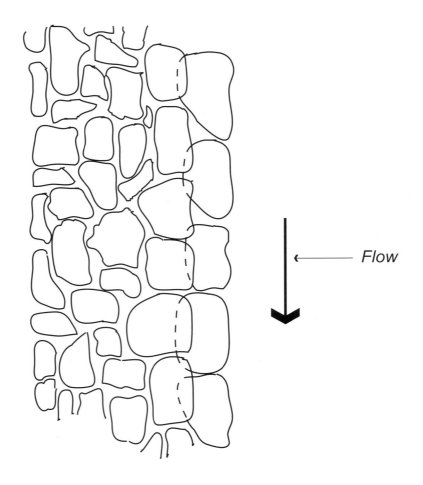

PLAN

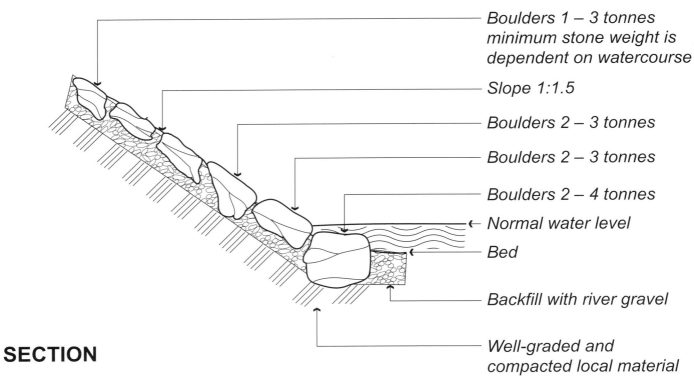

Boulders 1 – 3 tonnes
minimum stone weight is
dependent on watercourse

Slope 1:1.5

Boulders 2 – 3 tonnes

Boulders 2 – 3 tonnes

Boulders 2 – 4 tonnes

← Normal water level

Bed

Backfill with river gravel

Well-graded and
compacted local material

Flow

SECTION

Scale 1:100

POND CONSTRUCTION
Liner/bricks

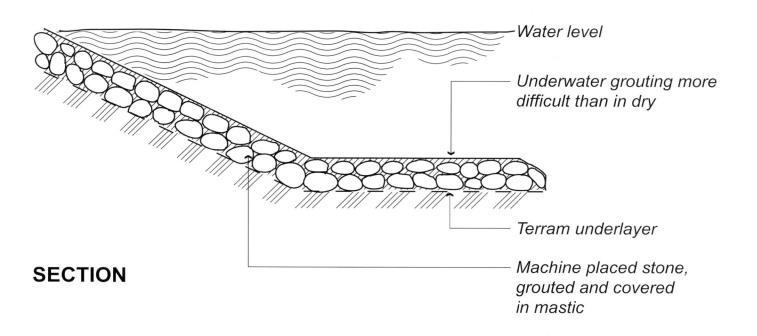

Water level

Underwater grouting more
difficult than in dry

Terram underlayer

Machine placed stone,
grouted and covered
in mastic

SECTION

SECTION   **Scale 1:50**

REVETMENT
Mastic-grouted stone

DAMS, WEIRS AND SLUICES

DAMS

Dams are not easy to build, as great care is needed to ensure stability and water-tightness. Small on-stream ponds can be created by building a bank no more than 1 metre high across a stream, but these are of limited value as they are unlikely to be very deep and will silt up rapidly.

A dam generally impounds the waters of a stream and converts an area into a pond, lake or a reservoir. It can be built of earth, masonry, concrete etc., but in an earth dam, flood waters are never allowed to overtop the crest and must be carried off by an overflow channel. The construction of high earth dams is a work requiring technical skill and experience and should not be undertaken lightheartedly. These notes deal with the smaller dams, say up to 6 m in height.

There are two types of dam – on-stream and off-stream. On-stream dams block existing watercourses to form lakes and this requires a high-quality (high-cost) spillway to accommodate heavy storm flows.

Off-stream dams are built in isolation and supplied with water from an outside source. Their advantage is that they are independent of the natural drainage pattern and so of less concern to water authorities. They are cheaper.

Before undertaking a design for a dam, a survey is necessary to determine all the natural environmental data such as geology, soils, climate, hydrology, etc. as well as all the physical factors such as existing services, hard surfaces, etc.

The following are essential to design:

- The dam must be strong enough to sustain the pressure of water behind it, which is greatest at the base and this must be the strongest part. Non-porous installations must be keyed into impervious strata. 'The rule of thumb is to make concrete or brickwork at least half as thick as the head, i.e. if the head is 'h' the weir or sluice must be $\frac{1}{2}h$ thick. The maximum head over non-porous weirs and sluices of the sort which volunteers can easily construct is about 1.2–1.5 m (4–6 inches). Even at this head, concrete or brickwork must be 610–760 mm (2 ft–2 ft 6 inches) thick' (BTCV, 1992). The risk of failure lies in the liability of the earthwork itself to slip.

- The ends and bottom of the dam must be so constructed that the water does not seep around or under it.

- The overflow or waste water channel must be large enough to allow the heaviest flood to run off. Flood water must not be allowed to flow over the top of an earthen dam under any circumstances.

- The system of drawing off the water must be simple and accessible.

Site selection

A site giving the maximum natural basin for the minimum of expenditure should be selected. A natural water course or stream bed is ideal where its gradient is low and where it widens out behind some natural restriction. If such a natural area is not available then a dam of the 'horseshoe' type can be used.

Particular attention must be given to the hydrology of the catchment area, reservoir and drainage system with special emphasis to the measurements of the greatest flood flow that the dam spillway must be designed to pass.

Consideration of the suitability of the site for a spillway should be undertaken.

Natural or uncut spillways are generally to be preferred, particularly if a rocky outcrop could be utilised. Badly decomposed rock or granite is unsuitable. In soil, a cut spillway will need to be constructed and covered with grass. Attention must be given to the route that the water will follow back to its natural course.

Construction

There are various methods of and materials available for the building of dams, but the most common one is 'earth' or 'gravity' dams. Their stability depends upon their weight and consequent resistance to moving under pressure from the water impounded. The design of dams is beyond the scope of this book but properly designed and constructed dams are amply sufficient to withstand the maximum water pressure for which they have been designed.

Dams are also referred to as homogeneous, zoned diaphragm and blanket. Homogeneous dams are constructed of impermeable soil throughout and can be placed on an impermeable or permeable soil base.

Zoned and diaphragm dams are made of permeable soil with an impermeable core, which is the seepage barrier, on either a permeable or impermeable base.

Blanket dams are used where limited amounts of impermeable soil are available and which can be used in the centre core, surrounded by permeable soil with a waterproof blanket on the wet slope.

Foundations

The essential conditions for the foundation of an earth dam are that the soil should be compact, that it will not yield when wet, and that it will not settle nor slip under the weight of the dam. The best foundation for a dam is:

- Hard compact rock. The surface should be level, or sloping slightly downward from the downstream side towards the upstream side of the dam.

The next best foundations are in the order named:

- The softer rocks
- Hard, compact and solid gravelly soil
- Hard clay soil
- Brown and red soils
- 'Black cotton' soil.

The embankment

The embankment should comprise a subsoil of 20–30 per cent clay mixed with sand and gravel, and can be constructed of one material throughout, which when compacted produces a dense waterproof material. The diagram shows a typical cross-section of an earth dam.

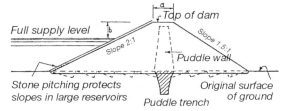

CROSS-SECTION – EARTH DAM

The main features are a core consisting of clay or some selected impervious material in the heart of the dam and keyed into the foundation material in a trench. The rest of the embankment material is then placed on both sides and above the core.

The side slopes of the embankment should not be steeper than 2:1 (2 m horizontal to 1 m vertical) on the upstream side and 1.5:1 on the downstream side. If the embankment is made of very sandy or non-cohesive material, slopes should be made flatter.

The width of the dam at the top or crest should never be less than 2.0 m and the height of the crest should always be higher than the maximum anticipated water level under extreme flood conditions. This is known as the 'freeboard' and the amount depends upon the height of the dam and other design factors – usually it is around 1.0 m.

The normal method of construction, after removal of all vegetation and topsoil, is to excavate down until a firm natural soil is found. An impervious clay core is usually included in the design commencing in a trench approximately 2.0 m wide along the axis of the dam.

The core material, which is the best clay available, is first made plastic with water, and the trench is then filled with plastic clay, or 'puddle'. The puddle is then carried up through the dam as the rest of the embankment material is placed.

The material for the dam is often excavated on the upstream side of it, and the excavation should be well clear of the toe of the slope (a distance of three times height of dam from it).

The material, free of all clods, lumps, large stones and rubbish, is spread in layers 150 mm thick over the entire width of dam and well rammed. If the material is too dry it should be damped before being placed in the work.

The site of large dams is drained by means of dry stone drains. The drains carry away any infiltration from lake reservoir and thus preserve the dam.

Where the dam impounds a stream, the waters should be carried through the outlet pipe during the construction.

Grass seed should be sown immediately upon finishing the earthworks for the dam as this will help to stabilise the soil and minimise erosion as well as prevent growth of other undesirable plants.

The best grasses are strains of creeping bent *(Agrostes stolonifera)* and rough stalk meadow grass *(Poa trivalis)*. These are fairly low growing and will tolerate wet or dry conditions. Fencing the area may be necessary, especially during the establishment phase.

Non-earth dams

A small low dam could be constructed of stones and cement mortar, provided it was built solidly and on sound foundations of concrete or stone. The proportions usually adopted for the construction are:

$$t_1 = 0.2h, \ t_2 = 0.7h$$

Therefore in a wall 2 m high the thickness at the base would be 0.7 x 2 = 1.4 m and at the top 0.2 x 2 = 0.4 m.

Dams and weirs are also built of uncemented stones ('rock fill dams'). The stones are carefully piled much as earth in an earthen dam (i.e. with appropriate slopes). The water face of the dam is made as watertight as possible, either by covering it with masonry in cement or even a mass of clay. Rock fill dams are not water tight but can be made so if an impervious core is incorporated in their construction. They can also be constructed with the use of gabions. The function of a gabion is to provide an easily constructed unit that is large enough and heavy enough to remain stable in moving water.

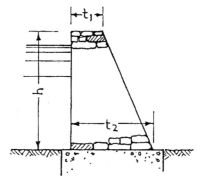

SMALL MASONRY DAM

As gabions are permeable and flexible they generally do not require complex structural design, but if they are to be submerged in water, calculations should be made for their stability under flood conditions. Evenly graded stones should be used so that the gabions are well packed with few empty spaces, and the largest stone should not be more than two-thirds of the minimum gabion dimension. As gabions are usually filled by hand, the manpower available will determine the maximum size of stone used.

Dams can also be constructed of ex-railway sleepers and timber boards, for shallow streams 1–1.2 m (2–4 ft) deep. They can also function as a weir with a breakwater placed on top.

While they are easy to construct they are prone to leaking and both the sleepers and the boards must be well bedded into the banks and/or set against posts to ensure permanent stability.

Filled sacks of sand, clay or concrete can be used to make dams, piled up and protected on both sides with galvanised sheeting and wooden or iron stakes driven into the ground.

Overflow outlet

Overflows are not required for off-stream dams provided that the inflow can be controlled. On-stream dams must have adequate overflows to prevent overtopping and failure during periods of heavy rain and floods. The calculations of catchment run-off and overflow capacity are very complicated and expert advice will be necessary.

The spillway

A spillway is necessary as it releases water so that the dam is not over-topped, which could very quickly lead to failure.

The spillway is usually similar to a weir that is over-topped as soon as the water level rises above the planned storage level.

Natural spillways, especially of rock, are preferred to excavated spillways.

The design of the spillway must ensure that it is of sufficient size to carry the maximum amount of water and that it is secure against any erosion. The location of the spillway is usually at one end of the dam.

In certain situations the spillway can be made part of the dam structure or earth bank provided its slope is not steeper than 1:3, the surface has a satisfactory grass area, and the head over the spillway is never more than 75–100 mm (3–4 inches).

WEIRS

Weirs are constructed for holding back a certain volume of water for a specific purpose, such as creating pools of deeper water for fish and other aquatic life. Weirs may be part of the overflow system of a dam or placed on their own in an area of flowing water but where they can be over-topped, depending on the surrounding rainfall catchment.

A simple weir can be made by inserting a solid barrier (known as a spillboard) between the existing banks of a stream or ditch or partly cutting off a water course with an earth bank containing a spillboard. Various materials can be used such as wooden planks, old railway sleepers (timber or concrete), old wharf or jetty bulk timbers and round logs. The spillboard needs to be keyed into a groove in each bank with any gaps plugged with clay crib weirs of rough tree trunks, stones/clay and boards are economical in both materials and labour, yet produce a strong structure.

Logs of 100–150 cm diameter are placed 600–900 cm apart and spiked to other logs placed at right angles (similar to a vertical crib wall but horizontal). The spaces between the logs are filled and consolidated with stones and/or clay with both the upstream and downstream faces covered with boards sealed with clay to prevent seepage (caulking as on the decks of ships may be more effective and longer lasting).

Alternatively, the downstream side could be stepped to provide a more effective appearance and a break in the force of the water. The downstream channel will need protection by rocks/boulders, gabions or other appropriate materials to prevent erosion. Weirs can also be constructed of in situ concrete, concrete blocks, or rough stones. The design should ensure that the base thickness is 50 per cent greater than the height. A small apron should be included at the base on the downstream side to turn the water slightly upwards. This will break the force of the water and assist in preventing erosion.

SLUICES

Sluices are used as a means of controlling water or for conducting water through regulating valves or gates.

When the water level of a small pond is high and needs to be lowered, boards can be removed or a gate lowered to allow water to escape. When a dry period is prevalent the outflow can be blocked to keep the water at the appropriate level.

A system of ditches or dykes with sluices have often been used in water management to ensure adequate water to a series of fish ponds or to ensure certain areas are kept in a fen where a high diverse flora is protected and encouraged. Sluices can also control tidal waters and prevent them from flowing into freshwater areas. A box gate is a suitable method, as shown in the diagram.

There are various forms of sluices but the plank gate set in a metal or precast concrete channel is the best design because of its simplicity. Oak boards 25 x 100 mm (1 x 6 inches) are the most durable.

Solid gates use heavy duty hardware with ratchets, turnscrews or other mechanisms to make lifting easier. Single or double gates can be used depending upon the degree of control required.

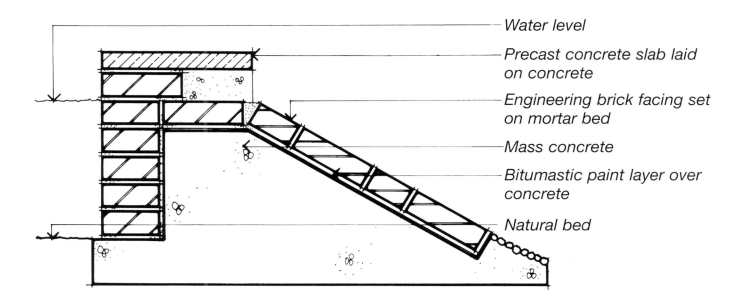

SECTION

Water level

Precast concrete slab laid on concrete

Engineering brick facing set on mortar bed

Mass concrete

Bitumastic paint layer over concrete

Natural bed

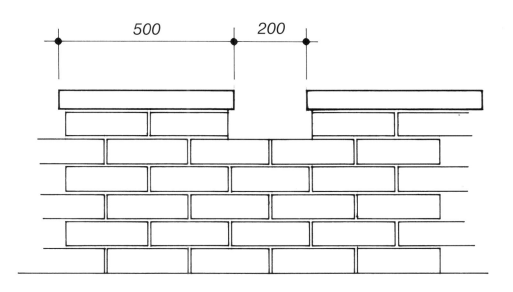

500   200

ELEVATION

Scale 1:10

WEIR
Brick

175

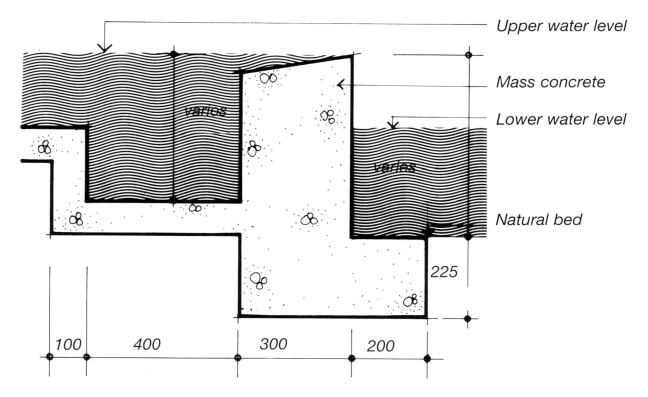

Upper water level

Mass concrete

Lower water level

Natural bed

varies

varies

225

100   400   300   200

SECTION 1:10

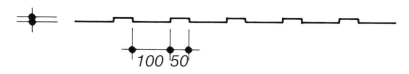

100 50

PLAN 1:10

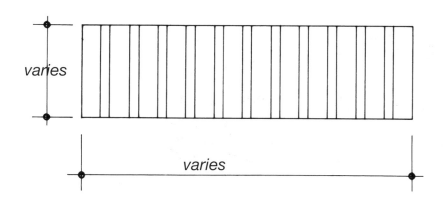

varies

varies

ELEVATION 1:20

Scale A·S

WEIR
Concrete

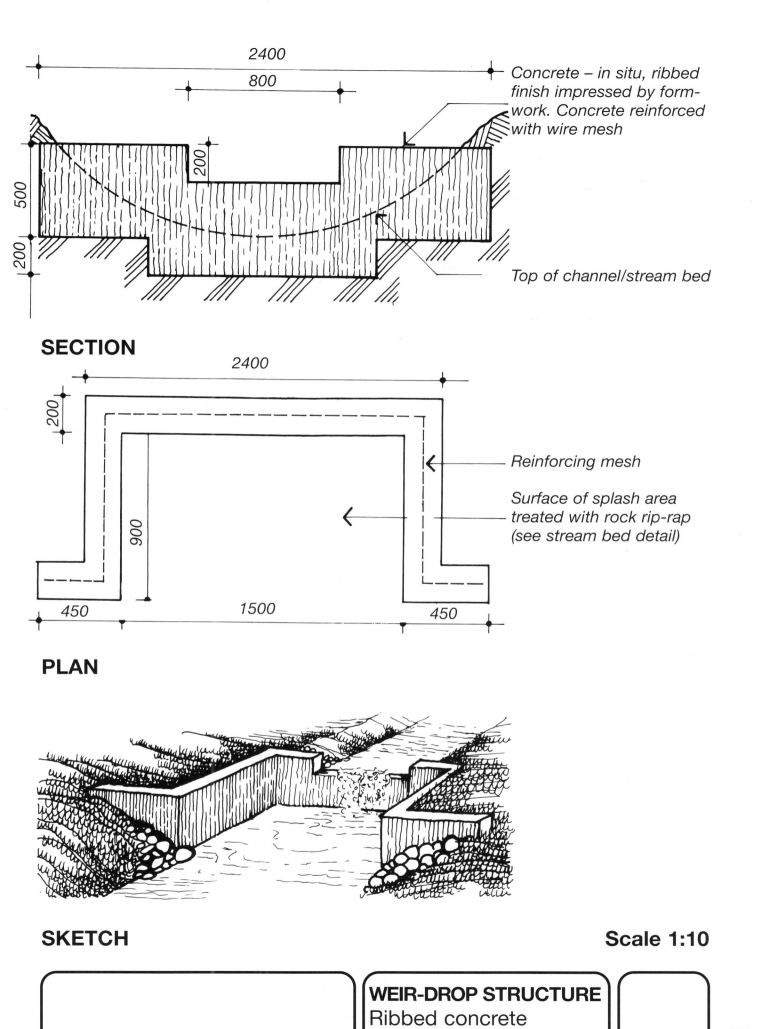

SECTION

2400

800

200

500

200

Concrete – in situ, ribbed finish impressed by form-work. Concrete reinforced with wire mesh

Top of channel/stream bed

PLAN

2400

200

900

450

1500

450

Reinforcing mesh

Surface of splash area treated with rock rip-rap (see stream bed detail)

SKETCH

Scale 1:10

WEIR-DROP STRUCTURE
Ribbed concrete

177

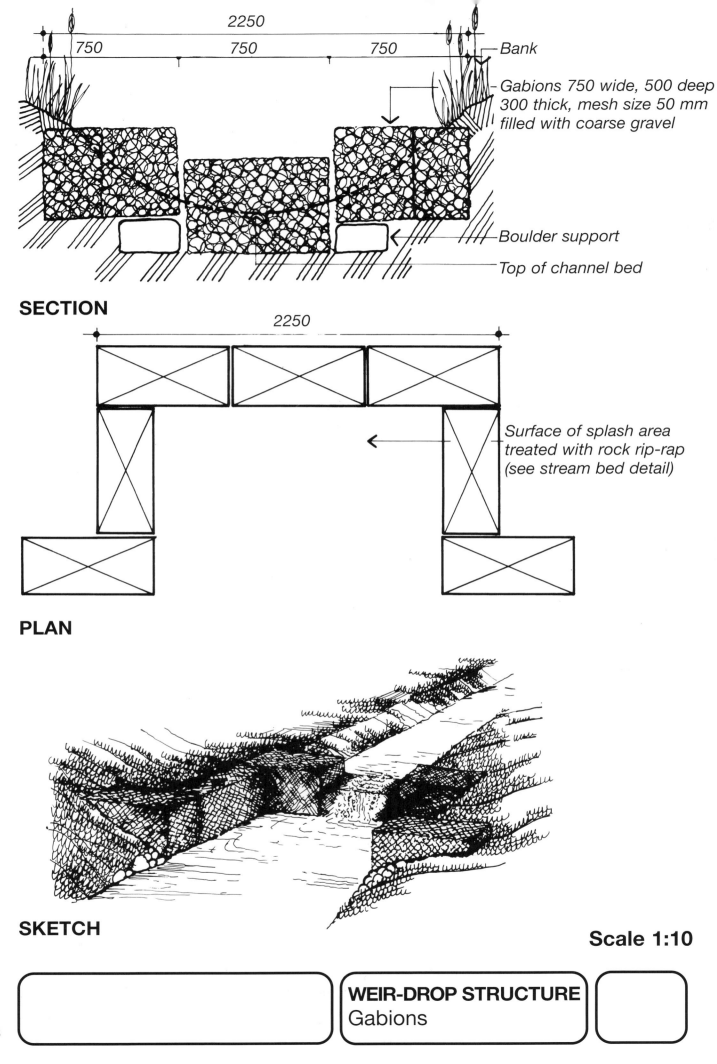

2250

750   750   750

Bank

Gabions 750 wide, 500 deep
300 thick, mesh size 50 mm
filled with coarse gravel

Boulder support

Top of channel bed

SECTION

2250

Surface of splash area
treated with rock rip-rap
(see stream bed detail)

PLAN

SKETCH

Scale 1:10

WEIR-DROP STRUCTURE
Gabions

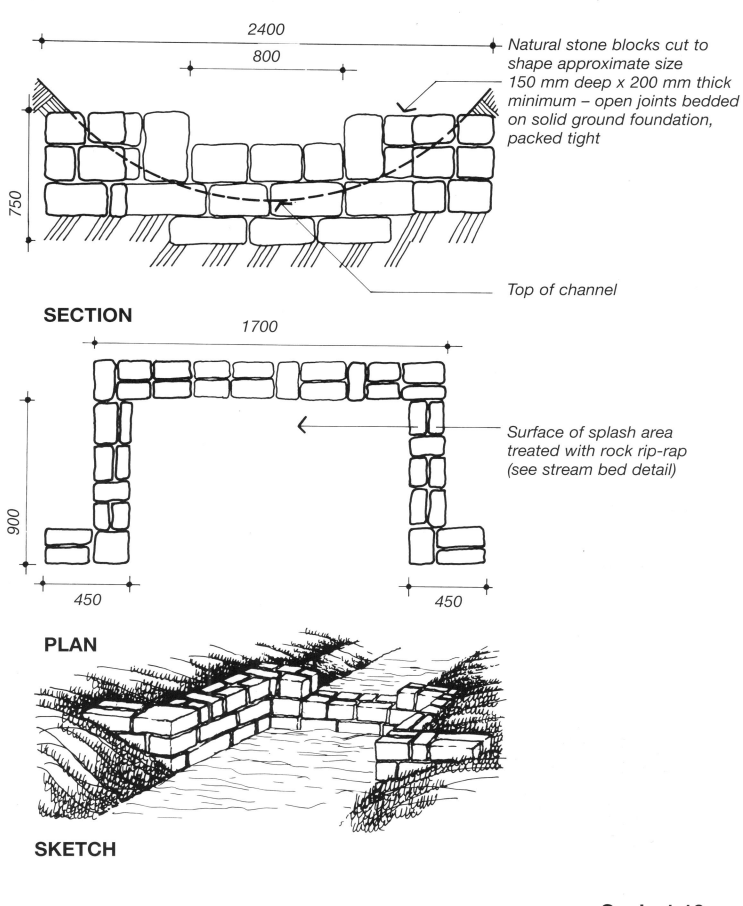

2400

800

750

Natural stone blocks cut to shape approximate size 150 mm deep x 200 mm thick minimum – open joints bedded on solid ground foundation, packed tight

Top of channel

SECTION

1700

900

450

450

Surface of splash area treated with rock rip-rap (see stream bed detail)

PLAN

SKETCH

Scale 1:10

WEIR-DROP STRUCTURE
Natural stone

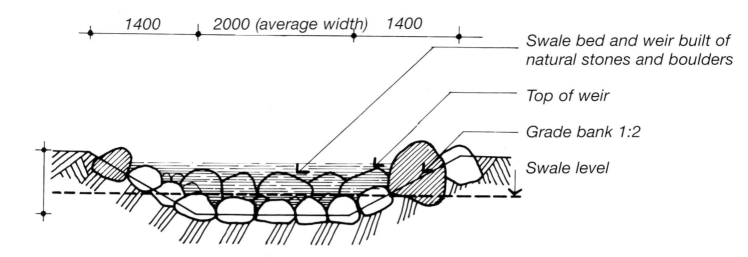

1400 | 2000 (average width) | 1400

Swale bed and weir built of natural stones and boulders

Top of weir

Grade bank 1:2

Swale level

CROSS SECTION

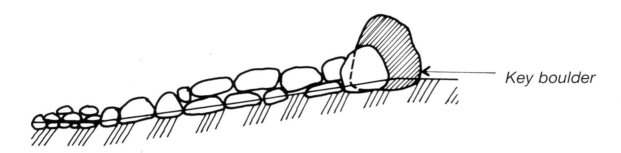

Key boulder

LONG SECTION

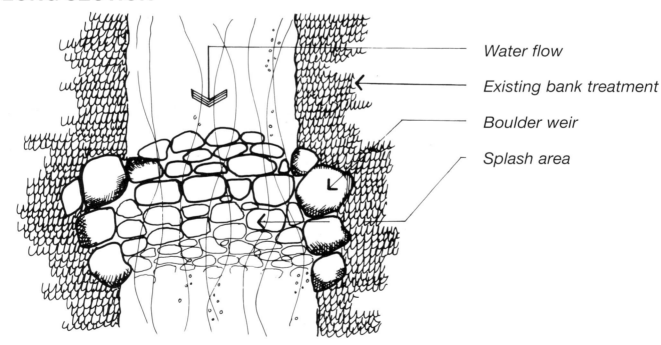

Water flow

Existing bank treatment

Boulder weir

Splash area

PLAN   **Scale 1:20**

WEIR
Natural stone (multiple)

180

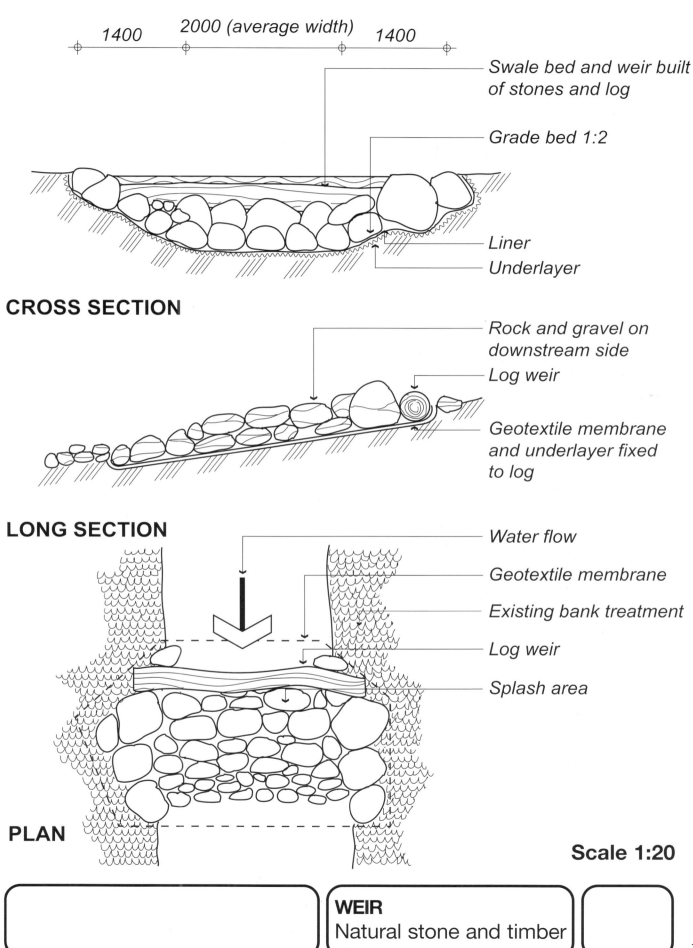

1400　2000 (average width)　1400

Swale bed and weir built of stones and log

Grade bed 1:2

Liner

Underlayer

CROSS SECTION

Rock and gravel on downstream side

Log weir

Geotextile membrane and underlayer fixed to log

LONG SECTION

Water flow

Geotextile membrane

Existing bank treatment

Log weir

Splash area

PLAN

Scale 1:20

WEIR
Natural stone and timber

181

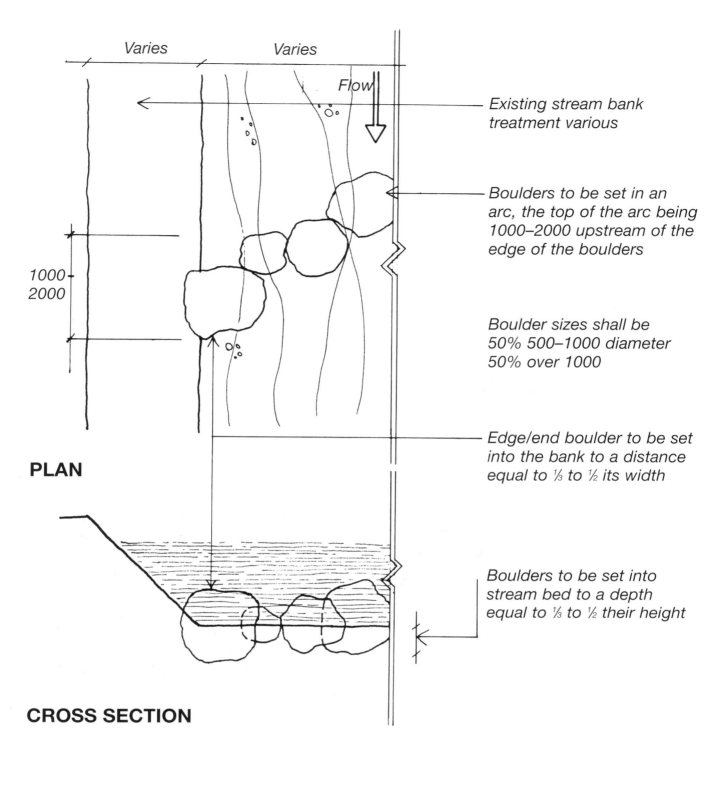

Varies Varies

Flow

—— Existing stream bank treatment various

—— Boulders to be set in an arc, the top of the arc being 1000–2000 upstream of the edge of the boulders

1000–2000

Boulder sizes shall be 50% 500–1000 diameter 50% over 1000

PLAN

—— Edge/end boulder to be set into the bank to a distance equal to ⅓ to ½ its width

Boulders to be set into stream bed to a depth equal to ⅓ to ½ their height

CROSS SECTION

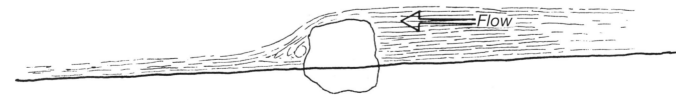

Flow

LONG SECTION **Scale 1:50**

	BLOCKSTONE ARCH WEIR Single stone	

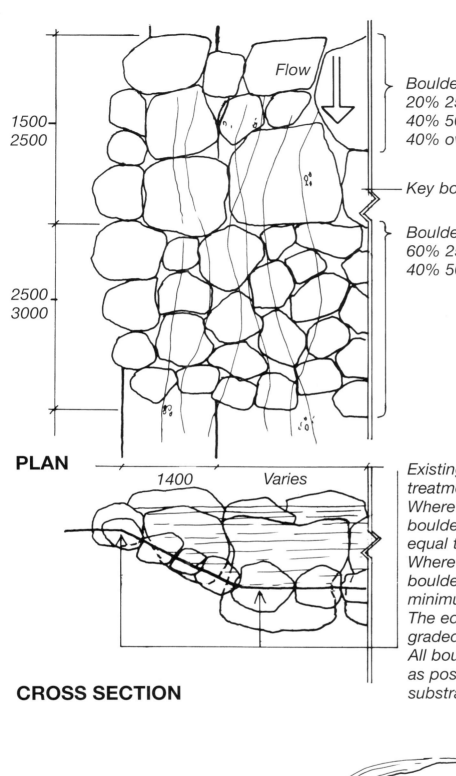

PLAN

Flow

1500–2500

2500–3000

Boulders upstream of key boulders
20% 250–500 diameter
40% 500–1000 diameter
40% over 1000 diameter

Key boulders to be over 1000 dia.

Boulders in splash area
60% 250–500 diameter
40% 500–1000 diameter

1400   Varies

CROSS SECTION

Existing stream bank and bed
treatment varies.
Where treatment is loose substrate
boulders to be set into a depth
equal to ½ to ⅓ their height.
Where treatment is concrete
boulders to be set into 100
minimum depth of wet concrete.
The edges of the concrete shall be
graded down to existing levels.
All boulders shall be placed as close
as possible to minimise exposure of
substrate.

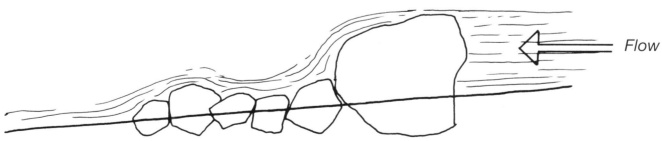

Flow

LONG SECTION

Scale 1:50

WEIR
Natural stone (Multiple)

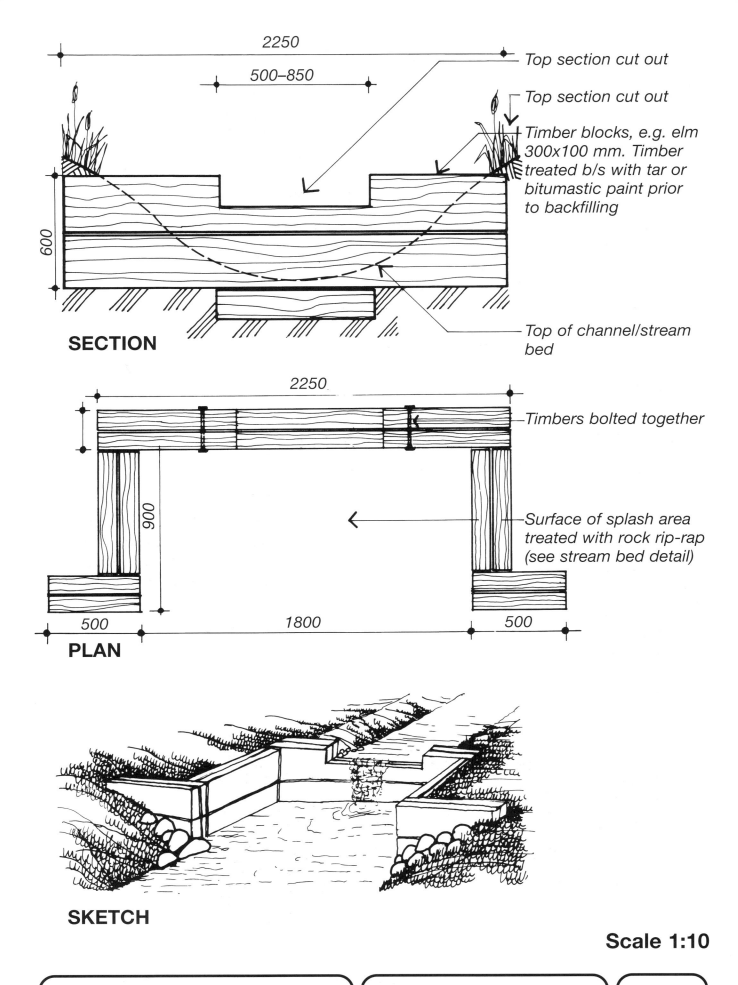

2250

500–850

Top section cut out

Top section cut out

Timber blocks, e.g. elm 300x100 mm. Timber treated b/s with tar or bitumastic paint prior to backfilling

600

SECTION

Top of channel/stream bed

2250

Timbers bolted together

900

Surface of splash area treated with rock rip-rap (see stream bed detail)

500   **1800**   **500**

PLAN

SKETCH

Scale 1:10

WEIR-DROP STRUCTURE
Timber

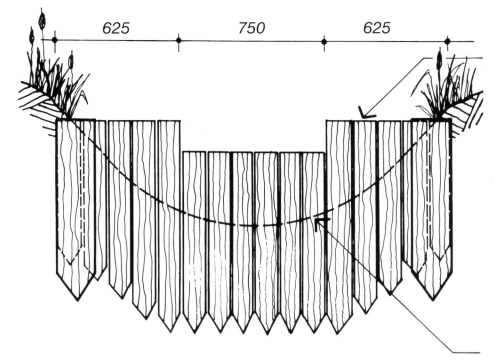

625   750   625

*Timber – ex-railway
sleepers 200x125 mm
driven into augered
holes to 600 mm depth.
Timber to be given one
coat of tar or bitumastic
paint prior to backfilling*

Top of channel

SECTION

200

825

500   1625   500

*Surface of splash
area treated with
rock rip-rap (see
stream bed detail)*

PLAN

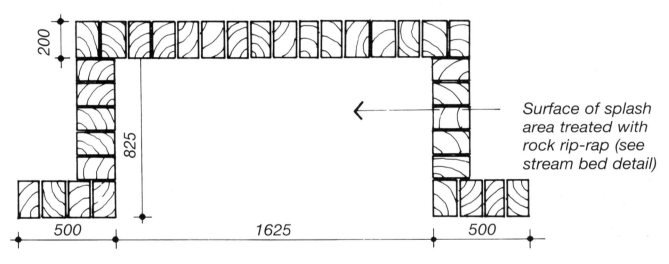

SKETCH

WEIR-DROP STRUCTURE
Timber sleepers

185

ISLANDS, RAFTS AND JETTIES

ISLANDS

The design of an island is determined by its purpose – for example, as a habitat for birds and other wildlife, for visual appeal, or as a retreat for people. For wildlife to be safe on an island it has to be located a minimum of 27 m (30 yards) from shore and even this is no guarantee against mink.

Frozen water in winter will provide a bridge for many predators such as rats, stoats and weasels. These will have to be trapped every spring otherwise they will cause havoc.

There are two ways to form an island – one is to have an area of land after excavation of the pond or lake, and the second is to bring in suitable materials.

There are situations where the restrictions for the operation's large machinery may make it impossible to do either and the cost may make the island prohibitive in these circumstances.

Where an island is being made in situ the sides will need to be in a series of steps for stability, depending upon the type of soil. Where the soil is not stable, the shape of the island should be indicated by stakes with the sides being made secure by an appropriate edge treatment.

For islands made from materials brought into the site a check should be made that they are free of any polluting substances. Various types of materials can be used, for example builders' rubble and hardcore, which can be compacted, followed by a topping of earth, gravel, mud – depending upon the purpose of the island. Old turf should be retained for the surface.

The sides of the island should be formed to ensure that they will not erode and, where necessary, appropriate materials used.

Very small islands can be made from precast concrete pipes of a large diameter, set onto the bottom of the pond or lake filled with a layer of gravel followed by soil. A grouping could be formed which, when filled with plants, would look most effective. These pipe islands are also useful for containing plants that normally spread over a large area.

As an alternative to concrete pipes, corrugated sheets held in place by treated timber posts could be used. With this material various shapes, besides the circle, can be achieved.

With a concrete pond liner it is preferable to build the island after constructing the pond using concrete blocks or other solid material. For the latter, a concrete raft approximately 150 mm (6 ft) deep is laid on the pond bed. Then the walls can be built up, using blocks, rocks or stone, with reinforcement in the blockwork if the walls are over 600 mm (2 ft). In certain circumstances a stepped wall with blocks at the bottom and rocks at the top could be built to provide contained planting areas. It would also reduce the cost and amount of natural stone or rock required.

RAFTS

Rafts are invaluable for birds, especially if located in deep water. They provide a safer harbour island as they are free from any mammalian predators. Rafts, like islands, have to be designed for a purpose. For birdlife there are several variations for consideration, depending upon the location and species.

When designing a raft (non-people) many aspects have to be considered such as:

- The deck must float above the water line.
- It should have the ability to rise and fall easily.

• It should have stability, a dry, protected area for nesting and be harmonious with the environment.

Rafts are made in a variety of materials and in many sizes. It has been found that all timber rafts absorb water and sink; a combination of materials such as timber, polystyrene and empty metal drums are much more successful.

Rafts must be anchored; two are preferable to one and they should be attached in opposite corners to prevent the raft from swaying in the wind. The anchors must be placed on the bottom and not on the shore to stop any vandalism and to keep rats, weasels, etc. from gaining access. Anchors can be made from any heavy material: blocks, bricks attached to heavy metal chains, etc. For a large raft a weight of 50 kg (1 cwt) would be suitable. Concrete can be utilised by using a suitable container as a mould.

To encourage ducks, a small house could be added to the raft, made from a wine/spirit cask laid on its side with an entrance made at one end. Ramps would need to be added for access to the water, preferably a solid plank with treads made of battens added for ease of use by the ducks.

Floating islands or rafts used by people for recreational purposes will differ from those designed as wildlife habitats in the selection of the surface and edge material. This must be of good quality, smooth and free from any item in its construction that could cause any harm or danger. The buoyancy factor must also be considered, ensuring that the raft cannot be overturned in any way when people pull themselves up out of the water onto the surface.

JETTIES

Jetties are used mainly by pedestrians to reach deep water for access to boats or for fishing, or just to observe the activities and scenery.

A jetty, or dock, can be built in sections and assembled on-site. This type of construction is durable and provides a constant height above the water line so that boats can be tied up. Changes in water height will have no effect as the dock moves with the boat. Side panels and extensions longer than 4 m will need to be anchored to the shore in order to take some of the stress from the base hinge.

All timber used should be rough-sawn and treated, if softwood. All metalwork should be galvanised. A large concrete base is necessary to keep the jetty stable against wind and wave action. The base of this should be below the frost line or at least 900 mm in depth on the water side.

Placement of flotation blocks is important for a more stable dock. The blocks should be placed as near the dock edge as possible, and heavy timbers should be added if the dock still is not stable. The timbers add weight to hold the dock in the water and stabilise bobbing up and down. When the dock is placed into the water, it must be anchored to the shore by cables as long as possible. Anchor both sides to the shore to a 'dead-man' or pilings; the anchorage must be able to hold sideways currents, waves, winds, and high water during storms.

FISHING PLATFORMS AND BOAT MOORINGS

Summary of requirements

Issued by the Environment Agency

Fishing platforms

Fishing platforms shall be parallel to the river flow and shall not project out from the river bank more than 1 m. They shall be solidly staked down and be constructed so as not to pose a maintenance problem and to minimise the obstruction to flow.

Platforms of pallets tied back to small pegs in the bank are not permitted as these can be torn away during a flood and cause an obstruction at a downstream bridge or culvert.

The access ramps/steps/ladder to the platform shall also be designed so as not to create erosion or obstruct flow.

Siting of platforms shall be carefully considered to avoid undue impact on the environment.

Boat moorings

Any works constructed in association with the moorings of vessels on a main river shall not interfere with the flood carrying section of the river. Where possible, they shall be set back into the bank of the river.

Where a river has a large range of levels, due to either tidal variation or fluvial floodings, moorings and jetties shall be designed to allow for this range of levels without the necessity for loosening or tightening mooring ropes. Ideally, they shall consist of a vertical pole with a sliding ring attached in order to reduce the risk of boats breaking away in times of high flood or high tide, and damaging river structures.

Where the construction of moorings has resulted in bank disturbance, bank protection shall be provided beyond the disturbed width, which is adequately keyed into both bed and banks. This shall be in keeping with the surrounding environment.

The above requirements shall be read in conjunction with 'Land Drainage Consents'.

The information given is subject to review.

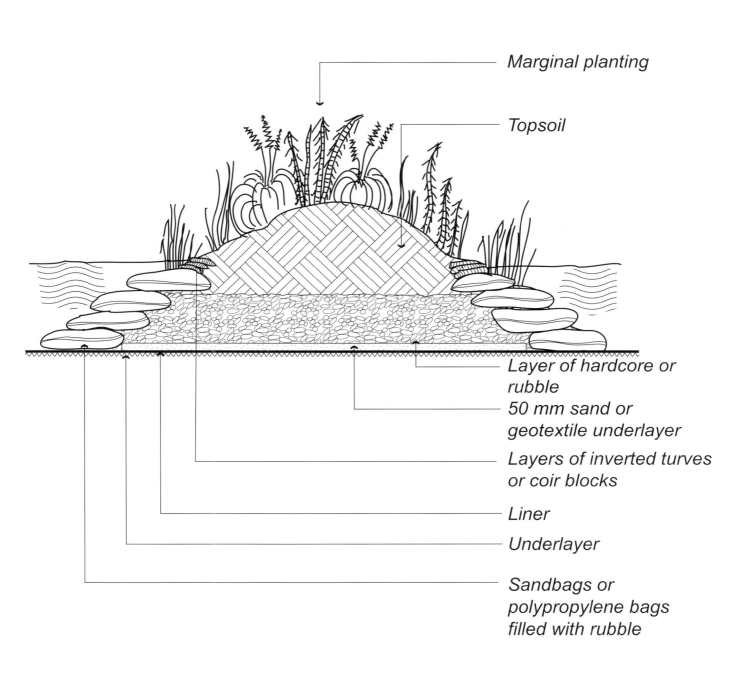

Marginal planting

Topsoil

Layer of hardcore or rubble

50 mm sand or geotextile underlayer

Layers of inverted turves or coir blocks

Liner

Underlayer

Sandbags or polypropylene bags filled with rubble

SECTION

Scale 1:50

ISLANDS
Wet type

189

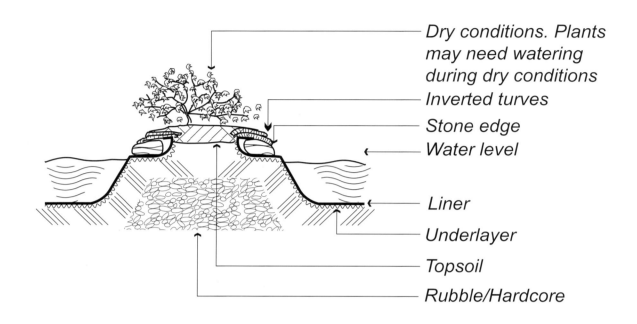

Dry conditions. Plants
may need watering
during dry conditions

Inverted turves

Stone edge

Water level

Liner

Underlayer

Topsoil

Rubble/Hardcore

SECTION

Scale 1:50

ISLANDS
Dry type

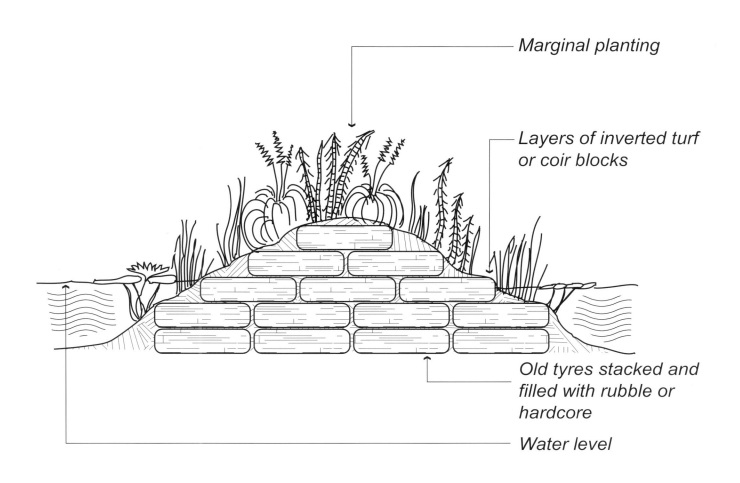

Marginal planting

Layers of inverted turf or coir blocks

Old tyres stacked and filled with rubble or hardcore

Water level

SECTION

Scale 1:50

ISLANDS
Tyre

191

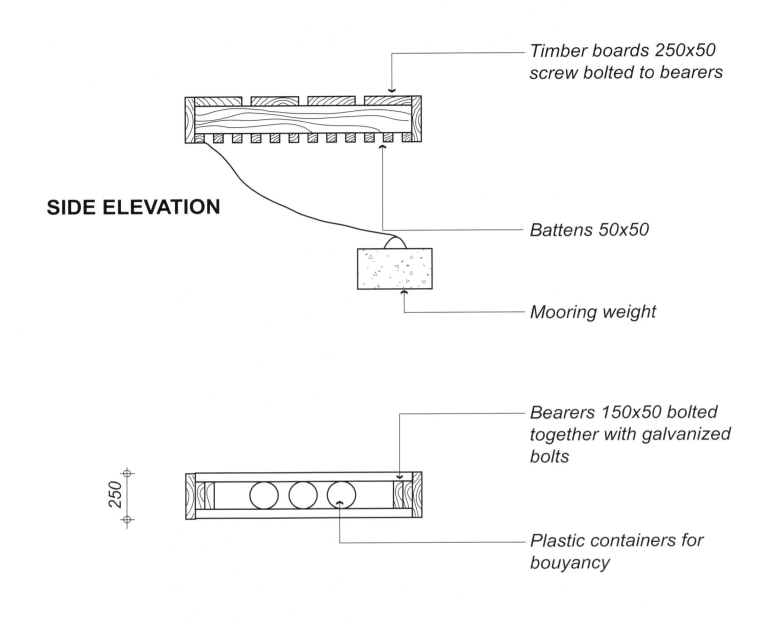

SIDE ELEVATION

Timber boards 250x50 screw bolted to bearers

Battens 50x50

Mooring weight

250

Bearers 150x50 bolted together with galvanized bolts

Plastic containers for bouyancy

SECTION

Note: All softwood to be pressure treated

Scale 1:20

ISLANDS
Raft

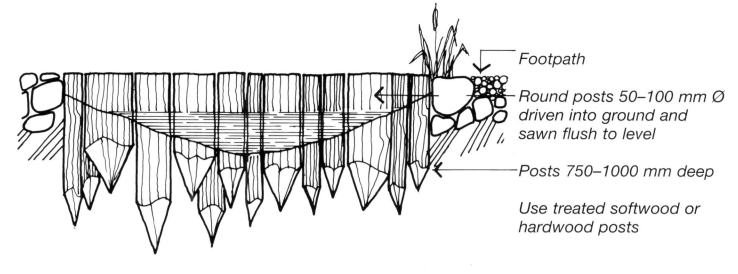

Footpath

Round posts 50–100 mm Ø driven into ground and sawn flush to level

Posts 750–1000 mm deep

Use treated softwood or hardwood posts

SECTION

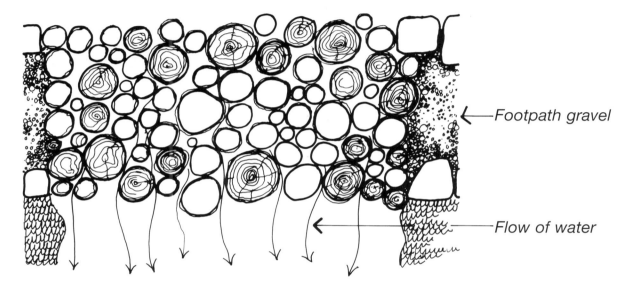

Footpath gravel

Flow of water

PLAN

SKETCH

Scale 1:10

CAUSEWAY
Log pile

193

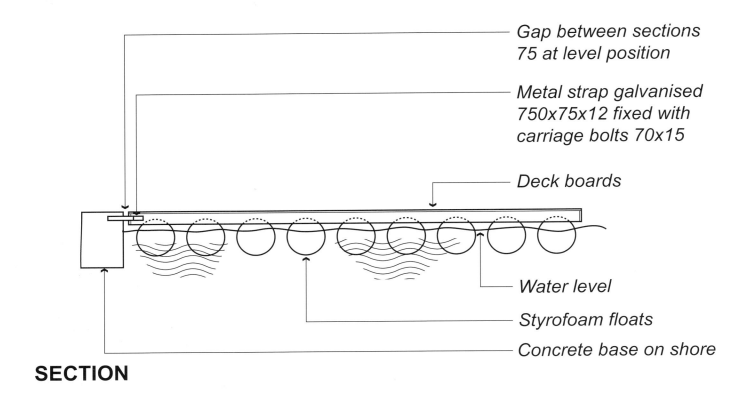

Gap between sections 75 at level position

Metal strap galvanised 750x75x12 fixed with carriage bolts 70x15

Deck boards

Water level

Styrofoam floats

Concrete base on shore

SECTION

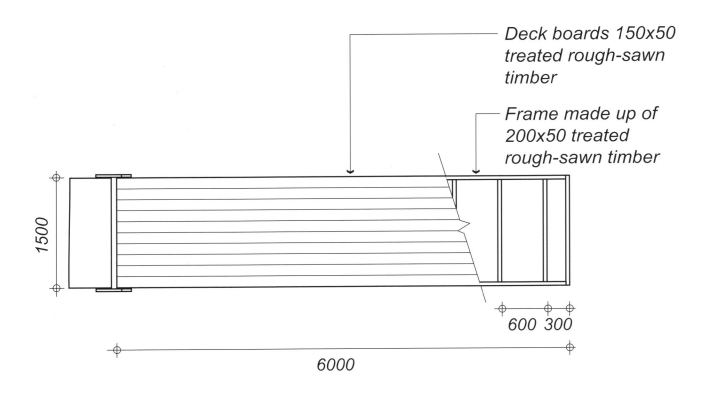

Deck boards 150x50 treated rough-sawn timber

Frame made up of 200x50 treated rough-sawn timber

1500

600 300

6000

PLAN

Scale 1:50

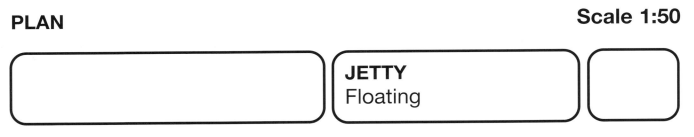

JETTY
Floating

DRAINAGE

Drainage is concerned with the removal of surplus water from rural and urban lands, both natural and paved surfaces, derived initially from precipitation.

From natural surfaces

The removal of water from areas in order to ensure dry conditions for the many activities that occur in the man-made landscape has tremendous implications for the designer. While expert advice from consulting engineers is appropriate for calculations and contract drawing, the designer should have a good all round knowledge of the drainage requirements for his or her design, be it a small residential project or a large commercial undertaking.

Knowledge of the rational formula could prove very useful as a first step. The usual one is $Q = C.I.A.$ where:

Q = peak run-off/rate of flow m³/sec.
C = run-off coefficient
      Roofed buildings and concreted areas 0.95–0.99
      Roads 0.75–0.90
      Pathways 0.50–0.75
      Gardens, lawns and wooded areas 0.10–0.15
I = rainfall intensity mm/hr
A = site area (hectares/square metres).

Controlling run-off using above ground methods

To control surface run-off, ground modelling can be used by the following:

- reducing the peak intensity
- decreasing the size of the watershed
- grass lined waterways, swales and grass areas
- pipe systems.

Reducing the peak intensity. This can be achieved by delaying the discharge of surface water from an area being developed by constructing, impounding or diverting dams or ponds. These will reduce the main fluctuating discharge from the watershed to a lower and safer rate of release to the main channel.

Decreasing the size of the watershed. By decreasing the size of the area which collects the water it will also reduce the peak intensity of the run-off. However, it will also lead to a greater number of structures necessary to cope with the total run-off from an area, although the dimensions of each structure may be reduced.

Grass lined waterways. A grass sward can impede the surface flow of water in existing waterways, increasing the time of concentration. Where there is run-off from cultivated land, a grass sward provides a more stable soil surface capable of withstanding higher water velocities. Covering the land with vegetation is a vitally important factor in controlling soil erosion because it safely absorbs the force of the rainfall as well as slowing run-off. Other techniques include special seepage areas of well-drained soils.

Pipe systems. Using pipes either full or half-round may be necessary in certain locations to ensure removal of surface water more quickly than that occurring naturally. The design of the final discharge point must be given attention, especially to ensure that no erosion occurs.

Piped drainage

Underground drainage pipes, sometimes referred to as 'trench drains', can be used to intercept surface water run-off near the source.

These drains can be used in high to low density developments; the higher densities and less well-drained soils will require an underdrain. Well-drained medium density sites may be able to absorb a greater degree of run-off, allowing the top of the drain to act as a swale for the larger design storms. The depth to bedrock and water table should be greater than 1 m.

A trench drain is typically constructed with a base layer of crushed stone, which may or may not surround a perforated pipe serving as an underdrain. It is then covered with coarse sand and finished with a surface of pavers, gravel, grass, or a grate. A longitudinal fall along the surface lets the drain act as an infiltration swale.

The advantages of trench drains include:

- possible recharge to the groundwater
- reduction in later system size
- an increased amount of available soil moisture for plants in paved areas.

Cost considerations include:

- high maintenance of the surface (to prevent clogging by debris)
- possible pollution of groundwater by substances from paved surfaces
- a possible higher cost of materials than for a straight conventional system.

Trench drains are most useful near paved surfaces or at the edge of gutterless roofs. They can be used near playing fields or other areas that generate run-off and have too little room for a detention pond.

Typical types are:

- clay tiles
- French drains
- controlled plastic
- ridged plastic
- ditches.

Clay tiles. The clay tile has been used for many years and is still one of the best materials for trench drains. These are made of unglazed baked clay in 300 mm lengths and the usual diameters used are 75 mm for laterals and 100 mm or 150 mm for main lines.

For best results the tiles are laid with small gaps in a bed of coarse stone in order to speed drainage and lengthen the life of the system. It is good practice to cover the top of the tile joints with a tar paper or terram to prevent sediment from entering the tile and eventually cutting off the flow of water.

The ideal drop or slope in which to place these systems is 2 per cent minimum and 4 per cent maximum. This will allow for a good deep flow in the tile and passage of any debris that might enter the line.

This slight grade helps prevent erosion into and around the tile, thereby preventing it collapsing. Concrete tiles should be used to withstand heavy weights of vehicles under roads or driveways. Concrete tiles can also be used for the entire system, but are much more costly and have a shorter life.

French drains. These are used to prevent the sides of a ditch from collapsing, to control seepage on road and railside cuttings, to reduce maintenance and to improve access to an area. A steep sided ditch is filled with coarse stone or gravel to provide a French drain.

French drains are a useful system to use in planting sites with a good slope. The system can be put in at planting time or later if problems of poor drainage develop. The French drain is simply a narrow trench filled with coarse stone that will allow the planting pit to drain quickly. The trench can be left open or, if appearance is important, it can be covered with a few inches of soil and turf. This system can be either used on one plant or joined in a network of plants.

Controlled plastic. Rolled corrugated plastic is quick and easy to install and works very well. Water enters the pipe from the soil through specially cut slots 30 mm long at 50 mm intervals and the pipe is currently available in 6 m lengths and 120 m coils.

The grade for this material is 2 per cent and the pipe should be laid with a bed of gravel with terram to reduce soil infiltration. The gravel also protects the pipe during the soil settlement period after laying.

This system will not last as long as the tile. Where possible, place the tile below the frostline in order to extend its life.

Ridged plastic. This is mainly used for golf greens or any area where near the surface drainage is required. This system is a little harder to lay, and it is also more expensive than the corrugated material. It has a line of holes in a row down one side. These should be placed on the bottom of the trench to allow only water to enter the pipe.

The grade should be 2 per cent and gravels used as for the controlled (or rolled) plastic.

Ditches. These are important in removing large volumes of water from an area of adjacent land or collected from piped drainage systems. The size and shape of a ditch will generally be influenced by the site conditions.

For a well-proportioned ditch the top width will be equal to the bottom plus the depth, with the sides sloped at 45° but varied to suit the ground conditions. The gradient of a ditch will depend upon the discharge level required with variations for different rates being taken into account.

Disposal of run-off

Artificial drainage increases the volume of water that the rivers have to carry unless special provision is made to delay the flow of water to the rivers in times of heavy rainfall. An example of this is the provision of balancing ponds and lakes along the watercourse. Without such provision artificial drainage tends to increase the risk of flooding from the overflow of rivers and streams.

Authority

The Environmental Agency is responsible for all land drainage and for the control of discharges into rivers and certain streams. They should be consulted on any project involving water.

Fact sheets are available such as:

Land drainage consents

Landfilling adjacent to or over a watercourse

Approved methods of erosion protection to river banks

Summary of requirements for pipe crossings

Summary of requirements for culverts

Summary of requirements for fishing platforms

Summary of requirements for cattle drinks and boat moorings.

Legislation

There is a considerable volume of legislation relating to the problems of the disposal of run-off. Some of the relevant statutory publications of HMSO are:

The Land Drainage Act, 1930

The Water Act, 1948

The Rivers (Prevention of Pollution) Act, 1951

The Land Drainage Act, 1961

The Rivers (Prevention of Pollution) Act, 1961

The Water Resources Act, 1963

The Water Act, 1973.

Drainage structures

These structures are used to direct the flow of storm water in a concentrated form.

Head walls and end walls. These are used as retaining walls and transition areas between the flow of a natural channel and a pipe or a culvert. The head wall must make the change with a minimum of head loss and its size will depend upon the pipe size.

End walls are outlets of piped flow. Their function, in discharging to a natural channel, is to slow down stream velocity, which in turn will limit scour.

Inlets/catch basins. Surface water run-off can be collected and transferred to underground pipes by the use of inlets. There are two types:

* drop inlet
* catch basin.

Cisterns. Surface water can be contained underground in large containers or cisterns for reuse or even as temporary storage for slow discharge.

Soakaways/seepage pits. These consist of a pit containing large crushed stone over which run-off is directed and allowed to percolate slowly.

Pits are typically less than 3 m deep and must be located on well-drained soils with the water table no less than 1.0 m. The slopes should not exceed 2 per cent.

While soakaways are an advantage on sites, which have limited surface detention capacity, they do need to be maintained on a regular basis. The silt removal system must be checked for its continued effectiveness of the soakaway.

A drop inlet has a smooth bottom, which allows immediate flow into the pipe while a catch basin has a sediment basin at the bottom, which collects heavy material before it can enter the pipe. A catch basin can collect water from the surface of other drains and from several drain pipes and drop all of the water through one large pipe.

Hard surface – water disposal. The main aim of the drainage is to ensure the removal of surface water as quickly and as efficiently as possible. This is generally achieved by means of falls (and cambers for roads/paths) through gutters, channels and gullies linked to the disposal system.

These can be made attractive elements, as part of the overall design, or made as unobtrusive as possible.

The permissible falls in channels or pavings govern the spacing of gullies – for flat roads these are approximately every 45 m.

Channels are described in Landscape Detailing: Surfaces, Volume 2.

Rainwater from roofs via downpipes does, in certain locations, discharge onto the footpaths, through grooved or small rounded, shallow channels and then into the gutter. Surface water from paved areas, especially roads, should be discharged to an interceptor tank to remove oils and other similar materials. This is especially important if the water is to be reused, in which case storage tanks will be necessary, either underground, or a retention pond in an urban or rural landscape. If the latter, then plants could be used to assist in cleaning up the water prior to its reuse or discharge into a natural waterway.

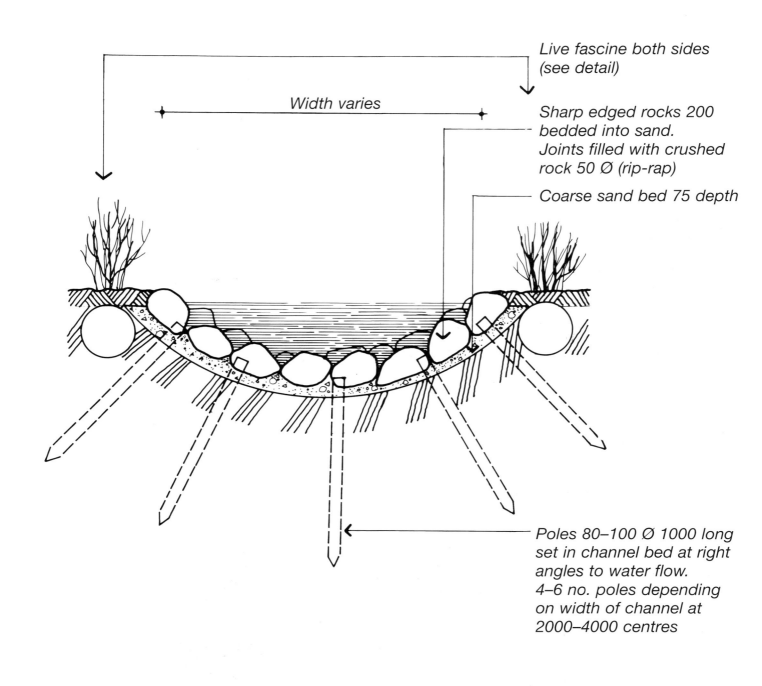

Live fascine both sides
(see detail)

Width varies

Sharp edged rocks 200
bedded into sand.
Joints filled with crushed
rock 50 Ø (rip-rap)

Coarse sand bed 75 depth

Poles 80–100 Ø 1000 long
set in channel bed at right
angles to water flow.
4–6 no. poles depending
on width of channel at
2000–4000 centres

NOTE
If ground underneath is
permeable use plastic
sheeting/liner or layer of
heavy clay consolidated

SECTION

Scale 1:10

OPEN DRAINAGE SWALE
Stone bed channel

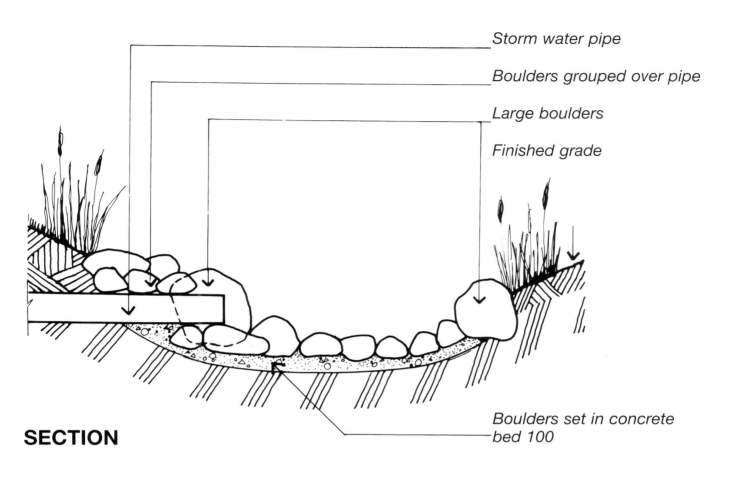

Storm water pipe

Boulders grouped over pipe

Large boulders

Finished grade

Boulders set in concrete bed 100

SECTION

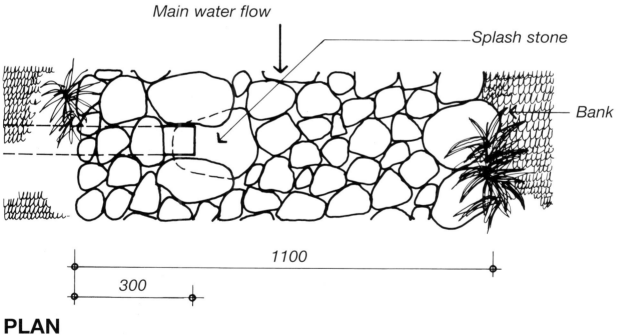

Main water flow

Splash stone

Bank

1100

300

PLAN

Scale 1:10

STORM DRAIN OUTLET

201

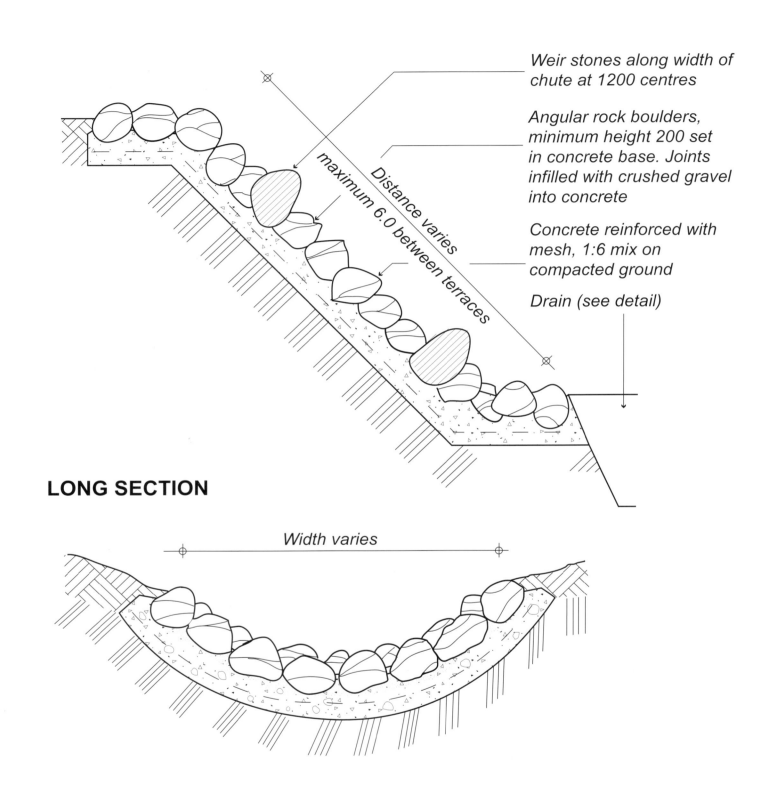

Weir stones along width of chute at 1200 centres

Angular rock boulders, minimum height 200 set in concrete base. Joints infilled with crushed gravel into concrete

Concrete reinforced with mesh, 1:6 mix on compacted ground

Drain (see detail)

Distance varies

maximum 6.0 between terraces

LONG SECTION

Width varies

CROSS SECTION

Scale 1:10

SLOPE DRAINAGE
Stone bed chute

202

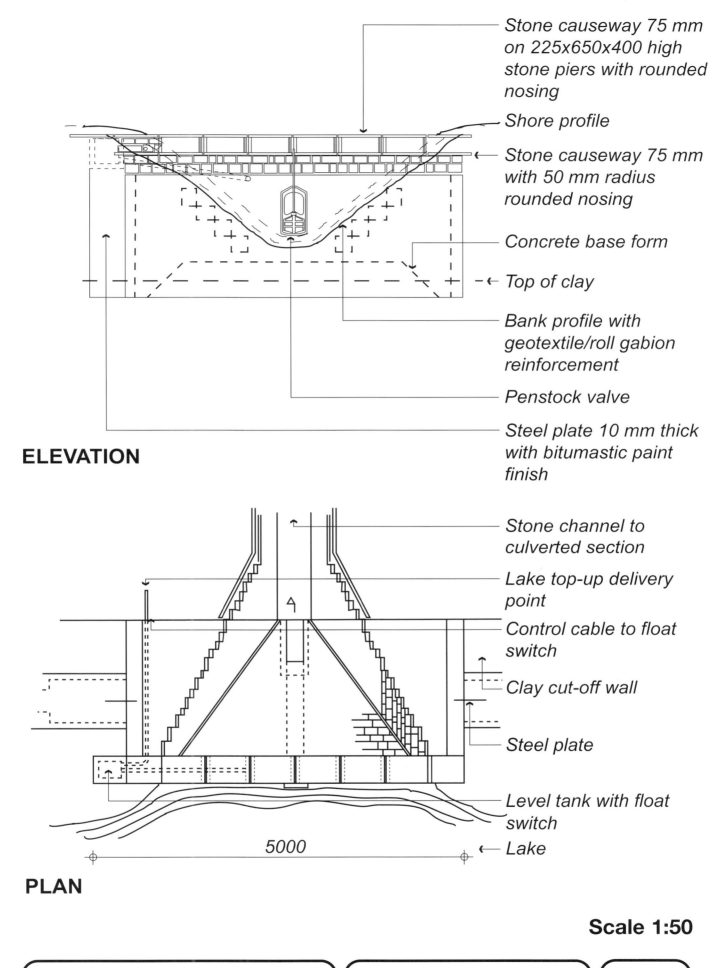

ELEVATION

Stone causeway 75 mm on 225x650x400 high stone piers with rounded nosing

Shore profile

Stone causeway 75 mm with 50 mm radius rounded nosing

Concrete base form

Top of clay

Bank profile with geotextile/roll gabion reinforcement

Penstock valve

Steel plate 10 mm thick with bitumastic paint finish

Stone channel to culverted section

Lake top-up delivery point

Control cable to float switch

Clay cut-off wall

Steel plate

Level tank with float switch

Lake

5000

PLAN

Scale 1:50

DRAINAGE
Lake outfall (1)

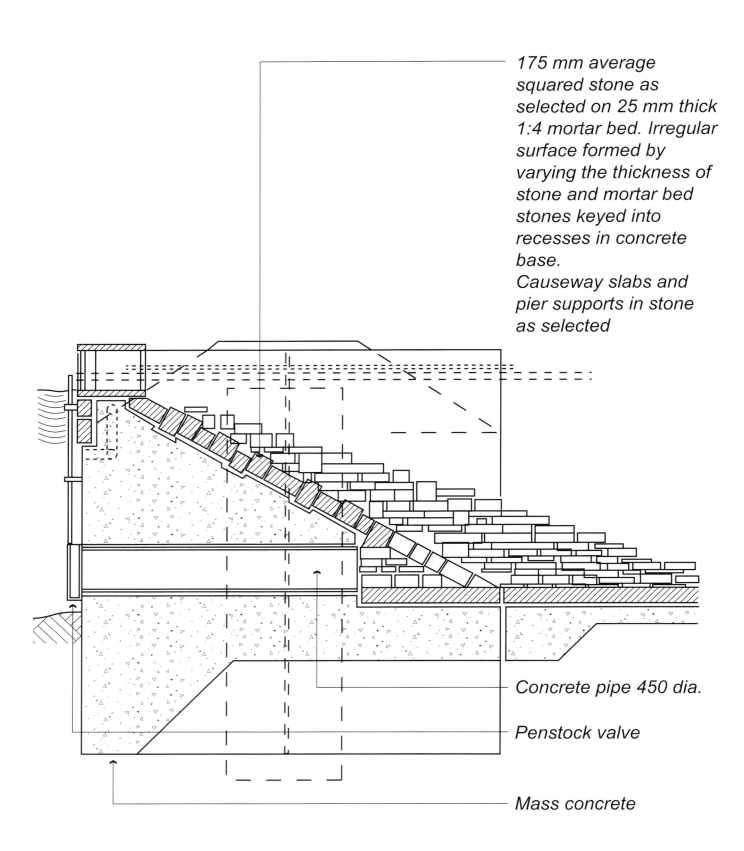

175 mm average squared stone as selected on 25 mm thick 1:4 mortar bed. Irregular surface formed by varying the thickness of stone and mortar bed stones keyed into recesses in concrete base.
Causeway slabs and pier supports in stone as selected

Concrete pipe 450 dia.

Penstock valve

Mass concrete

SECTION

Scale 1:50

DRAINAGE
Lake outfall (2)

204

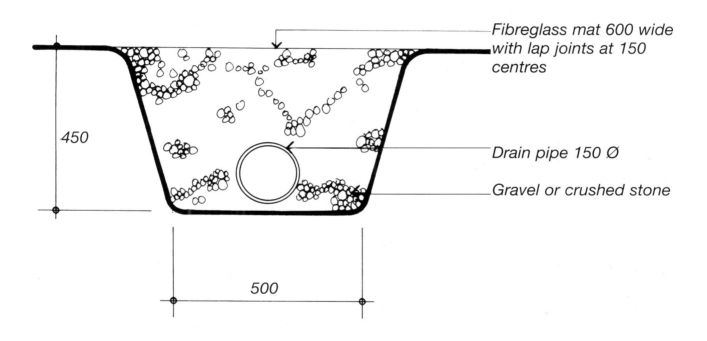

Pavement and base as selected

Fibreglass mat 600 wide with lap joints at 150 centres

450

Drain pipe 150 Ø

Gravel or crushed stone

500

SECTION

Scale 1:10

UNDERDRAIN
Pavement area

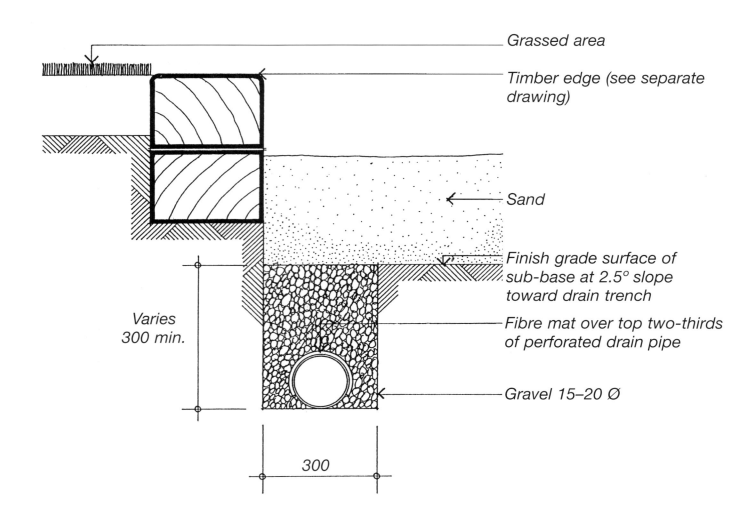

Grassed area

Timber edge (see separate drawing)

Sand

Finish grade surface of sub-base at 2.5° slope toward drain trench

Fibre mat over top two-thirds of perforated drain pipe

Gravel 15–20 Ø

Varies
300 min.

300

SECTION

Scale 1:10

UNDERDRAIN
Sand play area

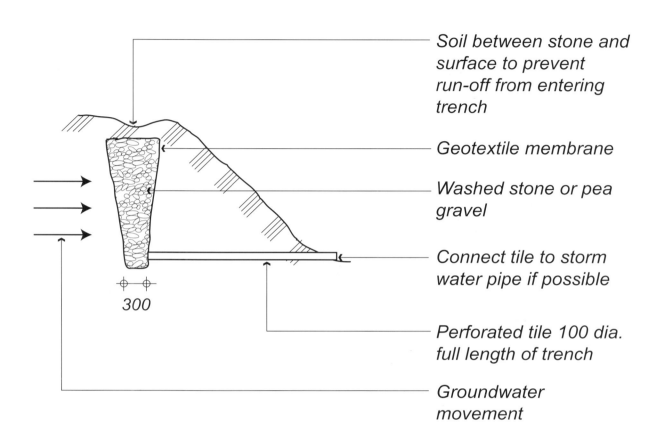

Soil between stone and surface to prevent run-off from entering trench

Geotextile membrane

Washed stone or pea gravel

Connect tile to storm water pipe if possible

Perforated tile 100 dia. full length of trench

Groundwater movement

300

SECTION   **Scale 1:50**

DRAINAGE
Interceptor for bank

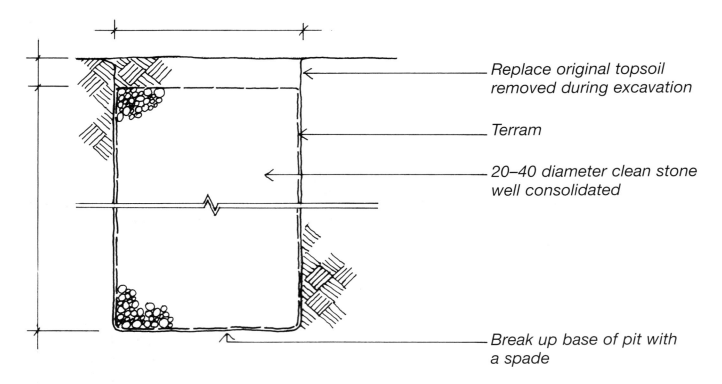

Replace original topsoil
removed during excavation

Terram

20–40 diameter clean stone
well consolidated

Break up base of pit with
a spade

TYPE 1

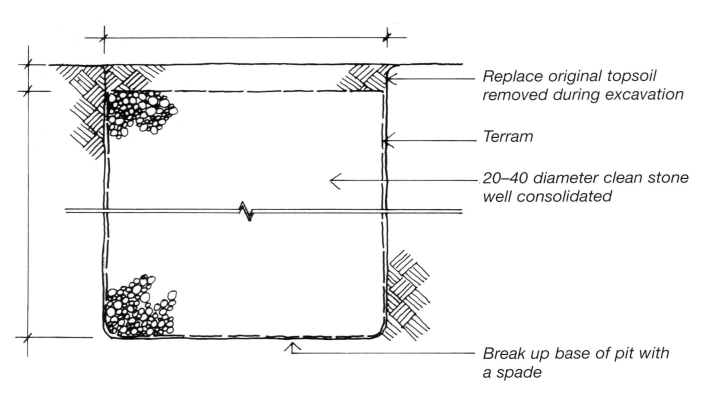

Replace original topsoil
removed during excavation

Terram

20–40 diameter clean stone
well consolidated

Break up base of pit with
a spade

TYPE 2

Scale 1:20

SOAKAWAY
Types 1 & 2

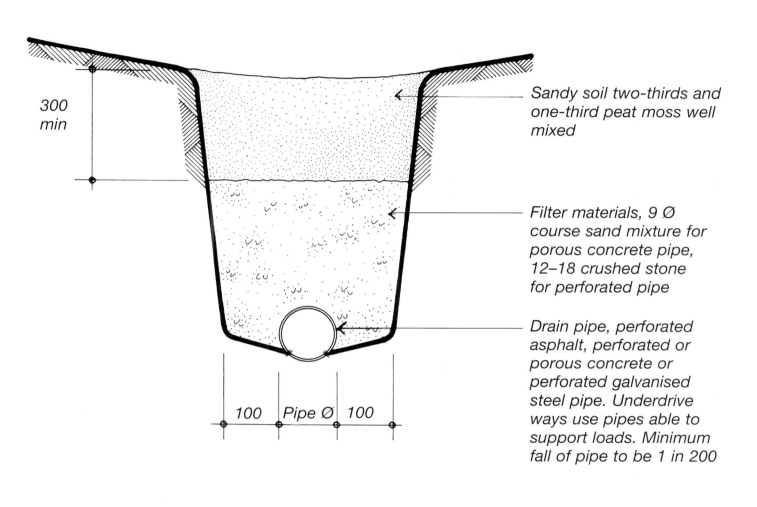

300 min

Sandy soil two-thirds and one-third peat moss well mixed

Filter materials, 9 Ø course sand mixture for porous concrete pipe, 12–18 crushed stone for perforated pipe

Drain pipe, perforated asphalt, perforated or porous concrete or perforated galvanised steel pipe. Underdrive ways use pipes able to support loads. Minimum fall of pipe to be 1 in 200

100   Pipe Ø   100

SECTION

Scale 1:10

FIELD DRAIN

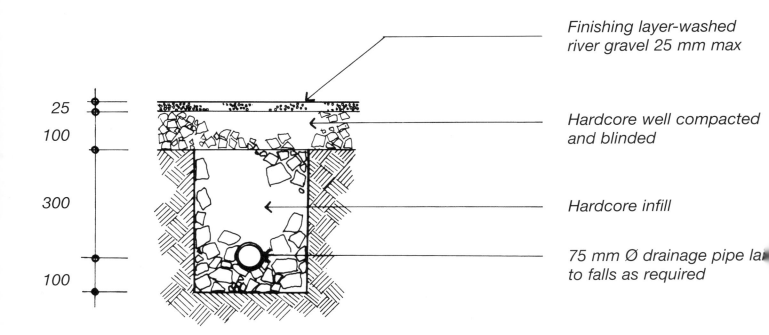

25
100

300

100

Finishing layer-washed
river gravel 25 mm max

Hardcore well compacted
and blinded

Hardcore infill

75 mm Ø drainage pipe la[...]
to falls as required

SECTION

Scale 1:10

VEHICULAR PAVING
French drain

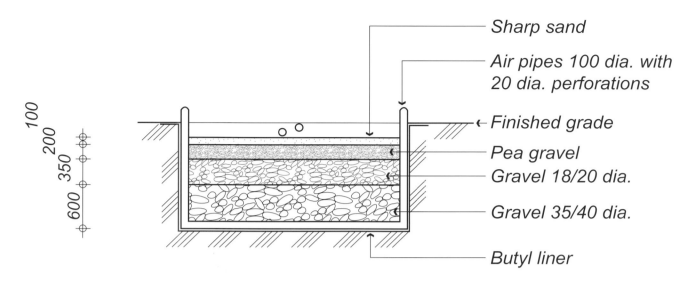

SECTION

100
200
350
600

Sharp sand

Air pipes 100 dia. with 20 dia. perforations

Finished grade

Pea gravel

Gravel 18/20 dia.

Gravel 35/40 dia.

Butyl liner

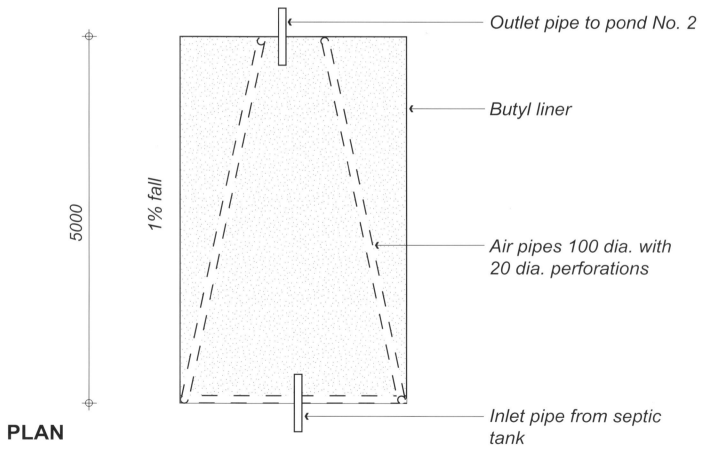

PLAN

5000

1% fall

Outlet pipe to pond No. 2

Butyl liner

Air pipes 100 dia. with 20 dia. perforations

Inlet pipe from septic tank

Scale 1:20

DRAINAGE
Sludge bed

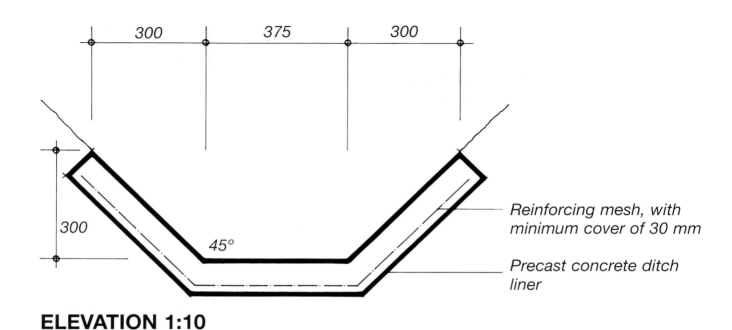

| 300 | 375 | 300 |

300

45°

Reinforcing mesh, with
minimum cover of 30 mm

Precast concrete ditch
liner

ELEVATION 1:10

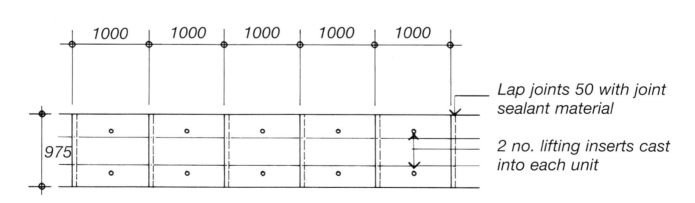

| 1000 | 1000 | 1000 | 1000 | 1000 |

975

Lap joints 50 with joint
sealant material

2 no. lifting inserts cast
into each unit

PLAN 1:50

Scale A·S

DITCH LINER
Concrete

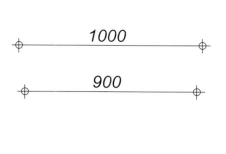
1000
900

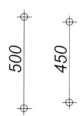
500
450

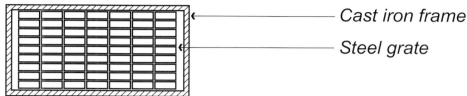
Cast iron frame

Steel grate

PLAN

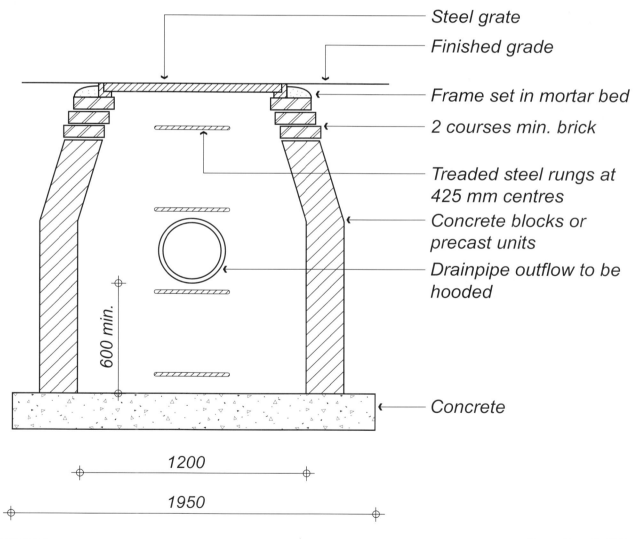

Steel grate

Finished grade

Frame set in mortar bed

2 courses min. brick

Treaded steel rungs at 425 mm centres

Concrete blocks or precast units

Drainpipe outflow to be hooded

Concrete

600 min.

1200

1950

SECTION

Scale 1:20

CATCH BASIN
Paved areas (1)

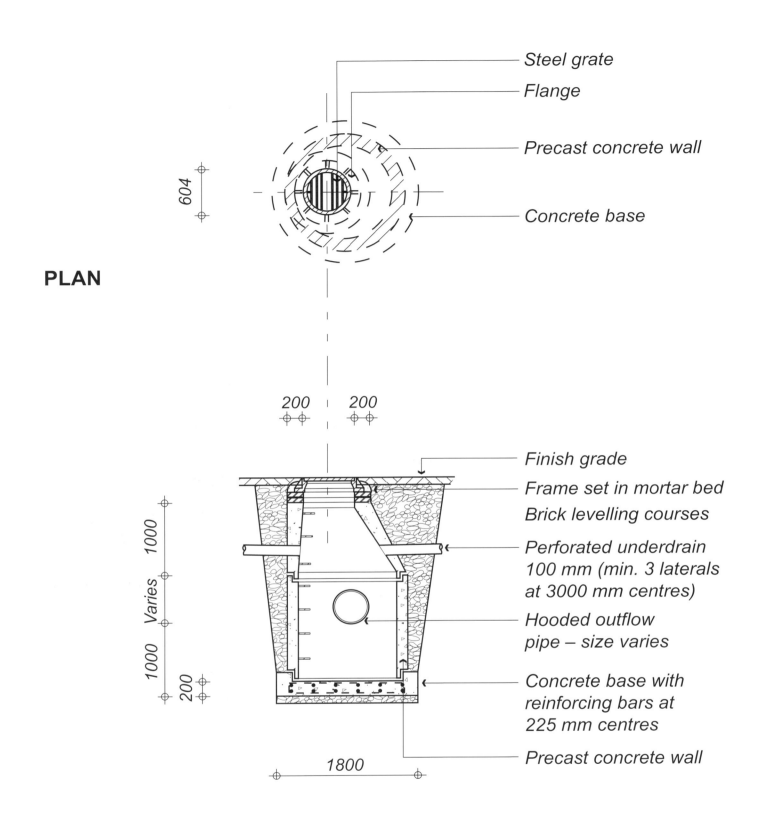

PLAN

604

200 | 200

1000
1000   Varies   1000
200

1800

Steel grate

Flange

Precast concrete wall

Concrete base

Finish grade

Frame set in mortar bed
Brick levelling courses

Perforated underdrain
100 mm (min. 3 laterals
at 3000 mm centres)

Hooded outflow
pipe – size varies

Concrete base with
reinforcing bars at
225 mm centres

Precast concrete wall

SECTION

Scale 1:50

CATCH BASIN
Paved areas (2)

214

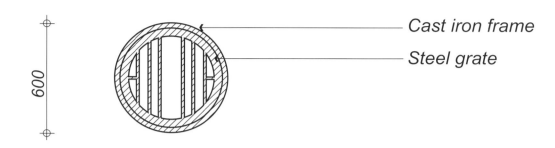

PLAN

600

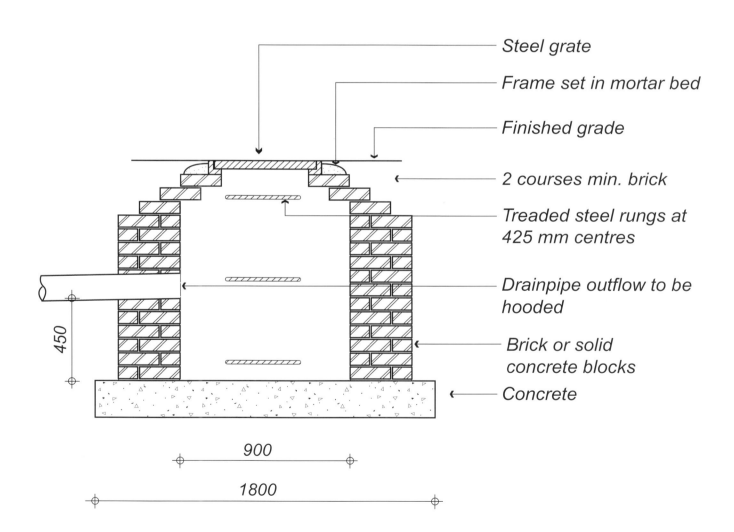

Cast iron frame

Steel grate

Steel grate

Frame set in mortar bed

Finished grade

2 courses min. brick

Treaded steel rungs at 425 mm centres

Drainpipe outflow to be hooded

Brick or solid concrete blocks

Concrete

450

900

1800

SECTION

Scale 1:20

CATCH BASIN
Lawn area

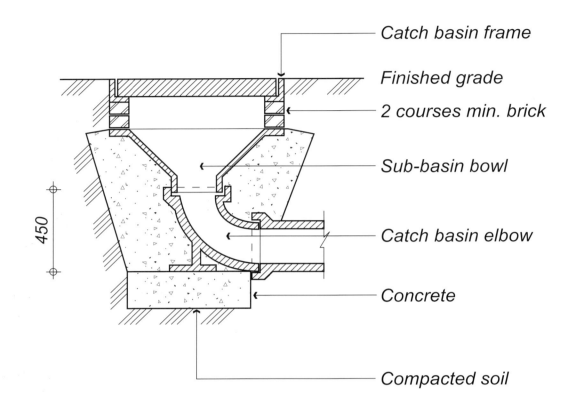

Catch basin frame

Finished grade

2 courses min. brick

Sub-basin bowl

Catch basin elbow

Concrete

Compacted soil

450

SECTION

Scale 1:20

DRAINAGE INLET
Steel grate (1)

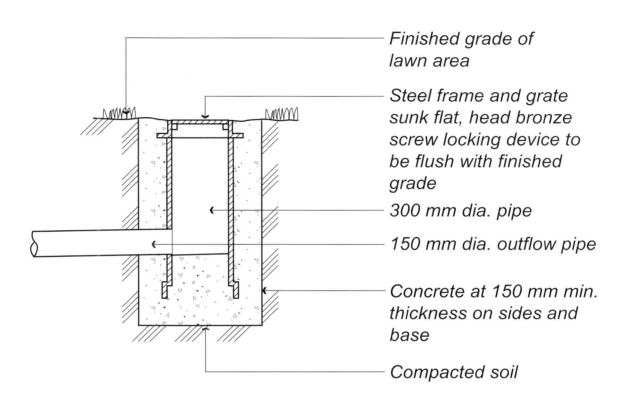

Finished grade of
lawn area

Steel frame and grate
sunk flat, head bronze
screw locking device to
be flush with finished
grade

300 mm dia. pipe

150 mm dia. outflow pipe

Concrete at 150 mm min.
thickness on sides and
base

Compacted soil

SECTION

Scale 1:20

DRAINAGE INLET
Steel grate (2)

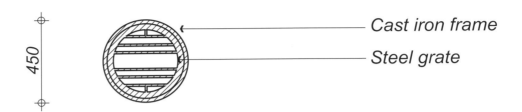

450

PLAN

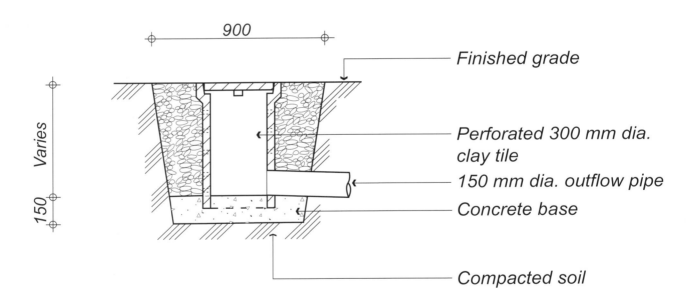

900

Varies

150

Cast iron frame

Steel grate

Finished grade

Perforated 300 mm dia. clay tile

150 mm dia. outflow pipe

Concrete base

Compacted soil

SECTION

Scale 1:20

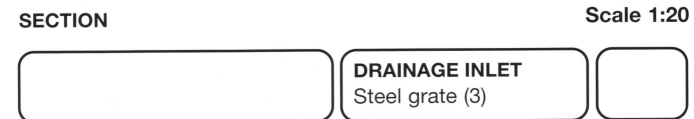

DRAINAGE INLET
Steel grate (3)

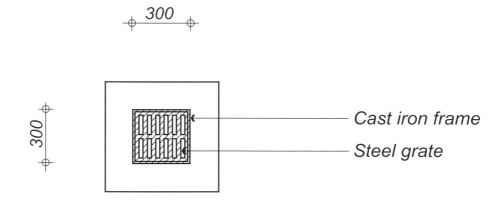

300

300

PLAN

Cast iron frame

Steel grate

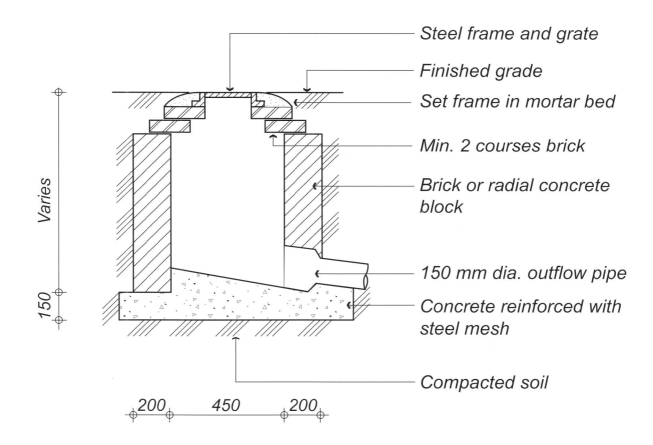

Steel frame and grate

Finished grade

Set frame in mortar bed

Min. 2 courses brick

Brick or radial concrete block

150 mm dia. outflow pipe

Concrete reinforced with steel mesh

Compacted soil

Varies

150

200   450   200

SECTION   **Scale 1:20**

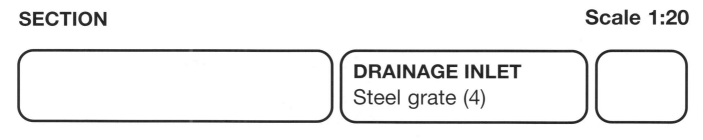

DRAINAGE INLET
Steel grate (4)

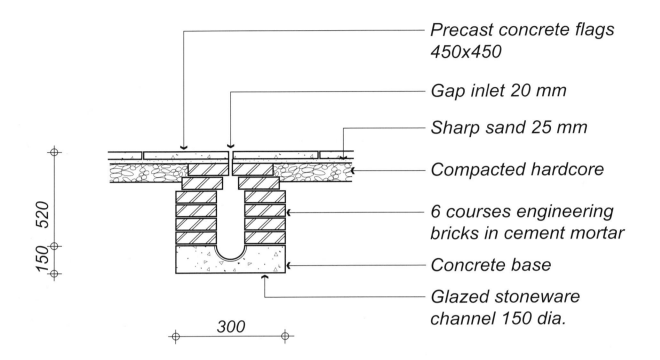

Precast concrete flags
450x450

Gap inlet 20 mm

Sharp sand 25 mm

Compacted hardcore

6 courses engineering
bricks in cement mortar

Concrete base

Glazed stoneware
channel 150 dia.

520

150

300

SECTION

Scale 1:10

DRAINAGE INLET
Drain channel

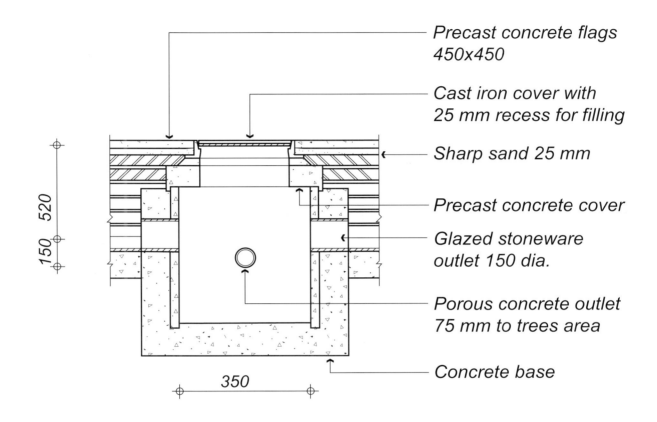

Precast concrete flags
450x450

Cast iron cover with
25 mm recess for filling

Sharp sand 25 mm

Precast concrete cover

Glazed stoneware
outlet 150 dia.

Porous concrete outlet
75 mm to trees area

Concrete base

520

150

350

SECTION   **Scale 1:10**

DRAINAGE INLET
Catchpit

221

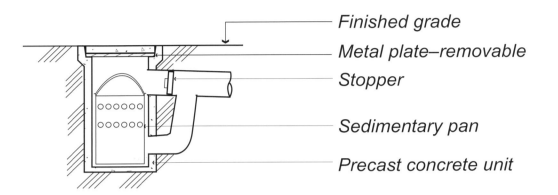

Paving units–removable

Finished grade

Metal plate–removable

Stopper

Sedimentary pan

Precast concrete unit

SECTION

Scale 1:20

222

DRAINAGE INLET
Silt trap

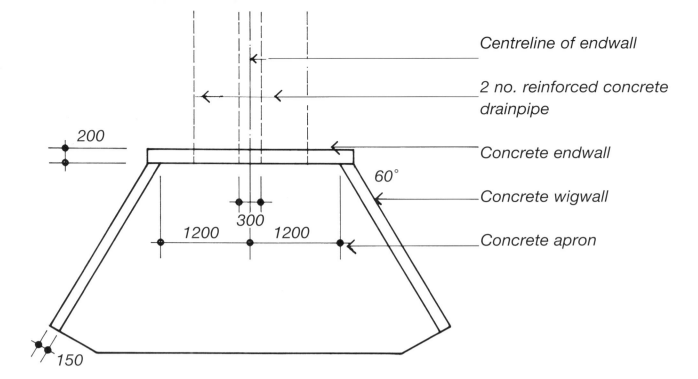

Centreline of endwall

2 no. reinforced concrete drainpipe

Concrete endwall

Concrete wigwall

60°

Concrete apron

200

300

1200   1200

150

PLAN 1:2

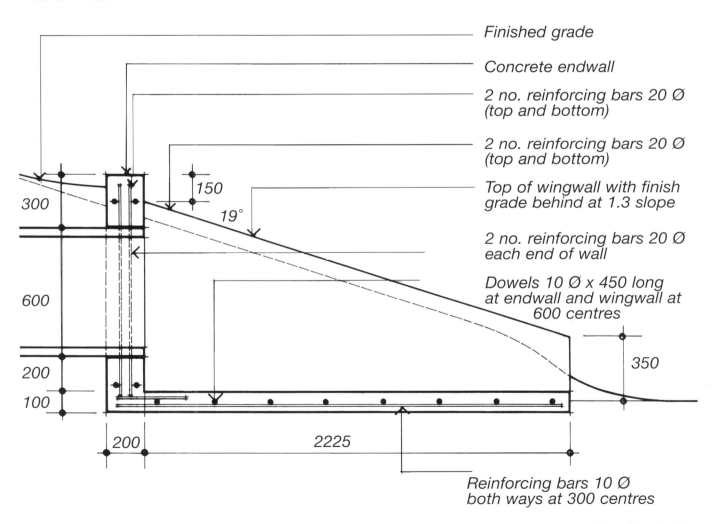

Finished grade

Concrete endwall

2 no. reinforcing bars 20 Ø (top and bottom)

2 no. reinforcing bars 20 Ø (top and bottom)

Top of wingwall with finish grade behind at 1.3 slope

2 no. reinforcing bars 20 Ø each end of wall

Dowels 10 Ø x 450 long at endwall and wingwall at 600 centres

300

150

19°

600

350

200

100

200

2225

Reinforcing bars 10 Ø both ways at 300 centres

SECTION 1:2   **Scale A·S**

ENDWALL
Concrete

223

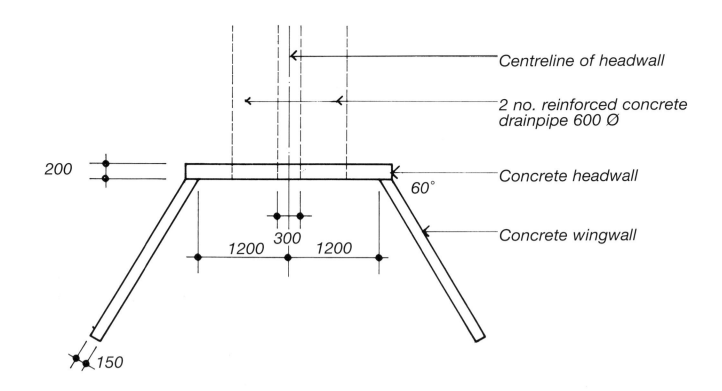

Centreline of headwall

2 no. reinforced concrete drainpipe 600 Ø

Concrete headwall

Concrete wingwall

200

60°

300

1200   1200

150

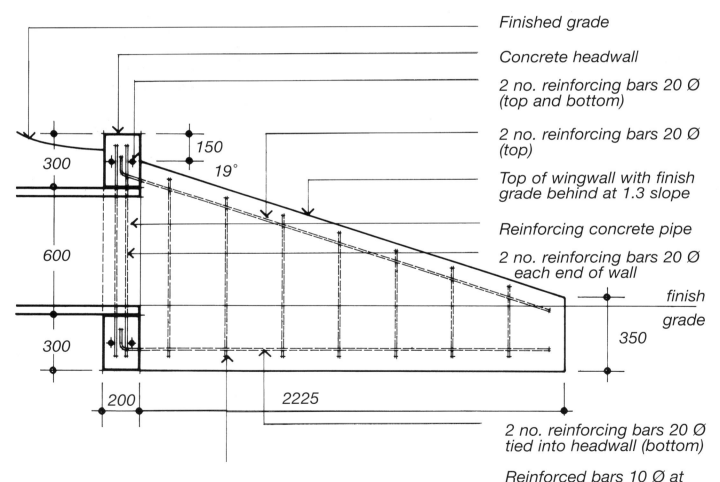

Finished grade

Concrete headwall

2 no. reinforcing bars 20 Ø (top and bottom)

2 no. reinforcing bars 20 Ø (top)

Top of wingwall with finish grade behind at 1.3 slope

Reinforcing concrete pipe

2 no. reinforcing bars 20 Ø each end of wall

150

19°

300

600

300

finish grade

350

200

2225

2 no. reinforcing bars 20 Ø tied into headwall (bottom)

Reinforced bars 10 Ø at 300 centres

SECTION

Scale A·S

HEADWALL
Concrete

224

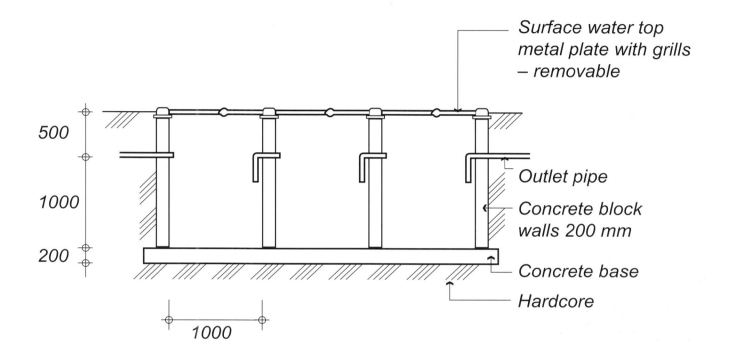

Surface water top
metal plate with grills
– removable

500

1000

200

1000

Outlet pipe

Concrete block
walls 200 mm

Concrete base

Hardcore

SECTION

Scale 1:40

INTERCEPTOR
Petrol and oil

225

BIBLIOGRAPHY & REFERENCES

APPENDIX A

Bibliography

Anthony Archer-Wills, *The Water Gardener*, Francis Lincoln Ltd, London, 1993

C. Douglas Aurand, *Fountains and pools, construction guidelines and specifications*, Spon, 1987

E. Beazley, *Designed for recreation*, Faber & Faber, 1969

Alan Blanc, *Landscape construction and detailing*, Batsford, London, 1996

British Trust for Conservation Volunteers, *Waterways and wetlands*, 1992

British Waterways, *The waterway environment and development plans*, British Waterways, Rugby, 1993

Craig C. Campbell, *Water in landscape architecture*, New York, Van Nostrand Reinhold, 1982

P.H. Chaplin, *Waterway conservation*, Whittet Books, 1989

Ralph Cobham, *Amenity landscape management: a resources handbook*, Spon, London, 1990

J. Doherty and J. Pilkington, *Hampshire's countryside heritage 3: Rivers and wetlands*, Hampshire County Planning Department, Winchester, 1963

M.F. Downing, *Landscape construction*, Spon, 1977

Forestry Commission, *Forests and water guidelines*, HMSO, London, 1991, 011-710296-2

Floyd Giles, *Landscape construction procedures, techniques and design*, Stipes Publishing Co., Champaign, Illinois, USA, 1991

S.M. Haslam and P.A. Wolseley, *River vegetation: its identification, assessment and management. A field guide to the macrophytic vegetation of British watercourses*, Cambridge University Press, 1981

R.W. Hemphill and M.E. Bramley, *Protection of river and canal banks, a guide to selection and design*, Butterworths, 1989 (for CIRIA)

G. Jekyll, *Wall and water gardens, 2nd edition*, Country Life and George Newnes, n.d.

S. and G. Jellicoe, *Water: the use of water in landscape architecture*, Adam and Charles Black, 1971

K. Kabisch, *Ponds and pools – oases in the landscape*, Croom Helm, London, 1984

H.C. Landphair and F. Klatt, *Landscape architecture construction*, New York, Elsevier, 1979

London Docklands Development Corporation, *Waterside design guidelines*, LDDC, London, 1993

Derek Lovejoy & Partners (eds), *Spon's landscape handbook*, E. & F.N. Spon, London

Tim Matson, *Earth ponds: the country pond maker's guide to building, maintenance and restoration*, 2nd edn, revised and expanded, Countryman Press, Woodstock, Vermont, USA, 1991

Travers Morgan, *Changing river landscapes. A study of river valley landscapes*, Countryside Commission CCP 238, Cheltenham, 1987

National Rivers Authority, *River landscapes assessment, methods and procedures*, NRA Bristol 1993, 1-873160-45-3

Anthony Paul and Yvonne Rees, *The water garden: a complete illustrated guide to creating and planting pools and water features*, Guild Publishing, 1986

George Plumptree, *The water garden, styles, designs and visions*, Thames & Hudson, London, 1993

V. Porter, *The pond book*, Bromley, Christopher Helm, 1988

Chris Probert, *Pearls in the landscape*, Farming Press

J. Purseglove, *Taming the flood: a history and natural history of rivers and wetlands*, Oxford University Press (with Channel 4 TV), 1988

Peter Robinson, *Water gardening,* Royal Horticultural Society, Dorling Kindersley, London, 1997

S. Russell, *Stapeley book of water gardens*, David & Charles, Newton Abbot

Robert Schafer, *Designing and living with water*, Garten und Landschaft, 1989, 7, 40–45

Stephen Scrivens, *Water features. 1: Design and informal water. 2: Pools, cascades, fountains.* Architects' Journal, 2 and 9 Nov, 1988, 69–74, 67–71

Marilyn Symmes, *Fountains, splash and spectacle: water design from the renaissance to the present*, Thames & Hudson (in association with Smithsonian Institution), London, 1998

A.E. Weddle (editor), *Techniques of landscape architecture*, Heinemann, 1967

References

D.W. Adie, Marinas, *A working guide to their development and design* (3rd edn), Architectural Press, 1984

Don Anderson, *Ponds, lakes and landscape architecture*, Landscape Australia, May 1990, 162–166 (includes instruction methods)

Penny Anderson, *Ponds from first principles,* Landscape Design, March 1999, 208, 12–14

Stuart Anderson, *Charting new currents in waterfront regeneration*, The Urban Street Environment, Sept/October 1993, 11, 10–17

Kevin & Briese, Kym Beattie, *The Cliffs Broadwalk: Brisbane's new riverside esplanade*, Landscape Australia, August 1993, 3, 249–255

Stephen Birch, *How to cope with a problem lake*, Landscape Design, March 1992, 208, 42–43

British Trust for Conservation Volunteers, *Waterways and wetlands*, 1992

Paolo Burgi, *Path by the lake*, Anthos, 1991, 3, 23–27

P. Carling, *The well-being of Britain's water*, Landscape Design, July/August 1989, 23–24

Jon Etchells, *A balancing act*, Landscape Design, March 1992, 208, 29–32

External Works, Endat Group, Stirling (annual)

Bruce K. Ferguson, *The failure of detention and the future of stormwater design*, Landscape Architecture, December 1991, 76–79

GGF '88, *Water and maritime competition*, Landscape Scotland Quarterly, Winter 1986–7, 9–14

Jan de Graff, *Cockles and mussels at Eastern Scheldt*, Topos, May 1993, 3, 85–92

E.F. Granfield, *Design, construction and maintenance of earth dams and excavated ponds*, HMSO, Forestry Commission Forest Record No. 75

Hank Haff, *Cardiff Bay, the inner harbour*, Urban Design Quarterly, April 1993, 46, 48–51

David Hares, *Lakes from wasteland*, Landscape Design, February 1992, 207, 24–26

Lyndall Horton-James, *Gaging the tiger (danger of pools for children)*, Landscape Australia, May, 160–161, 1990

A. Huckson, *The water industry in the countryside*, Landscape Design, July/August 1989, 13–15

Philip Jonker, *Geomembranes and other geosynthetics in water features*, Landscape in Southern Africa, March/April 1988, 24–26, 28

Dan Kiley, *A way with water*, Landscape Design, March 1992, 208, 33–36

E.C.S. Little, *Floating nest for wildfowl*, Birds, RSPB, March–April 1971, 176

Guide to small dam and reservoir siting, design and construction, 1977

Kevin Mann, *Castlefield's canalside*, Landscape Design, April 1992, 209, 33, 35, 37

John Merivale, *Amenity lakes and the Reservoirs Act*, November 1991, 205, 19–20

Janet Lennox Moyer, *Lighting water features*, Landscape Architecture, September 1992, 72–76

Michael Littlewood, *Tree detailing*, Butterworth Architecture, 1988

Ministry of Agriculture, Fisheries and Food, *Water for Irrigation*, HMSO, MAFF Bulletin No. 202

Debbie Roberts and Ian Smith, *Creating garden ponds and water features*, Harper Collins, 2001

Rick Rowbotham, *The Lake, Sutton Place, Guildford*. Landscape Design, October 1983 12–13

Anne Sansom, *Ponds and conservation*, The Environment Agency, 1998

Robert Schafer, *Designing and living with water*, Garten und Landschaft, 1989 (7) 40–45

Rainer Schmidt, *Construction of water bodies*, Garten und Landschaft, 1989 (7) 22–29

Stephen Scrivens, *Water features 1: Design and informal water, 2: Pools, cascades, fountains,* Architects' Journal, 1988, 188 (44) 67–74

D.E. Shirley, *An Introduction to concrete: notes for students*, Cement and Concrete Association, 1980

I.R. Smith and A.A. Lyle, *Distribution of freshwaters in Great Britain*, Institute of Terrestrial Ecology, Grange-over-Sands

David Stronach, *Partners and stone watercourses at Pasargadae: notes on the Achaemerid contribution to garden design,* Journal of Garden History, Jan–March 1994, 3–12

John Swift, *Ducks, ponds and people*, WAGBI, 1976

John D. Taylor, *Take back the water*, Landscape Architecture, May 1992, 50–55

Water Space Amenity Commission, *Conservation and Land Drainage Guidelines*, 1980

J. Whalley, *Water in the landscape*, Landscape and Urban Planning, October 1988, 145–162 (LUP special issue on Water).

Frank Wilson, *Heart of the matter (use of pumps in water features)*, Landscape Design, March 1992, 208, 40–41

Robin Winogrond, *Garden of water and light*, Anthos, 1992, 4, 24–26

R. Winter, *New lake under construction at Redditch new town*, Landscape Design, February 1972, 18–21

N.A. Young, *The management of ponds*, Birmingham Polytechnic, School of Planning and Landscape, 1977

INSTITUTIONS AND ASSOCIATIONS

APPENDIX B

Agricultural Development and Advisory Service (ADAS)*
MAFF, Great Westminster House
Horseferry Road
London SW1P 2AE

Agricultural Engineers Association
6 Buckingham Gate
London SW1

Agricultural Training Board (ATB)*
Bourne House
32–34 Beckenham Road
Beckenham
Kent BR3 4PB

Angling Trade Association
Prudential House
10th Floor
East Wing
Wellesley Road
Croydon CR0 9XY

Arboricultural Association
The Secretary
38 Blythwood Gardens
Stanstead, Essex

Biological Records Centre
Monks Wood Experimental Station
Abbots Ripton
Cambridgeshire PE17 2LS

Botanical Society of the British Isles
c/o Department of Botany
British Museum (Natural History)
Cromwell Road
London SW7

British Association for Shooting and Conservation (BASC)
(a) Marford Mill
     Rossett
     Wrexham
     Clwyd LL12 0HL
(b) Michael McMeekin
     7 Douglas Road
     Glenwherry
     Ballymena, NI

British Ecological Society
Burlington House
Piccadilly
London W1V 0LQ

British Herpetological Society
c/o The Zoological Society of London
Regents Park
London NW1 4RY

British Standards Institution (BSI)
Head Office: 2 Park Street
London W1A 2BS
Tel: (0207) 629 9000
Fax: (Group 2/3) (0207) 629 0506

British Trust for Conservation Volunteers (BTCV)
Head Office: 36 Mary's Street
Wallingford
Oxfordshire OX10 0EU

British Trust for Ornithology
Beech Grove
Tring
Hertfordshire HP23 5NR

British Waterways Board
Melbury House
Melbury Terrace
London NW1

Building Research Station
Bucknalls Lane
Garston
Watford
Hertfordshire

Cement and Concrete Association
Wexham Springs
Wexham
Slough SL3 6PL

Civic Trust
17 Carlton House Terrace
London SW1Y 5AW

**Council for Environmental Conservation
(CoEnCo)**
Zoological Gardens
Regents Park
London NW1

Council for Environmental Education
School of Education
University of Reading
London Road
Reading RG1 5AQ

Council for National Parks
4 Hobart Place
London SW1W 0HY

**Council for the Preservation of Rural
England**
4 Hobart Place
London SW1

**Council for the Preservation of Rural
Wales**
Yplas
Machynlleth
Montgomeryshire

**Council for the Protection of Rural
England**
4 Hobart Place
London SW1W 0HY

Council for the Protection of Rural Wales
31 High Street
Welshpool
Powys SY21 8PQ

Country Landowners' Association
7 Swallow Street
London W1

Country Naturalists Trusts
(Headquarters in each county)

Countryside Agency
John Dower House
Crescent Place
Cheltenham
Gloucestershire GL50 3RA

Countryside Agency for Scotland
Battleby
Redgorten
Perthshire PH1 3EW

Crafts Council
12 Waterloo Place
London SW1Y 4AU

Crown Estate Commissioners
Crown Estate Office
Whitehall
London SW1

**Department of Agriculture and Fisheries
for Scotland (DAFS)***
Chesser House
500 Gorgie Road
Edinburgh EH11 3AW

Department of Agriculture for Northern Ireland (DANI)*
Water Drainage and Conservation Section
Hydebank
4 Hospital Road
Belfast BT8 8JP

Department for the Environment (NI)
(a) Archaelogical Survey
   66 Balmoral Avenue
   Belfast BT9 6NY
(b) Conservation Branch
   Hut 6, Castle Grounds
   Stormont
   Belfast BT9 6NY
(c) Countryside and Wildlife Branch
   Calvert House
   Castle Place
   Belfast BT1 1FY

DEFRA (Department for Environment, Food and Rural Affairs)
Rural Development Service
Burghill Road
Westbury on Trym
Bristol BS10 6NJ

English Nature
Northminster House
Peterborough PE1 1UA

Environment Agency*
See telephone directory for address of local office

Farm Buildings Information Centre
National Agricultural Centre
Stoneleigh
Kenilworth
Warwicks CV8 3JN
Tel: (01203) 22345/6

Farming and Wildlife Advisory Group
The Lodge
Sandy
Bedfordshire SG19 2DL

Farming and Wildlife Trust (for FWAGS)*
National Agricultural Centre
Stoneleigh
Kenilworth
Warwickshire CV8 2LZ

Field Studies Council
62 Wilson Street
London EC21 2BU

Forestry Agency
231 Corstorphine Road
Edinburgh EH12 7AT

Freshwater Biological Association
Ferry House
Ambleside
Cumbria LA22 0LP

Friends of the Earth
377 City Road
London EC1V 1NA

Geological Society of London
Burlington House
Piccadilly
London W1V 0JU

Health and Safety Executive
Magdalen House
Stanley Precinct
Bootle
Merseyside L20 3QZ

Horticultural Education Association
65 Tilehurst Road
Reading
Berkshire

Hydraulics Research Ltd
Wallingford
Oxfordshire OX10 8BA
Tel: 01491 35381

Inland Waterways Association
114 Regents Park Road
London NW1 8UQ

Institute of Civil Engineers
25 Eccelston Square
London SW1V 1NX

Institute of Highways and Transportation
3 Lygon Place
Ebury Street
London SW1W 0JS

Institute of Terrestrial Ecology
68 Hills Road
Cambridge CB2 1LA

Institute of Water Pollution Control
53 London Road
Maidstone
Kent ME16 8JH

The Landscape Institute
6/7 Barnard Mews
London SW11 1QU

Mammal Society of the British Isles
(Business Office)
141 Newmarket Road
Cambridge CB5 8HA

Ministry of Agriculture, Fisheries and Food (MAFF)*
Whitehall Place
London SW1A 2HH

National Association of Local Councils
100 Great Russell Street
London WC1B 3LD

National Council for Voluntary Organisations
26 Bedford Square
London WC1

National Farmers Union
Agriculture House
25–31 Knightsbridge
London SW1X 7NJ

National Farmers Union of Scotland
17 Grosvenor Crescent
Edinburgh EH12 5EN

National Federation of Young Farmers' Clubs
YFC Centre
National Agricultural Centre
Kenilworth CV8 2LG

National Building Association Services Ltd
Mansion House Chambers
The Close
Newcastle-upon-Tyne NE1 3RE

The National Trust
36 Queen Anne's Gate
London SW1H 9AS

National Trust for Scotland
5 Charlotte Square
Edinburgh EH2 1UA

Pure Rivers Society
74 Dagenham Avenue
Dagenham
Essex

Royal Society for Nature Conservation (RSNC)*
(for Country Wildlife Trusts)
The Green
Nettleham
Lincoln LN2 2NR

Royal Society for the Protection of Birds (RSPB)
The Lodge
Sandy
Bedfordshire SG19 2DL

Scottish Conservation Projects Trust
Balallan House
24 Allan Park
Stirling FK8 2QG

Scottish Inland Waterways Association
25 India Street
Edinburgh E3

Scottish Landowners Federation
18 Abercrombie Place
Edinburgh EH3 6TY

Scottish River Purification Boards Association
City Chambers
Glasgow G2 1DU

Scottish Wildlife Trust
25 Johnston Terrace
Edinburgh EH1 2NH

Shell Better Britain Campaign (England, Wales & Northern Ireland)
Red House
Hill Lane
Great Barr
Birmingham B43 6LZ

Shell Better Britain Campaign (Scotland)
Balallan House
24 Allan Park
Stirling FK8 2QG

Town Planning Institute
26 Portland Square
London W1

Tree Council
Agriculture House
Knightsbridge
London SW1X 7NJ

Water Authorities Association
1 Queen Anne's Gate
London SW1H 9BT

Water Research Centre
Medmenham Laboratory
PO Box 16
Henley Road
Medmenham
Marlow
Buckinghamshire

Waterway Recovery Group
c/o 39 Westminster Crescent
Burn Bridge
Harrogate
North Yorkshire HG3 1LX

The Waterways Trust
The Trust House
Church Road
Watford
WD17 4QA

Welsh Office Agriculture Department (WOAD)*
Crown Offices
Cathays Park
Cardiff

Wildfowl Trust
New Grounds
Slimbridge
Gloucestershire GL2 7BT

Woodland Trust
Autumn Park
Dysart Road
Grantham
Lincolnshire NG31 6LL

World Wildlife Fund
Panda House
11–13 Ockford Road
Godalming
Surrey GU7 1QU

* Address given is of headquarters or head office from which addresses of regional/country offices can be obtained.

MANUFACTURERS AND SUPPLIERS

Water quality equipment

Anglo Aquarium Plant Co
Strayfield Road
Enfield
Middlesex EN2 9JE

Butyl Products
11 Radford Crescent
Billericay
Essex CM12 0DW

DRC Polymer Products
1 Regal Lane
Soham, Ely
Cambs CB7 5BA

Fairwater
Lodge Farm
Malthouse Lane
Ashington
West Sussex RH20 3BU

Flowform Marketing
Ruskin Mill
Nailsworth
Glos. GL6 0LA

Fountainhead
9 Station Approach
Kew Gardens
Surrey TW9 3QB

Fountains Direct
The Office
41 Dartnell Park
West Byfleet
Surrey KT14 6PR

Heissner UK
The New Regency Business Centre
Common Lane Industrial Est
Kenilworth
Warcs CV8 2EL

Hydroscape Group
10 Carvers Industrial Est
Ringwood
Hants BH24 1JS

Interpet/Blagdon
Interpet
Vincent Lane
Dorking
Surrey RH4 3XX

Karma
Unit 5
Babdown Airfield
Tetbury
Glos.

Kingcombe Aquacare
St Francis Farm
Hooke
Dorset DT8 3NX

Land and Water Services
Weston Yard
Aldbury
Surrey GU5 9AF

Leaky Pipe Systems
Frith Street
Dean Street
East Farleigh
Maidstone
Kent ME15 0PR

Lurgi Invent
Dell Road
Shawclough
Rochdale
Lancs OL12 6BZ

Mayer Environmental
Transport Avenue
Brentford
Middlesex TW8 9HA

Merton Hall Pond
Merton
Thetford
Norfolk IP25 6QH

Mickfield Watergarden Centre
Debenham Road
Mickfield
Nr Stowmarket
Suffolk IP14 5LP

Miles Waterscapes
School House
Great Ashfield
Bury St Edmonds
Suffolk IP31 3HJ

Simon Moore Water Services
Unit 2
Poundbury West
Dorchester
Dorset DT1 2PG

Symbio
38 Bookham Industrial Park
Bookham
Surrey KT23 3FU

Teviot Water Gardens
Kirkbank
Nr Eckford
Kelso
Roxburghshire
Scotland TD5 8LE

The Fountain Workshop
The Admiral's Offices
The Historic Dockyard
Chatham
Kent ME4 4TZ

Water Gardening Direct
Hards Lane
Frognall
Deeping St James
Peterborough

Water Sculptures
St Georges Studios
St Georges Quay
Lancaster LA1 5QJ

Water Techniques
Downside Mill
Cobham Park Road
Cobham
Surrey KT11 3PF

Yarningdale Nurseries
16 Chapel Street
Warwick
CV34 4HL

Fountains

Arcadian Garden Features
The Forge House
East Haddon
Northampton NN3 7SH

Fairwater
Lodge Farm
Malthouse Lane
Ashington
West Sussex RH20 3BU

Fibre Flora
Unit 26
Penley Industrial Estate
Penley
Wrexham LL13 0LQ

Flowform Marketing
Ruskin Mill
Nailsworth
Glos. GL6 0LA

Fountainhead
9 Station Approach
Kew Gardens
Surrey TW9 3QB

Fountains Direct
The Office
41 Dartnell Park
West Byfleet
Surrey KT14 6PR

Fountain Installers
Shamrock House
Elsenwood Drive
Camberley
Surrey GU15 2AZ

Haddonstone
The Forge House
East Haddon
Northampton NN6 8DB

Heissner UK
The New Regency Business Centre
Common Lane Industrial Estate
Kenilworth
Warcs CV8 2EL

Hydroscape Group
10 Carvers Industrial Est
Ringwood
Hants BH24 1JS

Interpet/Blagdon
Interpet
Vincent Lane
Dorking
Surrey RH4 3XX

James Designs
The Old Tannery
Kelston
Bath BA1 9AN

Kingcombe Aquacare
St Francis Farm
Hooke
Dorset DT8 3NX

Lurgi Invent
Dell Road
Shawclough
Rochdale
Lancs OL12 6BZ

Mickfield Watergarden Centre
Debenham Road
Mickfield
Nr Stowmarket
Suffolk IP14 5LP

Miles Waterscapes
School House
Great Ashfield
Bury St Edmonds
Suffolk IP31 3HJ

Simon Moore Water Services
Unit 2
Poundbury West
Dorchester
Dorset DT1 2PG

Teviot Water Gardens
Kirkbank
Nr Eckford
Kelso
Roxburghshire
Scotland TD5 8LE

The Fountain Workshop
The Admiral's Offices
The Historic Dockyard
Chatham
Kent ME4 4TZ

Water Gardening Direct
Hards Lane
Frognall
Deeping St James
Peterborough

Water Sculptures
St Georges Studios
St Georges Quay
Lancaster LA1 5QJ

Water Techniques
Downside Mill
Cobham Park Road
Cobham
Surrey KT11 3PF

Water liners

Alkor Plastics (UK) Ltd
Odhams Trading Est
St Albans Road
Watford WD2 5DG

Allen Plastics Ltd
1 Edison Road
Churchfields Industrial Est
Salisbury
Wiltshire SP2 7NU

Anaplast
Lundholm Road
Ardeer
Ayrshire KA20 3NQ

Anglo Aquarium Plant Co
Strayfield Road
Enfield
Middlesex EN2 9JE

Ardon International
PO Box 111
Tunbridge Wells TN4 0PZ

Butyl Products Ltd
11 Radford Crescent
Billericay
Essex CM12 0DW

DRC Polymer Products
1 Regal Lane
Soham, Ely
Cams CB7 5BA

Fairwater
Lodge Farm
Malthouse Lane
Ashington
West Sussex RH20 3BU

Fountainhead
9 Station Approach
Kew Gardens
Surrey TW9 3QB

Fountains Direct
The Office
41 Dartnell Park
West Byfleet
Surrey KT14 6PR

Gordon Lowe Plastics Ltd
Flexible Liners and Geotextile Underlays
Dragonfly House
Rookery Road
Wybaston
Bedfordshire MK44 3UG

Heissner UK
The New Regency Business Centre
Common Lane Industrial Est
Kenilworth
Warcs CV8 2EL

Interpet/Blagdon
Interpet
Vincent Lane
Dorking
Surrey RH4 3XX

Karma
Unit 5
Babdown Airfield
Tetbury
Glos.

Kingcombe Aquacare
St Francis Farm
Hooke
Dorset DT8 3NX

Land and Water Services
Weston Yard
Aldbury
Surrey GU5 9AF

Landline Ltd
1 Bluebridge Industrial Est
Halstead
Essex CO9 2EX

LEC Geosynthetics
Nags Corner
Wiston Road
Nayland
Colchester
Essex CO6 4LT

Lurgi Invent
Dell Road
Shawclough
Rochdale
Lancs OL12 6BZ

Mickfield Watergarden Centre
Debenham Road
Mickfield
Nr Stowmarket
Suffolk IP14 5LP

Midlands Butyl
Windmill Farm
Biggie Lane
Nr Hulland Ward
Derbyshire DE6 3FN

Miles Waterscapes
School House
Great Ashfield
Bury St Edmonds
Suffolk IP31 3HJ

Monarflex
Geomembranes Ltd
Lyon Way
St Albans
Herts AL4 0LB

Monomet Ltd
50 Beddington Lane
Croydon
Surrey CR0 4TE

Phi Group Ltd
72–74 Bath Road
Cheltenham
Glos GL53 7JT

Rawell Marketing Ltd
Carr Lane
Hoylake
Merseyside L47 4AZ

Rawell Water Control Systems
Carr Lane
Hoylake
Wirral
Merseyside CH47 4FE

Robb of St Ives (Water Ltd)
Unit 3c
Cromwell Business Park
New Road
St Ives
Huntingdon PE17 4BG

Russetts Developments
27 Burners Lane
Kiln Farm
Milton Keynes MK11 3HA

Simon Moore Water Services
Unit 2
Poundbury West
Dorchester
Dorset DT1 2PG

Stephens Plastics
Hawthorn Works
Corsham
Wilts SN13 9RD

T Harrison Chaplin
The Old Garage
The Green
Great Milton
Oxford OX44 7NP

Teviot Water Gardens
Kirkbank
Nr Eckford
Kelso
Roxburghshire
Scotland TD5 8LE

The Fountain Workshop
The Admiral's Offices
The Historic Dockyard
Chatham
Kent ME4 4TZ

Water Gardening Direct
Hards Lane
Frognall
Deeping St James
Peterborough

Water Sculptures
St Georges Studios
St Georges Quay
Lancaster
LA1 5QJ

Water Engineering Pumps

ABS Pumps Ltd
58 Beddington Lane
Croydon CR9 4PT

Beresford Pumps
Carlton Road
Foleshill
Coventry CV6 7FL

British Guinard Pumps Ltd
29–30 Kernan Drive
Swingbridge Industrial Est
Loughborough LE11 0JF

Cyprio Ltd
Eastgate Mews
131–133 Eastgate
Deeping St James
Peterborough PE6 8RB

Fairwater
Lodge farm
Malthouse Lane
Ashington
West Sussex RH20 3BU

Fountainhead
9 Station Approach
Kew Gardens
Surrey TW9 3QB

Fountains Direct
The Office
41 Dartnell Park
West Byfleet
Surrey KT14 6PR

IEM Wallingford
Wallingford
Oxon OX10 8BA

Heissner UK
The New Regency Business Centre
Common Lane Industrial Est
Kenilworth
Warcs CV8 2EL

Interpet/Blagdon
Interpet
Vincent Lane
Dorking
Surrey RH4 3XX

Javelin Water Engineering
The Pump House
Belvoir Way
Fairfield Industrial Est
Louth, Lincs. LN11 0YA

Karma
Unit 5
Babdown Airfield
Tetbury
Glos.

Kingcombe Aquacare
St Francis Farm
Hooke
Dorset DT8 3NX

Lake Aid Systems (Europe) Ltd
Bridge House
St Germans
King's Lynn
Norfolk PE34 3ES

Land and Water Services
Weston Yard
Aldbury
Surrey GU5 9AF

Lurgi Invent
Dell Road
Shawclough
Rochdale
Lancs OL12 6BZ

Miles Waterscapes
School House
Great Ashfield
Bury St Edmonds
Suffolk IP31 3HJ

Papa
14a Kingshill Industrial Est
Bude
Cornwall EX23 8QN

W Robinson & Sons (EC) Ltd
3 Redchurch Street
London E2 7DJ

Selwood Pumps
Bournemouth Road
Chandlers Ford
Eastleigh
Hampshire

Simon Moore Water Services
Unit 2
Poundbury West
Dorchester
Dorset DT1 2PG

Teviot Water Gardens
Kirkbank
Nr Eckford
Kelso
Roxburghshire
Scotland TD5 8LE

The Fountain Workshop
The Admiral's Offices
The Historic Dockyard
Chatham
Kent ME4 4TZ

Water Sculptures
St Georges Studios
St Georges Quay
Lancaster LA1 5QJ

Water Techniques
Downside Mill
Cobham Park Road
Cobham
Surrey KT11 3PF

Water display products

Abbey Waters Ltd
North Wyke Farm
Guildford Road
Normandy
Surrey GU3 2AN

Aqua Company Ltd
Abbott House
14a Hale Road
Farnham
Surrey GU9 9QH

Ayelco
Drayton House
Stede Quarter
Biddenden
Kent TN27 8JQ

Blagdon Water Garden Products Ltd
Unit 6 & 7
Commerce Way
Walrow Industrial Est
Highbridge
Somerset TA9 4AG

**Fordwater Pumping
Supplies**
49–51 Stratford Road
Birmingham B11 1RU

T Harrison Chaplin Ltd
Meadhurst Park Nursery
Cadbury Road
Sunbury-on-Thames
Middlesex

Hozelock Aquatics Ltd
Haddenham
Aylesbury
Buckinghamshire HP17 8JD

Lotus Water Gardens
PO Box 36
Junction Street
Burnley
Lancashire BB17 0NA

Remanoid Ltd
Unit 44
Number One Industrial Est
Medomsley Road
Consett
Co Durham DH8 6SZ

Stapeley Water Gardens Ltd
92 London Road
Stapeley
Nantwich CW5 7LM

Trident Water Gardens
Carlton Road
Foleshill
Coventry CV6 7FL

Waveney Fish Farm Ltd
Park Road
Diss
Norfolk IP22 3AS

Water feature displays, design and construction

Aquality-Aquatic Project Consultants
9 Crookston Road
London SE9 1YD

Aquatic Installation Supplies
15 Hallflat Lane
Balby
Doncaster DN4 8QA

Arcadran Garden Features
The Forge House
East Haddon
Northamptonshire NN3 7SH

Artscape Gardening
Twin Roofs
43 Golden Ball Lane
Pinkeys Green
Maidenhead
Berks SL6 GNW

Beaver Water Plants
Beaver Aquatic Nursery
Eastbourne Road
Lingfield
Surrey RH7 6HL

Bernard Crook Garden Services
Sherington Nurseries
Sherington
Newport Pagnell
Bucks MK16 9NQ

Blackburn Fraser
6 Choir Street
Salford M7 9ZD

Butyl Products
11 Radford Cresent
Billericay
Essex CM12 0DW

Chameleon Garden Products
BCP House
Basselsbury Lane
High Wycombe
Bucks HP11 1HT

Christine-Ann Richards
Chapel House
High Street
Wanstrow
Nr Shepton Mallet
Somerset BA4 4TE

DH Water Gardens
Wildmore Lane
Sherfield-on-London
Basingstoke
Hants RG27 0HA

Dodson Macrae
Unit 11
Kelliebank Industrial Est
Alloa
Scotland FK10 1NT

DRC Polymer Products
1 Regal Lane
Soham, Ely
Cambs CB7 5BA

Fairwater
Lodge Farm
Malthouse Lane
Ashington
West Sussex RH20 3BU

Fibre Flora
Unit 26
Penley Industrial Est
Penley
Wrexham LL13 0LQ

Flowform Marketing
Ruskin Mill
Nailsworth
Glos. GL6 0LA

Fountainhead Ltd
9 Station Approach
Kew Gardens
Surrey TW9 3QB

Fountains Direct
The Office
41 Dartnell Park
West Byfleet
Surrey KT14 6PR

Fountain Installers
Shamrock House
Elsenwood Drive
Camberley
Surrey GU15 2AZ

Gordon Low Products
Rookery Road
Wyboston
Beds MK44 3UG

HLD
The Old Shipyard
Gainsborough
Lincs DN21 1NG

Haddonstone
The Forge House
East Haddon
Northampton NN6 8DB

Heissner UK
The New Regency Business Centre
Common Lane Industrial Est
Kenilworth
Warcs CV8 2EL

IEM Wallingford
Wallingford
Oxfordshire OX10 8BA

Interpet/Blagdon
Interpet
Vincent Lane
Dorking
Surrey RH4 3XX

Invent Water Treatment Ltd
Grove Dairy Farm
Bobbing Hill
Bobbing
Sittingbourne
Kent ME9 8NY

IRIS Water and Design
Langburn Bank
Castleton
Whitby YO21 2EU

James Designs
The Old Tannery
Kelston
Bath BA1 9AN

Kingcombe Aquacare
St Francis Farm
Hooke
Dorset DT8 3NX

Lakescapes
144 Curley Hill
Ilkley
West Yorkshire

Land and Water Services
Weston Yard
Aldbury
Surrey SU5 9AF

Lurgi Invent
Dell Road
Shawclough
Rochdale
Lancs OL12 6B2

LWL Landscapes
3–4 Sudley Road
Bognor Regis
West Sussex PO21 1EU

Merton Hall Pond
Merton
Thetford
Norfolk IP25 6QH

Mickfield Watergarden Centre
Debenham Road
Mickfield
Nr Stowmarket
Suffolk IP14 5LP

Midlands Butyl
Windmill Farm
Biggie Lane
Nr Hulland Ward
Derbyshire DE6 3FN

Miles Waterscapes
School House Farm
Great Ashfield
Bury St Edmonds
Suffolk IP31 3HJ

Neaco
Norton Grove Industrial Est
Norton, Malton
N Yorks YO17 9HQ

Rock Themes International
Unit 1
Hawks Way
Tree Beach industrial Est
Gunnerleigh
Devon EX32 7NZ

Room for a View
Castlebay
Parkstone Avenue
Wickford
Essex SS12 0JE

Simon Moore Water Services
Unit 2
Poundbury West
Dorchester
Dorset DT1 2PG

Stuart Garden Centre
Burrow Hill Parm
Wiveliscombe
Somerset TA4 2RN

Symbio
Sutton Business Centre
Restmor Way
Wallington
Surrey SM6 7AH

T Harrison Chaplin
The Old Garage
The Green
Great Milton
Oxford OX44 7NP

Terra Products
21 Clifton Road
London N22 7NX

Teviot Water Gardens
Kirkbank
Nr Eckford
Kelso
Roxburghshire
Scotland TD5 8LE

The Fountain Workshop
The Admiral's Offices
The Historic Dockyard
Chatham
Kent ME4 4TZ

Ustigate Ltd
3 Berkley Crescent
Gravesend
Kent DA12 2AD

Water Features
Redbourne
Herts AL3 7AE

Water Gardening Direct
Hards Lane
Frognall
Deeping St James
Peterborough

Water Management
Rutherford House
43 Terrace Road
Walton-on-Thames
Surrey KT12 2JP

Water Sculptures
St Georges Studios
St Georges Quay
Lancaster LA1 5QJ

Water Techniques
Downside Mill
Cobham Park Road
Cobham
Surrey KT11 3PF

Waterland Productions
Mississippi House
41 Balcombe Road
Haywards Heath
West Sussex RH15 1PA

Yarningdale Nurseries
16 Chapel Street
Warwick
CV34 4HL

Ornamental/sculpture

Angela Conner
George & Dragon Hall
Mary Place
London W11 4PL

Brookbrae Ltd
53 St Leonard's Road
London SW14 7NQ

Cast Iron Company
Ashley House
18–20 George Street
Richmond
Surrey TW9 1HD

Crowther of Syon Lodge Ltd
Syon Lodge
Bush Corner
London Road
Isleworth TW7 5HB

The David Sharp Studio
201A Nottingham Road
Somercotes DE55 4JG

Dorothea
Pearl House
Hardwick Street
Buxton
Derbyshire SK17 6DH

Furniture International Ltd
Seager Buildings
Brookmill Road
London SE8 4HL

Haddonstone Ltd
The Forge House
East Haddon
Northampton

Kingswood Services Ltd
170 Alfreton Road
Sutton in Ashfield
Nottinghamshire NG17 1JB

The Landscape Ornament Co
Long Barn
Palney
Devizes
Wilts SN10 3RB

Minsterstone (Wharf Lane) Ltd
Station Road
Ilminster
Somerset

Ornate Products
26–27 Clivemont Road
Cordwallis Est
Maidenhead
Berkshire SL6 7BZ

Ornate Products
Limecroft Road
Knaphill,
Medomsley Road Consett
Co Durham DH8 6SZ

Peter Thursby
Oakley House
28 Oakley Close
Pinhoe
Exeter EX1 3SB

Rawstone Associates
Dunsdale
Forest Row
East Sussex RH18 5BD

Shedlow Harrisons Joinery
Stratford St Andrew
Saxmundham
Suffolk IP17 1LF

Stone Heritage Ltd
Portaway Mine
Off Dunwood Lane
Elton
Derbyshire DE3 2BD

Walcot Sculptures
108 Walcot Street
Bath
Avon BA1 5BG

Water Sculptures
St Georges Studios
St Georges Quay
Lancaster LA1 5QJ

William Pye Ltd
43 Hamball Road
Clapham
London SW4 9EQ

Artificial rock

Bernard Crook Garden Services
Sherington Nursery
Bedford House
Sherington
Newport Pagnell
Buckinghamshire MK16 9NQ

Custom Rock Creations
Marwood Cottage
Kingford
Umberleigh
Devon EX37 9NB

Di Giacomo
612 South Duggan Avenue
Azusa
California 91702-5138
USA

Euro Wonder Rock Ltd
9 Allens Close
Boreham
Chelmsford
Essex CM3 3DR

Rockscapes
44 High Street
Malmesbury
Wiltshire SN16 9AT

Rockways
9 Allens Close
Boreham
Chelmsford
Essex CM3 3DR

Water lighting

Aqua Bean
PO Box 3
Willowland
Grantham
Lincs NG31 6AA

BBI Lighting
PO Box 2417
Coventry CV1 2YB

Fairwater
Lodge Farm
Malthouse Lane
Ashington
West Sussex RH20 3BU

Fountainhead
9 Station Approach
Kew Gardens
Surrey TW9 3QB

Fountains Direct
The Office
41 Dartnell Park
West Byfleet
Surrey KT14 6PR

Fountain Installers
Shamrock House
Elsenwood Drive
Camberley
Surrey GU15 2AZ

Garden and Security Lighting
39 Reigate Road
Hookwood
Horley
Surrey RH6 0HL

Garden Architecture
259 Munster Road
Fulham
London SW6 6BW

Heissner UK
The New Regency Business Centre
Common Lane Industrial Est
Kenilworth
Warcs CV8 2EL

Interpet/Blagdon
Interpet
Vincent Lane
Dorking
Surrey RH4 3XX

Kingcombe Aquacare
St Francis Farm
Hooke
Dorset DT8 3NX

Lightscape Projects
23 Jacob Street
London SE1 2BG

Lightwater International
8 Harshwood Road
Lightwater
Surrey GU18 5QZ

Lumisphere Products
Hardings Lane
Mill Green
Ingatestone
Essex CM4 0HZ

Lurgi Invent
Dell Road
Shawclough
Rochdale
Lancs OL12 6BZ

Marwood Electrical Company
Maidstone Road
Paddock Wood
Tonbridge
Kent TN12 6DR

Mickfield Watergarden Centre
Debenham Road
Mickfield
Nr Stowmarket
Suffolk IP14 5LP

Miles Waterscapes
School House
Great Ashfield
Bury St Edmonds
Suffolk IP31 3HJ

Monarflex Geomembranes
Lyon Way
St Albans
Herts AL4 0LB

Nexus Lighting
68 Great Cullings
Romford
Essex CM5 9EF

OTSS
PO Box 39
Grantham
Lincolnshire NG31 6AA

Simon Moore Water Services
Unit 2
Pondbury West
Dorchetser
Dorset DT1 2PG

Teviot Water Gardens
Kirkbank
Nr Eckford
Kelso
Roxburghshire
Scotland TD5 8LE

The Fountain Workshop
The Admiral's Offices
The Historic Dockyard
Chatham
Kent ME4 4TZ

Water Gardening Direct
Hards Lane
Frognall
Deeping St James
Peterborough

Water Sculptures
St Georges Studios
St Georges Quay
Lancashire LA1 5QJ

Water Techniques
Downside Mill
Cobham Park Road
Cobham
Surrey KT11 3PF

Timber structures

Concrete & Timber Services Ltd
Colne Valley Workshops
Linthwaite
Huddersfield HD7 5QG

Hickson Leisure Developments
New Potters Grange
Goole
North Humberside DN14 6XF

Woodscapes Ltd
Upfield
Pike Lowre
Brinscall
Chorley PR6 8SP

GLOSSARY

APPENDIX D

Acidic: with a pH value of less than 7 (see pH)

Aerobic: characterised by the presence of free or molecular oxygen; requiring such conditions to live

Aggregate: similar to ballast, a loose mixture of crushed stone and sand used to reinforce concrete

Algal growth: growth of very small water plants which may help to reduce pollution in water but if they become too numerous cause difficulties in water treatment such as clogging filters, etc.

Alkaline: with a pH value above 7 (see pH)

Alluvium: fine sediments deposited by floods

Amphibious: able to live both on land and in water

Anaerobic: action which occurs out of contact with air or oxygen

Aquatic plant: any plant that can grow with its roots surrounded by water, either free-floating or in saturated soil

Armoured cabling: cabling with reinforced protective covering for safety

Armour layer: outer layer of a revetment; protects the underlying material against erosion by currents, waves and other external agents

Backfill: to fill in a hole around the object occupying it, for example a rigid pool unit or a plant root ball

Bacterial count: a method of estimating the number of bacteria present per unit volume of water

Ballast: a sand and gravel mix used in making concrete

Bankfull capacity: volume of water contained in a river channel when the water level is at, but not over, the top of the bank

Bar deposit: layer of river bed load material deposited on the inside of a bend

Batten: a narrow strip of wood

Batter: slope of a bank, expressed either as a ratio of horizontal distance to vertical distance (e.g. 1:2) or as the angle of a slope in degrees (e.g. 63°)

Bay: recess in the water margin of a pond or lake

Bearer: a supporting beam or plank on which joists rest

Bedding mortar: a mixture of sand and cement used for laying paving stones

Bentomat: a waterproof lining material containing bentonite

Bentonite: a powder derived from fossilised volcanic ash which, when mixed with water and added to clay, swells into a water-resistant gel

Berm: shelf or ledge in the bank of a watercourse or water body

Bilharzia: a disease caused by a very small free-swimming parasite

Bilharzia cercaria: the stage of the Bilharzia parasite when it is infective to humans. Infection is by penetration of the skin

Blanket bog: extensive area of acid mire found on flat and gently sloping ground where rainfall is high

Block rock: 'as-quarried' rock having roughly rectangular faces, the maximum length of side being no longer than twice the minimum

Bog: mire containing acid-loving plants

Bog garden: an area where the soil is permanently damp

Bog plant: plants that will grow and thrive with their roots in wet soil; many will also grow in shallow water, and are more properly called marginal plants

Bolster chisel: a steel chisel with a wide blade used with a cub hammer for cutting bricks, pavers or blocks

Breeze block: an undecorative, moulded concrete block

Butyl: strong, durable, waterproof material made of rubber

Canalised river: a river which is controlled by weirs and provided with locks to permit navigation

Carr: fen scrub

Catchment: area of ground which collects and feeds waterway or wetland

Chamfer: to bevel symmetrically a right-angled edge or corner

Circuit breaker: see Residual current device

Club hammer: a heavy, mallet-shaped hammer used with a bolster chisel to cut walling stones

Colloidal material: solid particles suspended in water of such a small size that they cannot be settled or filtered by simple means

Community: group of plants and/or animals living together under characteristic, recognisable conditions

Concrete: a mixture of sand, cement, water and small stones, which sets to form an extremely strong, durable building material; often used to make foundations

Conduit: a tube or duct conducting water or enclosing cables

Coping: the top course of stones or bricks in a wall; often flat or sloping stones that differ from those used in the wall, for decorative effect or to allow rainwater to run off

Correlation: a mathematical relationship

Countersunk screw: a screw with a head that, when fully screwed down, lies flush with the surface

Culvert: an aperture in, e.g., brickwork that allows water to flow out from a concealed header pool or tank

Datum peg: a wooden peg driven into the ground; the top of, or a mark on, the peg is used as a reference point to establish a horizontal level

Degradation: regional drop in bed level of a channel; opposite is termed aggradation

Delivery pipe: the pipe that runs from a pump to the water outlet in a recirculating feature

Desludging: the removal of accumulated sludge from settling tanks, aqua privies, septic tanks, etc. If this is not carried out properly the level of sludge will build up and seriously affect the action of the apparatus and may cause serious nuisance

Dissolved oxygen: oxygen dissolved in water

Drain: man-made open watercourse for receiving and conveying drainage flow

Draw-down: localised lowering of the water table around a groundwater abstraction point

Dyke: ditch or watercourse that functions, at least in part, as a barrier; in Scotland, a dry-stone wall

Dystrophic: water of no or extremely low productivity

Ecology: study of how living things relate to their environment or surroundings

Ecosystem: the totality in which any living organism finds itself

Ecotone: area between zones which may in itself constitute a zone with its own communities

Effluent: any liquid discharge

Elbow joint: a length of connecting pipe bent to form a right-angle

Embankment: man-made bank to raise natural bank level in order to prevent flooding, generally constructed of soil

Empirical: verifiable by observation and experiment

Engineering brick: a dense, hard, water-resistant brick, dark in colour and hence inconspicuous under water

Eutrophic: water of high productivity

Eutrophication: the process by which a water body becomes more productive over time

Excavated: dug in the soil

Faecal pollution: pollution or impurity caused by the excreta of animals and humans, may be a source of disease organisms

Faggot: bundle of cut branches

Faggoting: method of bank protection using bundles of long twigs (faggots) placed along the water's edge and pegged down

Fairway: the centre of the navigable part of a canal or waterway

Fen: mire containing neutral or alkaline-loving plants

Fetch: direct horizontal distance (in direction of the wind) over which wind generates waves

Fissured rock: rock containing many cracks which may behave as water channels

Flash: small depression with shallow water, which may be natural or excavated

Flexible liner: a waterproof butyl, PVC, or plastic liner

Flocculation and coagulation: processes in which chemicals are added to water to produce a precipitate which combines with solid material suspended in the water and enables it to settle to the bottom leaving a clear top layer

Flood meadow: pasture adjacent to a river that is regularly inundated by natural flooding

Flood plain: flat land on either side of a river over which flood waters spread, although this may be prevented by flood protection works

Flow adjuster: an adjustable valve used to control water flow

Flume: artificial channel built to maximise flow-through efficiency

Flush: area of soil in which nutrients accumulate due to water inflow or soil movement and breakdown

Fluvio-glacial: material transported and deposited by rivers and glaciers during the Ice Age

Footing: a narrow trench foundation, usually for a wall

Formation: prepared foundation surface on which a structure is constructed

Foundation: a solid base, often of concrete, on which a structure stands

Frictional headloss: a loss of pressure in a pipe caused by friction between the flow of liquid and the pipe itself. It is measured as the difference in head level required to overcome the headloss

Friable: dry and crumbly

Frog: the hollow in a brick

Gabions: rectangular or tubular baskets made from steel wire or polymer mesh and subsequently filled with stones

Galvanised: of metal objects such as nails, with a coating of zinc to protect them from rusting

Geotextile: permeable synthetic fabric used in conjunction with soil for the function of filtration, separation, drainage, soil reinforcement or erosion protection

Glacial till: unsorted clays, sands, gravels and stones left by melting glaciers

Gravity sewers: sewers utilising natural drainage without the use of pumps

Groundwater: water stored in the pores and voids of rocks in the saturated zone below the water table

Habitat: the recognisable area or type of environment in which an organism normally lives

Hardcore: broken bricks, concrete, or stones used to create a firm base for foundations or paving

Hardness: property of water reflecting the quantity of dissolved calcium (and magnesium) salts; in domestic usage, more soap is needed to make a lather with hard water than with soft

Hardpan: a virtually impermeable layer of compacted soil

Hard protection: collective term for bank protection with materials such as steel, concrete, etc., as distinct from protection with natural 'soft' materials such as vegetation

Hardwood timber: timber cut from deciduous trees

Head: the difference in the depth of water at any two points, or the measure of the pressure at the lower point expressed in terms of this difference

Header pool: the uppermost pool in a recirculating water feature

Headwater: part of a river system near to the source

Hill gripping: land drainage technique in upland areas involving cutting closely spaced, steep-sided, open drains

Hose connector: a moulded plastic joint used to join two pipes together

Humus: stable organic matter found in soil and necessary for good moisture retention, etc.

Hydraulic loads: forces due to action of water; may be hydrodynamic or hydrostatic

Hydraulic short-circuiting: takes place when the inlet and outlet of a tank or pond are close together and flow takes the shortest possible path allowing a large volume of the liquid to be undisturbed

Hydraulics: study of the behaviour of flowing water

Hydrogen potential (pH): a measure of the relative acidity or alkalinity of water or soil **(see pH)**

Hypertufa: a concrete mix incorporating some organic matter, encouraging mosses and algae to grow on its surface for an 'antique' effect

Imbricated: well-graded alluvial gravel deposit; critical shear stress is enhanced by ordered structure caused by gentle mode of deposition

Impervious: watertight

Impoundment: reservoir

Joist: a wooden supporting beam that runs beneath and usually perpendicular to planks, used, e.g., for flooring, decking or bridges

Leach: the process by which percolating water removes nutrients from the soil

Leat: artificial channel, the main purpose of which is to supply water to another waterway or to water-powered mills

Lifecycle costs: whole cost of a scheme, including investigation, design, construction, management (i.e. monitoring, inspection and maintenance) and eventual replacement or rehabilitation costs

Limestone: mineral consisting mainly of calcium carbonate ($CaCO_3$). It is not the same as lime, oxide of lime, quicklime or road-lime, which are all calcium oxide (CaO), or slaked lime, which is calcium hydroxide ($Ca(OH)_2$). These other substances can be used to correct acidity but they are more soluble in water and need to be dosed in the correct proportions.

Macrophyte: broad leaved plant

Marsh: area of mineral-based soil in which the summer water level is close to the surface but seldom much above it

Mat: geotextile comprising a relatively open, three-dimensional, random matrix of filaments

Mesotrophic: water of medium productivity

Methane gas: an inflammable gas produced by the anaerobic fermentation of organic material such as sludge

Mire: area of permanently wet peat

Moisture lovers: plants that thrive in moist soil. Unlike bog plants, moisture-lovers need some soil drainage and do not tolerate waterlogged conditions

Mole drain: unlined sub-surface enclosed channel made by a special tractor-pulled plough

Morphology: science of form and structure of, e.g., a river channel

Natural succession: the process by which one community of organisms gives way to another in an orderly series from colonisers to climax

Non-point sources: diffuse sources of water pollution that do not emanate from a single location

Non-return valve: a valve that allows water to flow in one direction only

Non-woven fabric: geotextile fabric produced by methods other than weaving, often with a complex fibre structure having a random matrix of filaments

Ochre: natural pigment caused by the bacterial oxidation of iron in previously water-logged soil following exposure to air, frequently as a result of land drainage. The colour may be brown, yellow or red

Oliogotrophic: water of low productivity, low in plant nutrients

Osier: willow (*Salix viminalis* and *S. purpurea*) traditionally grown to produce slender rods for basket making

Oxygenator: submerged aquatic plant which performs a key functional role in ponds; the leaves and stems release oxygen into the water as a by-product of photosynthesis

Pan: a hard, distinct soil layer caused by the precipitation of iron or other compounds

Pathogenic organisms: organisms responsible for disease

Peak demand: highest rate of consumption measured at any time, in practice the peak demand may last for no more than a few minutes. It may be found when all taps and other outlets in a system are operating fully open at the same time

Pea shingle: fine gravel, often used as a top dressing for soil

Peat: soil made up entirely of organic remains

Ped block: roughly rectangular block of material formed during break-up of bank comprising cohesive soil

Permeable strata: layers of soil or other minerals through which water can freely drain. Impermeable strata such as clay will retain water and prevent drainage

pH: quantitative expression denoting the acidity or alkalinity of a solution or soil. It has a scale of 0 to 14; pH7 is neutral, below 7 is acid and above 7 is alkaline

Photosynthesis: the behaviour of plants which liberate oxygen by day and carbon dioxide by night

Piped drain: underdrain lined with a pipe designed to collect and carry percolating water. Pipe materials include tiles (porous, clay pipe) perforated plastic pipe and also concrete, steel, etc.

Piping: internal erosion of a dam, usually by water seeping along a pipe or up from below

Plumb line: a length of string with a metal weight attached, used to determine vertical alignment

Poaching: trampling by livestock causing land to break up into wet muddy patches

Pointing: filling the joints in brickwork and stonework with mortar

Pollard: tree that has been cut 2–4 metres above ground level and then allowed to regrow

Polythene film: thin sheet of plastic material, preferably black in colour. This material is often used in coffee factories and may be known as coffee sheeting. Thicker material can be obtained and is more durable

Pool: area of deeper water within a watercourse; pond, especially within a wetland

Potable water: water that is fit to drink

Precipitation: a change which enables dissolved substances to separate from solutions as solid particles

Preformed unit: ready-made, rigid mouldings for pools and streams

Productivity: description of ecosystem in terms of 'biomass' (total mass of living organisms)

Pro rata: in proportion to the rate (of flow)

Puddled clay: traditional pond and waterway lining material, made by pounding clay and water to make a dense mass resistant to water penetration

PVC: a strong, durable waterproof material made of vinyl chloride

Quiescent: still or undisturbed

Reach: a length of channel

Reconstituted stone: natural stone aggregate cast in preformed shapes such as slabs or blocks

Regime channel: channel formed in erodible material but experiencing no long-term degradation, or aggradation. The cross-section may vary in the short term and the channel may move laterally due to continuing processes of erosion and deposition

Reinforcing fibres: synthetic fibres – based on polypropylene – which are mixed with cement-based materials to provide extra strength and elasticity

Render: to cover a surface with mortar or cement in order to produce a smooth finish

Reservoir pool: a pool at the lowest point of a water feature

Residual current device (RCD): often called a circuit breaker, used as a safety measure; an automatic switch halts electricity flow in the event of a short-circuit, or if the current exceeds a pre-set safe value

Respiration: process in which plants and animals derive energy by means of internal chemical reactions, generally using oxygen and giving out carbon dioxide

Retention time: time that flowing water is retained in tanks, filters, etc. It may be calculated from the volume of tank and the rate of flow: RT = Volume of tank/Rate of flow

Return current: current set up by a moving boat in a restricted waterway, flowing in the opposite direction to boat movement

Revetment: lining of wood, stone of any suitable material to prevent the walls of pits or channels collapsing in soft soil

Rhyne: Somerset name for a permanently wet ditch

Riffle: section of the watercourse where the bed gradient is steep locally, the flow usually being shallow and supercritical. Shallow area in a watercourse, usually in fairly fast-flowing water and with a stone or gravel substrate

Rilling: bank erosion caused by small surface gullies due to surface water run-off down the bank

Riparian owner: owner of the land alongside a channel. In the UK, ownership normally extends to the centreline of the channel

Rip-rap: randomly placed, loose rock armour

Run-up: vertical height above still water level that a wave will reach on an inclined structure or bank

Sand filtration: the process in which solid particles are allowed to fall to the bottom of a body of water in a sedimentation tank or settlement tank

Scour: removal of soil particles by current, propeller or wave-induced shear forces. Scour commonly refers to localised erosion of bed material such as, e.g., at the unprotected toe of the bank of a channel

Screw-race: a high velocity jet of water generated by a boat's propeller and capable of causing serious scour

Sealant: a proprietary compound used to waterproof cement, timber, etc.

Sedimentation (settlement): the process in which solid particles are allowed to fall to the bottom of a body of water in a sedimentation tank or settlement tank

Seepage: movement of water into or out of the channel bank

Sett: a granite paving block, often cuboid in shape

Shoal: shallow area in watercourse caused by deposition of sediment

Shoaling: build-up of erosion material in a watercourse

Sharp sand: a sand composed of hard, angular particles, used in specific mixes with cement and water for rendering walls and similar surfaces

Shingle: small, rounded stones

Shuttering: a timber frame forming a mould into which concrete is poured to create side-walls

Sieve: a perforated screen usually of wire mesh. There is a British Standard specification for the sizes of the holes in the mesh but as sizes are quoted in inches and mm, any suitable wire mesh or perforated metal sheet with the correct size holes may be used.

Significant wave: statistical term relating to the average of the highest one-third of the waves of a given wave record. Hence significant wave height and a significant wave period

Silt: fine sediments deposited in still water

Soft protection: opposite of hard protection – normally employing natural materials

Soft sand: fine sand

Softwood timber: timber cut from coniferous trees

Spill stone: a flat stone set at the point at which water falls from one level to another

Spirit level: a tool for checking horizontal levels

Spit: a rough unit of depth measurement used in digging, equal to the length of a spade blade; small promontory extending into a body of water

Staining: coloration of water by dissolved substances

Straight-edge: a straight length of timber on which to rest a spirit level

Submerged plants: plants that for the most part have totally submerged foliage and, in many cases, emergent flowers

Submersible pump: a water-recirculating pump that is housed, and runs, under water

Subsoil: the soil within the bank of a channel, or behind the bank protection, beneath topsoil

Substrate: literally underlayer; the material on the bottom of a river, pond, etc.

Succession: replacement of one type of community by another, shown by progressive changes in vegetation and animal life

Sump: a pool or container into which water drains

Surface pump: a water-recirculating pump housed and running on dry land

Suspended solids: particulate materials held in suspension by moving water; a standard test in water analysis to determine the weight of solids suspended in a known volume of water

Swamp: area of mineral soil normally flooded in the growing season and dominated in most cases by emergent macrophytes

Sward: above-ground components of grass

Tamp: to compress firmly

Topsoil: the top layer of soil, which contains plant nutrients

Transformer: an apparatus for reducing or increasing the voltage of electrical currents

Turbidity: the pollution of water by suspended matter

Turbulence: random, very short-term fluctuations in fluid velocity. Degree of turbulence is measured by the root mean square of the fluctuations from the mean

Ultraviolet light (UV): radiation with a wavelength less than that of visible light; a component of sunlight

Underlay: cushioning material laid under flexible liner as a form of protection

Underlayer: the layer in a revetment between the armour layer and the subsoil. It may consist of a geotextile or a granular material or both

Up-rush: the movement of water up an inclined structure or bank when a wave reaches it. Up-rush is followed by a downward movement – down-rush

UV filter and magnet: a combination system that prevents the build-up of minerals on which algae thrive

Waling: horizontal beam that supports a sheet-piled retaining wall

Wall tie: a metal strip or wire figure-eight mortared into brickwork to cross the gap between double walls, giving them more stability

Washland: area of frequently flooded flat land adjacent to a river

Watercourse: natural or man-made channel that conveys water

Water level drawdown: a relatively quick drop in water level in the channel, often causing excess pore water pressure in the bank. Associated in particular with the return current created by a boat

Water meadow: waterside meadow with a managed regime of flooding

Water table: level below which the soil is waterlogged

Waterway: channel used for navigation

Wick effect: tendency of water to move from a pond to surrounding soil, drawn by plants' root systems

Withy bed: term used in some regions to describe a bed of osier willow

Zonation: the occurrence of communities in distinct geographical areas or zones

CONVERSION TABLES

APPENDIX E

LENGTH
Approximate equivalents

Millimetres to inches		Inches to millimetres	
1	1/32	1/32	1
2	1/16	1/16	2
3	1/8	1/8	3
4	5/32	3/16	5
5	3/16	1/4	6
6	1/4	5/16	8
7	9/32	3/8	10
8	5/16	7/16	11
9	11/32	1/2	13
10 (1cm)	3/8	9/16	14
11	7/16	5/8	16
12	15/32	11/16	17
13	1/2	3/4	19
14	9/16	13/16	21
15	19/32	7/8	22
16	5/8	15/16	24
17	11/16	1	25
18	23/32	2	51
19	3/4	3	76
20	25/32	4	102
25	1	5	127
30	1 3/16	6	152
40	1 9/16	7	178
50	1 31/32	8	203
60	2 3/8	9	229
70	2 3/4	10	254
80	3 5/32	11	279
90	3 9/16	12 (1 ft)	305
100	3 15/16	13	330
200	7 7/8	14	356
300	11 13/16	15	381
400	15 3/4	16	406
500	19 11/16	17	432
600	23 5/8	18	457
700	27 9/16	19	483
800	31 1/2	20	508
900	35 7/16	24 (2ft)	610
1000 (1m)	39 3/8		

Metres to feet/inches		Yards to metres	
1	3' 3"	1	0.914
2	6' 7"	2	1.83
3	9' 10"	3	2.74
4	13' 1"	4	3.66
5	16' 5"	5	4.57
6	19' 8"	6	5.49
7	23' 0"	7	6.40
8	26' 3"	8	7.32
9	29' 6"	9	8.23
10	32' 10"	10	9.14
20	65' 7"	20	18.29
50	164' 0"	50	45.72
100	328' 1"	100	91.44

Category	Unit	Equivalent
Length	1 millimetre (mm)	= 0.0394 in
	1 centimetre (cm)/10 mm	= 0.3937 in
	1 metre/100 cm	= 39.37 in/3.281 ft/1.094 yd
	1 kilometre (km)/1000 metres	= 1093.6 yd/0.6214 mile
	1 inch (in)	= 25.4 mm/2.54 cm
	1 foot (ft)/12 in	= 304.8 mm/30.48 cm/0.3048 metre
	1 yard (yd)/3 ft	= 914.4 mm/91.44 cm/0.9144 metre
	1 mile/1760 yd	= 1609.344 metres/1.609 km
Area	1 square centimetre (sq cm)/ 100 square millimetres (sq mm)	= 0.155 sq in
	1 square metre (sq metre)/10,000 sq cm	= 10.764 sq ft/1.196 sq yd
	1 are/100 sq metres	= 119.60 sq yd/0.0247 acre
	1 hectare (ha)/100 ares	= 2.471 acres/0.00386 sq mile
	1 square inch (sq in)	= 645.16 sq mm/6.4516 sq cm
	1 square foot (sq ft)/144 sq in	= 929.03 sq cm
	1 square yard (sq yd)/9 sq ft	= 8361.3 sq cm/0.8361 sq metre
	1 acre/4840 sq yd	= 4046.9 sq metres/0.4047 ha
	1 square mile/640 acres	= 259 ha/2.59 sq km
Volume	1 cubic centimetre (cu cm)/ 1000 cubic millimetres (cu mm)	= 0.0610 cu in
	1 cubic decimetre (cu dm)/1000 cu cm	= 61.024 cu in/0.0353 cu ft
	1 cubic metre/1000 cu dm	= 35.3147 cu ft/1.308 cu yd
	1 cu cm	= 1 millilitre (ml)
	1 cu dm	= 1 litre see **Capacity**
	1 cubic inch (cu in)	= 16.3871 cu cm
	1 cubic foot (cu ft)/1728 cu in	= 28,316.8 cu cm/0.0283 cu metre
	1 cubic yard (cu yd)/27 cu ft	= 0.7646 cu metre
Capacity	1 litre	= 1.7598 pt/0.8799 qt/0.22 gal
	1 pint (pt)	= 0.568 litre
	1 quart (qt)	= 1.137 litres
	1 gallon (gal)	= 4.546 litres
Weight	1 gram (g)	= 0.035 oz
	1 kilogram (kg)/1000 g	= 2.20 lb/35.2 oz
	1 tonne/1000 kg	= 2204.6 lb/0.9842 ton
	1 ounce (oz)	= 28.35 g
	1 pound (lb)	= 0.4536 kg
	1 ton	= 1016 kg
Pressure	1 gram per square metre (g/metre^2)	= 0.0295 oz/sq yd
	1 gram per square centimetre (g/cm 2)	= 0.228 oz/sq in
	1 kilogram per square centimetre (kg/cm^2)	= 14.223 lb/sq in
	1 kilogram per square metre (kg/metre^2)	= 0.205 lb/sq ft
	1 pound per square foot (lb/ft^2)	= 4.882 kg/metre^2
	1 pound per square inch (lb/in^2)	= 703.07 kg/metre^2
	1 ounce per square yard (oz/yd^2)	= 305.91 g/metre^2
	1 ounce per square foot (oz/ft^2)	= 305.15 g/metre^2
Temperature	To convert °F to °C, subtract 32, then divide by 9 and multiply by 5	
	To convert °C to °F, divide by 5 and multiply by 9, then add 32	
Force	1 Newton	Force exerted by 0.225 lbs
	1 KN or 1000 Newtons	Force exerted by 1/10 ton
Stress	1 N/mm^2	147 lbs/sq. inch
	15.2 N/mm^2	1 ton/sq. inch
	1 KN/m^2	0.009 tons/sq. ft.
	107 KN/m^2	1 ton/sq. ft.
	1 KN/M	68.5 lbs/ft.
Speed	1 Metre/Sec.	2.2 m.p.h.

STANDARD GRAPHICS SYMBOLS

APPENDIX F

FLEXIBLE MATERIALS

 Gravel

 Hardcore

 Hoggin

 Rock

 Rubble

 Sand

 Topsoil

 Water

UNIT MATERIALS

 Brick paving

 Brickwork

 Cobbles

 Concrete-p.c. blockwork

Unit Materials continued

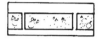 Concrete-pc paving units

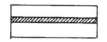 Metal

 Setts

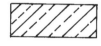 Stone-natural, cut

 Stone-reconstituted

 Rubble stone-random

 Rubble stone-coursed

 Timber-dressed (wrot)

 Timber-rough (unwrot)

IN SITU MATERIALS

 Asphalt

 Concrete – in situ

 Mortar

LEGEND
Section

FLEXIBLE MATERIALS

 Grass

 Gravel

 Hoggin

 Sand

 Soil

 Rock

 Rubble

 Water

UNIT MATERIALS

 Brick – stretcher bond

 Brick – basket weave

 Brick – stack bond

 Brick – herringbone

 Cobbles – random

 Cobbles – coursed

 Cobbles – flat, parallel laid

Unit Materials continued

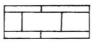 Concrete-p.c. paving slabs

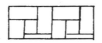 Concrete-p.c. blocks

 Concrete-p.c. hexagonal slabs

 Setts – stack bond

 Setts – stretcher bond

 Stone – natural

 Stone – reconstituted

 Stone – random paving

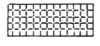 Tiled paving

 Timber

IN-SITU MATERIALS

 Asphalt

 Concrete – i.s.broom finish

 Concrete – i.s.exposed aggregate

 Concrete – i.s.trowelled finish

 Concrete – i.s.marked finish

LEGEND
Plan